EQUAL·JUSTICE·UNDER·LAW

A National Strategy to Reduce Crime

National Advisory Commission on Criminal Justice Standards and Goals

Foreword

This volume, *A National Strategy to Reduce Crime,* is one of six reports of the National Advisory Commission on Criminal Justice Standards and Goals.

The Commission was appointed by the Administrator of the Law Enforcement Assistance Administration (LEAA) on October 20, 1971, to formulate for the first time national criminal justice standards and goals for crime reduction and prevention at the State and local levels.

The views and recommendations presented in this volume are those of a majority of the Commission and do not necessarily represent those of the Department of Justice. Although LEAA provided $1.75 million in discretionary grants for the work of the Commission, it did not direct that work and had no voting participation in the Commission.

Membership in the Commission was drawn from the three branches of State and local government, from industry, and from citizen groups. Commissioners were chosen, in part, for their working experience in the criminal justice area. Police chiefs, judges, corrections leaders, and prosecutors were represented.

Other recent Commissions have studied the causes and debilitating effects of crime in our society. We have sought to expand their work and build upon it by developing a clear statement of priorities, goals, and standards to help set a national strategy to reduce crime.

Some State or local governments may already meet standards or recommendations proposed by the Commission; most in the Nation do not. In any case, each State and local government is encouraged to evaluate its present status and to implement those standards and recommendations that it deems appropriate.

The precise standards and recommendations of the Commission are presented in the other Commission reports. Those five volumes, entitled *Criminal Justice System, Police, Courts, Corrections,* and *Community Crime Prevention,* are addressed to the State and local officials and other persons who would be responsible for implementing the standards and recommendations. Synopses of all Commission standards and recommendations are presented in this volume to provide an overview of that material.

A seventh volume, *Proceedings of the National Conference on Criminal Justice,* is being published by the Commission. The *Proceedings* do not constitute a statement of the Commission, but they are included with the reports of the Commission for the convenience of the interested reader. They contain the edited transcripts of the National Conference on Criminal Justice, sponsored by LEAA and held in Washington, D.C., on January 23–26, 1973.

The purpose of *A National Strategy to Reduce Crime* is to present a broad picture of the Commission's work and its strategy for the reduction of crime in America. Many of the chapters of this volume are based on the companion reports. This volume also contains a substantial amount of material that does not appear in any other Commission report, including material in the chapters entitled National Goals and Priorities, Criminal Code Reform and Revision, Handguns in American Society, and A National Commitment to Change.

This Commission has completed its work and submitted its report. The Commission hopes that its standards and recommendations will influence the shape of the criminal justice system in this Nation for many years to come. And it believes that adoption of those standards and recommendations will contribute to a measurable reduction of the amount of crime in America.

The Commission thanks Jerris Leonard, Administrator of LEAA, and Richard W. Velde and Clarence M. Coster, Associate Administrators, for their efforts in authorizing and funding this Commission and for their support and encouragement during the life of the Commission.

The Commission expresses its sincerest gratitude to the task force chairmen and members and to the many practitioners, scholars, and advisers who contributed their expertise to this effort. We are also grateful to the Commission staff and to the staffs of the task forces for their hard and dedicated work.

On behalf of the Commission, I extend special and warmest thanks and admiration to Thomas J. Madden, Executive Director, for guiding this project through to completion.

Russell W. Peterson

RUSSELL W. PETERSON
Chairman

Washington, D.C.
January 23, 1973

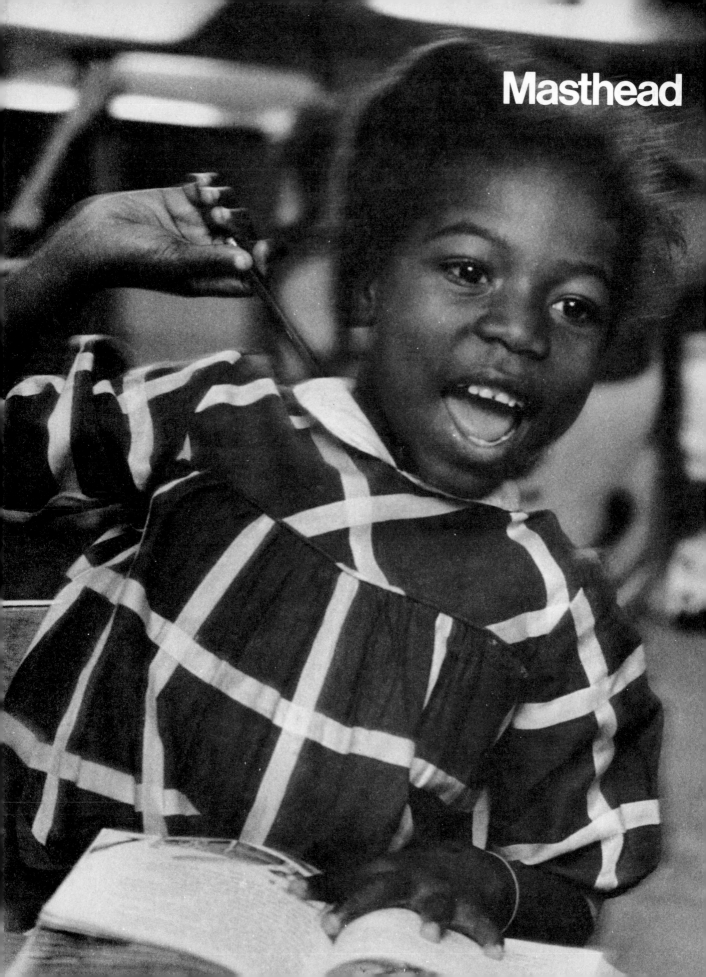

Masthead

**NATIONAL
ADVISORY
COMMISSION
ON
CRIMINAL
JUSTICE
STANDARDS
AND GOALS**

Chairman

Russell W. Peterson

Vice Chairman

Peter J. Pitchess

Richard R. Andersen	Henry F. McQuade
Forrest H. Anderson	Gary K. Nelson
Sylvia Bacon	Charles L. Owen
Arthur J. Bilek	Ray Pope
Frank Dyson	Elmer J. C. Prenzlow, Jr.
Caroline E. Hughes	Milton G. Rector
Howard A. Jones	Arlen Specter
Robert J. Kutak	Leon H. Sullivan
Richard G. Lugar	Donald F. Taylor
Ellis C. MacDougall	Richard W. Velde

Task Force Chairmen

Police

Edward M. Davis

Courts

Daniel J. Meador

Civil Disorders

Jerry V. Wilson

Community Involvement

George B. Peters

Drug Abuse

Sterling Johnson

Education, Training, and Manpower Development

Lee P. Brown

Corrections

Joe Frazier Brown

Community Crime Prevention

Jack Michie

Information Systems and Statistics

John R. Plants

Juvenile Delinquency

Wilfred W. Nuernberger

Organized Crime

William L. Reed

Research and Development

Peter J. McQuillan

Commission Staff

Executive Director

Thomas J. Madden

Deputy Director

Lawrence J. Leigh

Associate Director

Robert H. Macy

Assistant Directors

Hayden Gregory
Marilyn Kay Harris
Thomas M. O'Neil, Jr.

Special Assistant to the Chairman

Joseph M. Dell'Olio

Administrative Assistant to the Executive Director

Mary M. Curtin

Management Consultant

Frederick W. Giggey

Members

Kirby L. Baker
Malcolm Barr
Elizabeth E. Bates
Don Clasen
Joyce M. Cromer
Audrey L. Gaston
Kenneth D. Hines
Ellen Jasper
Michael D. Jones
Jerome Katz
Lillian Kharasch
Diane Liptack
Roma K. McNickle
Sandra M. Miller
Amil N. Myshin
Malcolm H. Oettinger, Jr.
Karen Peck
George W. Shirley

Publications Unit

Executive Editor

Joseph Foote

Associate Editor and Production Manager

Marilyn Marbrook

Associate Editors

Nina M. Graybill
DuPre A. Jones
David Mink
Newton T. Stark

Staff Writers

Patricia B. Fox
J. Andrew Hamilton
Richard C. Letaw

Copy Editors

Patricia Helsing
Joyce E. Latham
Jean A. McRae
John N. Rogers

F. R. Ruskin
Marilyn M. Sharkey

Staff Assistants

Therese L. Gibbons
Lucile M. Graham

Design

Nolan and White
Visual Communications

Design Coordinator

E. James White

Art Director

Robert B. Orban

Designer

Celia L. Strain

Table of Contents

Chapter 5
Police 71

This project was supported by the Law Enforcement Assistance Administration, U.S. Department of Justice, under the Omnibus Crime Control and Safe Streets Act of 1968, as amended. Points of view or opinions stated in this document are those of the National Advisory Commission on Criminal Justice Standards and Goals, and do not necessarily represent the official position of the U.S. Department of Justice.

A National Strategy to Reduce Crime

GOALS AND PRIORITIES

GOALS FOR CRIME REDUCTION

The Commission proposes as a goal for the American people a 50% reduction in high-fear crimes by 1983. It further proposes that crime reduction efforts be concentrated on five crimes. The goals for the reduction of these crimes should be:

- Homicide: Reduced by at least 25% by 1983
- Forcible Rape: Reduced by at least 25% by 1983
- Aggravated Assault: Reduced by at least 25% by 1983
- Robbery: Reduced by at least 50% by 1983
- Burglary: Reduced by at least 50% by 1983

PRIORITIES FOR ACTION

The Commission proposes four areas for priority action in reducing the five target crimes:

- Juvenile Delinquency: The highest attention must be given to preventing juvenile delinquency and to minimizing the involvement of young offenders in the juvenile and criminal justice system, and to reintegrating juvenile offenders into the community.
- Delivery of Social Services: Public and private service agencies should direct their actions to improve the delivery of all social services to citizens, particularly to groups that contribute higher than average proportions of their numbers to crime statistics.
- Prompt Determination of Guilt or Innocence: Delays in the adjudication and disposition of criminal cases must be greatly reduced.
- Citizen Action: Increased citizen participation in activities to control crime in their community must be generated, with active encouragement and support by criminal justice agencies.

KEY COMMISSION PROPOSALS

CRIMINAL JUSTICE SYSTEM

The Commission proposes broad reforms and improvements in criminal justice planning and information systems at the State and local levels. Key recommendations include:

- Development by States of integrated multiyear criminal justice planning.
- Establishment of criminal justice coordinating councils by all major cities and counties.
- Establishment by each State of a Security and Privacy Council to develop procedures and recommendations for legislation to assure security and privacy of information contained in criminal justice information systems.
- Creation by each State of an organizational structure for coordinating the development of criminal justice information systems.

COMMUNITY CRIME PREVENTION

The Commission proposes that all Americans make a personal contribution to the reduction of crime, and that all Americans support the crime prevention efforts of their State and local governments. Key recommendations include:

- Increased citizen contribution to crime prevention by making homes and businesses more secure, by participating in police-community programs, and by working with youth.
- Expanded public and private employment opportunities and elimination of unnecessary restrictions on hiring ex-offenders.
- Establishment of and citizen support for youth services bureaus to improve the delivery of social services to young people.
- Provision of individualized treatment for drug offenders and abusers.
- Provision of statewide capability for overseeing and investigating financing of political campaigns.
- Establishment of a statewide investigation and prosecution capability to deal with corruption in government.
- Development in the schools of career education programs that guarantee to every student a job or acceptance to an advanced program of studies.

KEY COMMISSION PROPOSALS

POLICE

The Commission proposes that the delivery of police services be greatly improved at the municipal level. Key recommendations include:

- Consolidation of all police departments with fewer than 10 sworn officers.
- Enhancement of the role of the patrolman.
- Increased crime prevention efforts by police working in and with the community.
- Affirmative police action to divert public drunks and mental patients from the criminal justice system.
- Increased employment and utilization of women, minorities, and civilians in police work.
- Enactment of legislation authorizing police to obtain search warrants by telephone.

COURTS

The Commission proposes major restructuring and streamlining of procedures and practices in processing criminal cases at the State and local levels, in order to speed the determination of guilt or innocence. Key recommendations include:

- Trying all cases within 60 days of arrest.
- Requiring judges to hold full days in court.
- Unification within the State of all courts.
- Allowing only one review on appeal.
- Elimination of plea bargaining.
- Screening of all criminal cases coming to the attention of the prosecutor to determine if further processing is appropriate.
- Diverting out of the system all cases in which further processing by the prosecutor is not appropriate, based on such factors as the age of the individual, his psychological needs, the nature of the crime, and the availability of treatment programs.
- Elimination of grand juries and arraignments.

KEY
COMMISSION
PROPOSALS

CORRECTIONS

The Commission proposes fundamental changes
in the system of corrections that exists in States,
counties, and cities in America—changes based on
the belief that correctional systems usually are
little more than "schools of crime." Key
recommendations include:

- Restricting construction of major State
  institutions for adult offenders.
- Phasing out of all major juvenile offender
  institutions.
- Elimination of disparate sentencing practices.
- Establishment of community-based correctional
  programs and facilities.
- Unification of all correctional functions within
  the State.
- Increased and expanded salary, education, and
  training levels for corrections personnel.

CRIMINAL
CODE
REFORM
AND
REVISION

The Commission proposes that all States
reexamine their criminal codes with the view to
improving and updating them. Key recommendations include:

- Establishment of permanent criminal code
  revision commissions at the State level.
- Decriminalization of vagrancy and drunkenness.

HANDGUNS
IN
AMERICAN
SOCIETY

The Commission proposes nationwide action at
the State level to eliminate the dangers posed by
widespread possession of handguns. The key
recommendation is:

- Elimination of importation, manufacture, sale,
  and private possession of handguns by
  January 1, 1983.

Chapter 1

A National Strategy To Reduce Crime

This report presents a national strategy to reduce crime. After almost 2 years of study and research, the National Advisory Commission on Criminal Justice Standards and Goals concludes that this Nation can markedly reduce crime over the next 10 years.

The Commission foresees a time, in the immediate future, when:

• A couple can walk in the evening in their neighborhood without fear of assault and robbery.
• A family can go away for the weekend without fear of returning to a house ransacked by burglars.
• A woman can take a night job without fear of being raped on her way to or from work.
• Every citizen can live without fear of being brutalized by unknown assailants.

America can and should make its cities and neighborhoods, its highways and parks, and its homes and commercial establishments safe places for all persons at all times.

America can and should begin to reduce crime of all sorts, and to erase those social conditions associated with crime and delinquency—poverty, unemployment, inferior education, and discrimination.

This can be done.

The National Advisory Commission concludes that this Nation can and should reduce the rate of "high-fear" crime by 50 percent in the next 10 years.

These are the crimes of murder, rape, aggravated assault, robbery, and burglary, when committed by strangers.

THE NEED FOR A PLAN

Americans know that crime reduction is imperative. They know the costs and consequences of crime. They know the fear of crime. They have been the victims of crime.

In early 1973, Dr. George Gallup released a poll showing that more than one of every five people across the Nation had been victimized by crime between December 1971 and December 1972. The figures for center cities showed that one of three people had been victims of crime. Respondents listed crime as the worst problem in their community. Fifty-one percent of the people questioned by Dr. Gallup said there was more crime in their area than there was a year ago. Only 10 percent said there was less crime.[1]

There has been considerable study of the criminal justice system in this Nation in recent years. Congress has examined the problems and developed laudable programs. The Department of Justice, the

---

[1] The Gallup Poll, January 13, 1973, and January 15, 1973.

Department of Health, Education, and Welfare, and the Special Action Office for Drug Abuse Prevention —to name just a few Federal agencies—have studied the crime situation and begun to move toward solutions. State and local governments have reacted to the growing public desire for crime reduction, and the press has focused attention on many of the most neglected areas of the criminal justice system.

What has been needed, however—and what this Commission now offers—is a plan of action that States, cities, and citizens can implement to reduce crime, protect society, and increase public safety.

The Commission's plan begins with the selection of goals—including the goal of reducing "high-fear" crime by 50 percent by 1983.

The Commission's plan emphasizes four basic priorities:

• Prevent juvenile delinquency.
• Improve delivery of social services.
• Reduce delays in the criminal justice process.
• Increase citizen participation.

The plan also emphasizes the need for all elements of the criminal justice system to plan and work together as a system and to plan and work together with the social service delivery system. The plan emphasizes the need for the police patrolman to

strengthen his ties to the community and to be given greater responsibility and authority for preventing and reducing crime in the community. The plan emphasizes the need for the prosecutor, defender, and judiciary to work toward insuring speedier trials while still protecting fundamental rights. The plan also emphasizes the need for corrections to develop effective programs and procedures for reintegrating offenders into the community as soon as possible consistent with the protection of the community.

To reach these goals, the Commission offers hundreds of standards and recommendations. These standards and recommendations establish performance levels for operation of the criminal justice system as a whole, for police, for courts, for corrections, and for service agencies of government.

The details are presented in this volume and in five companion volumes—*Community Crime Prevention, Criminal Justice System, Police, Courts,* and *Corrections.*

The six volumes were developed by the 22 members of the National Advisory Commission on Criminal Justice Standards and Goals and by the more than 180 members of its task forces as well as by an even greater number of advisers, consultants, and staff members. Represented on the Commission and task forces were men and women with practical working experience in the criminal justice and crime prevention fields who have

---

Citizen action project promoting opportunities for youth.

direct knowledge of the crime problems facing America and insight into contemporary society.

This volume contains summaries of the other volumes, as well as new material that does not appear in the other reports. The new sections cut across the entire subject matter of the Commission's work and include National Goals and Priorities, Criminal Code Reform and Revision, Handguns in American Society, and A National Commitment to Change.

A seventh volume contains the proceedings of the National Conference on Criminal Justice, where the basic plan of the Commission was introduced to and critiqued by more than 1,500 members of the criminal justice community.

PRINCIPLES GUIDING THE COMMISSION'S WORK

The first principle guiding the Commission's work is that operating without standards and goals does not guarantee failure, but does invite it.

Specific standards and goals enable professionals and the public to know where the system is heading, what it is trying to achieve, and what in fact it is achieving. Standards can be used to focus essential institutional and public pressure on the reform of the entire criminal justice system.

In setting standards and goals for the prevention and reduction of crime, this Commission was not constrained by the limits of the traditional criminal justice system, usually defined as comprising police, courts, and corrections. In addition to setting standards for police, courts, and corrections, it established a broad range of standards and recommendations for citizen action, for improving governmental integrity, and for improving and expanding the delivery of social services to the community.

In undertaking its work, the Commission began with an acceptance of the scope and extent of crime and the damaging effects it has on the social structure of America. These matters had been well documented by other commissions, including the Commission on the Causes and Prevention of Violence and the President's Commission on Law Enforcement and Administration of Justice. The reports of this Commission go directly to the beginning of a solution, to workable practical standards.

In developing its standards, the Commission directed its research in large part to existing programs and practices, to criminal justice planning documents, and to articles and reports on crime prevention and reduction programs.

Because the Commission was developing standards, the emphasis of its efforts was placed not only on what was desirable but also on what was workable and practical. Many standards are based upon successful models that are operational in one or more places in the country. Many models were found that had never been documented before. Where no model existed, standards were based upon concepts that the task forces and the Commission felt were necessary for crime reduction.

The scope of the Commission's work did not extend to the setting of standards and recommendations for agencies of the Federal Government. The reason is that the Commission's work was funded by LEAA, which is charged with improving law enforcement and criminal justice at the State and local levels. The Commission's membership therefore consisted of citizens from public and private life at the State and local levels; the one Federal official on the Commission had no voting participation.

The role of the Federal Government is discussed, however, in instances where Federal programs impact on or coincide with the law enforcement and criminal justice efforts of State and local agencies. In its *Report on Police,* for example, the Commission recommends that law enforcement agencies cooperate in the establishment of task force efforts with other criminal justice agencies on the local, State, and Federal levels. The organized crime strike forces operated by the United States Department of Justice are another activity in which local and Federal cooperation is encouraged.

Finally, some of the standards, upon initial reading, may not appear to be directly related to crime reduction. Examples include standards dealing with expansion of the constitutional rights of convicted offenders, elimination of plea bargaining, expansion of the right to counsel, the use of summons in lieu of arrest, and integrity in government. In setting such standards, it was the opinion of the Commission that to foster respect for the criminal laws and to win the respect and cooperation of all citizens, the agencies and officials of the criminal justice system and the governing authorities of this country must themselves respect the law and must act fairly and justly toward all citizens.

NEED FOR A NATIONAL COMMITMENT

This Commission calls for the establishment of a national strategy to reduce crime through the timely and equitable administration of justice; the protection of life, liberty, and property; and the efficient mobilization of resources.

Implementation is inherent in the development of any strategy. Central to the work of this Commission is the belief that crime in America can be reduced, that the goals in this report can be met if the standards and recommendations proposed in the reports on *Community Crime Prevention, Police, Courts, Corrections,* and *Criminal Justice System* are implemented.

The Commission is aware that the cost of implementing the standards could be substantial, at least in the short term. Yet, when the cost of crime reduction is weighed against the cost of crime itself, it is clear that the additional outlays by the system are more than justified. In addition, less crime will mean fewer victims of crime and will result in genuine, demonstrable savings, both to potential victims and to the whole society.

A critical step in the implementation process is a comprehensive evaluation of all standards and recommendations considered applicable in a given jurisdiction. Through careful evaluation, needless frustration and wasted time and effort can be avoided, as inevitably some measures that appear desirable are found after further study to be too ambitious, too costly, or otherwise inappropriate. The Commission's program for implementation and evaluation is presented in Chapter 10.

There are signs that leadership at the State level around the Nation is interested in the concept of establishing standards for law enforcement and criminal justice agencies. A majority of States already have plans to review and examine formally the standards and recommendations of this Commission with a view to implementing those that are appropriate. Details on these developments are provided in the Postscript to Chapter 10.

A commitment to change is vital to implementation. The citizens of this country and the agencies of government, individually and collectively, must work to bring about the necessary changes both inside and outside the criminal justice system. If the people of this country are committed to reducing crime, its rate will decrease dramatically.

Chapter 2

National Goals And Priorities

Crime is not a new phenomenon in American life. Scholars and commissions before this one have documented the growth and complexity of the crime problem in the United States, its causes, and its destructive effects on national life. The damage to persons, property, and spirit, and the fear of unprovoked, unpredictable violence are more than familiar.

This Commission does not offer easy solutions to those problems. But it does offer a beginning.

GOALS FOR THE DECADE AHEAD

The Commission believes that the American people can reduce the social and economic damage caused by all forms of crime. The Commission also believes that there are certain crimes that threaten the very existence of a humane and civilized society and that the rate of these crimes can be assessed and controlled. These are the violent crimes of murder and nonnegligent manslaughter, forcible rape, robbery, aggravated assault, and the property crime of burglary.

These five crimes are particularly serious when committed by a stranger on the streets and highways of the Nation. In such cases, an extra dimension is present—the dimension of fear. Thus, when these crimes are committed by strangers, the Commission labels them "high-fear" crimes and proposes a sharp reduction in their rate.[1]

Violent crime and burglary, however, are also serious when committed by relatives and acquaintances.

Generally, the Commission proposes a two-level attack on these five crimes:

First, the rate of "high-fear" (stranger-related) crimes should be cut in half by 1983.

Second, whether the crime is committed by a relative or acquaintance, or a stranger, the crime rates should be cut by 1983 as follows:
- Homicide (murder and nonnegligent manslaughter)—at least 25 percent.
- Forcible rape—at least 25 percent.
- Aggravated assault—at least 25 percent.
- Robbery—at least 50 percent.
- Burglary—at least 50 percent.

---

[1] The National Commission on the Causes and Prevention of Violence pointed out in 1969 that, although violent crimes form a relatively small percentage of all crimes known to the police, their effect is out of proportion to their volume. "In violent crime man becomes a wolf to man, threatening or destroying the personal safety of his victim in a terrifying act. Violent crime (particularly street crime) engenders fear—the deep-seated fear of the hunted in the presence of the hunter." National Commission on the Causes and Prevention of Violence, *To Establish Justice, To Insure Domestic Tranquility* (1969), p. 18.

Probation officer counseling youth.

The Commission is aware that the selection of these crimes and percentages of reduction [2] will arouse the doubts of skeptics, but the Commission submits that the proposed crime reduction goals are aspirations, not predictions. They define what could be, not what necessarily will be. To reach these goals will require a concentration of the national will and the best application of our capabilities. The Commission is confident that by improved effort, including use of the standards and recommendations presented elsewhere in its reports, the goals can be attained.

Why These Crimes?

The Commission decided to focus attention on the five target crimes because of their cost to society—economic cost to some degree but, more importantly, their cost to citizens in fear, psychic damage, and mistrust.

The economic loss resulting from the five crimes amounts to hundreds of millions of dollars.[3] According to the FBI, money and property taken from victims of robbery and burglary in 1971 totaled $87 million and $739 million respectively.[4] These figures do not show the undoubtedly large losses resulting from unreported offenses.

To add up economic costs alone would be to underestimate seriously the total cost of crime in America. No price tag can be put on the fear that, as much as any other factor, is speeding the exodus from the cities, strangling businesses, and causing people to mistrust each other.

Polls conducted by the Gallup organization indicate that fear may have become more widespread since the Violence Commission reported. In 1968, 31 percent of Gallup survey respondents said they were afraid to walk in their own neighborhoods at night. By the end of 1972, the number had risen to 42 percent.

Considerations similar to those above caused the Commission to include burglary among the target crimes. A Gallup poll late in 1972 found that one person in six does not feel safe in his own home at night.[5] While burglary is technically classified as a

[2] Crimes are defined and trends noted in Federal Bureau of Investigation, *Crime in the United States: Uniform Crime Reports—1971* (1972), pp. 6-21. Publication is referred to hereinafter as *UCR,* with the appropriate date. The rate of commission of these crimes is the number of actual and attempted offenses per 100,000 inhabitants.

[3] For discussion of several methods of estimating costs of crime, see Donald J. Mulvihill and Melvin M. Tumin, *Crimes of Violence,* a report of the National Commission on the Causes and Prevention of Violence (1969), pp. 394-404.

[4] *UCR—1971,* pp. 15, 21. These figures do not indicate how much stolen property was recovered.

[5] The Gallup Poll, "The Dimensions of Crime" (January 14, 1973), p. 3.

property crime rather than a crime of violence and might perhaps be expected to occasion less fear, widespread apprehension about personal safety in the home certainly indicates that fear of being burglarized is the subject of acute concern among many Americans.

By focusing attention on the target crimes, the Commission does not wish to suggest that other crimes are not serious problems for the Nation. Yearly arrests for shoplifting, fraud, embezzlement, forgery and counterfeiting, arson, and vandalism far exceed in number the arrests for the target crimes.

Nor do the target crimes produce the greatest direct economic loss. The President's Commission on Law Enforcement and Administration of Justice (the President's Crime Commission) estimated that in 1965 direct losses through crimes against persons, crimes against property, and the cost of illegal goods and services, amounted to about $15 billion a year. Of this loss, violent crimes and burglary were estimated to account for little more than $1 billion, or 7 percent of the total.[6]

The estimate of the President's Crime Commission did not include losses from crimes where victimization is often secondary, diffuse, and difficult

[6] President's Commission on Law Enforcement and Administration of Justice, *Task Force Report: Crime and Its Impact—An Assessment* (1967), pp. 44, 46.

to measure, such as violations of antitrust laws, building codes, pure food and drug laws, and statutes relating to the public trust (prohibiting bribery of public officials, for example). Whatever the cost of these crimes, it is certainly greater than direct economic losses from violent crimes and burglary.

The true cost of the target crimes lies in their capacity—their increasing capacity—to inspire fear. It is this fear that, in the words of the Violence Commission, "is gnawing at the vitals of urban America."

Why Set Quantitative Goals?

The use of numerical values gives a dimension to goal-setting that has been lacking in earlier proposals for reducing crime.

Previously, government reports and political leaders have spoken in broad terms, such as: crime should be controlled and reduced; administration of the criminal justice system should be improved; public expenditures on the system should be increased; Americans should redouble their efforts to eliminate the causes of crime, such as poverty, discrimination, urban blight, and disease; planning should be improved; additional research should be undertaken; citizens should become more involved; and so on.

Unfortunately, these broad statements are not easily translated into action. What, for example, does it mean to say that crime should be reduced? Which crimes? What is to be reduced—the rate, the actual number, the economic and social impact, or something else? How great a reduction is possible? How great a reduction is acceptable? How do State and local governments, criminal justice agencies, and citizens go about realizing these goals? And how is it possible to tell if a goal has been achieved?

These are not academic questions. They have practical implications in time, dollars, and lives. Goals are most useful when they are measurable, when at the end of a given period achievements can be compared with expectations and an assessment of the reasons for discrepancies made. For citizens, goals to reduce crime provide benchmarks for judging the effectiveness of criminal justice operations and other public programs. For legislators, they are guides to funding. For operating agencies, they are focal points for the allocation of men and equipment.

BASIC FACTORS IN SETTING GOALS FOR CRIME REDUCTION

In making its judgments on goals for crime reduction, the Commission considered in depth many factors. Although it is impossible to enumerate all of the factors, the Commission believes that among the most important are the following:
- Characteristics of the target crimes.
- Socioeconomic changes.
- Changes in public attitudes.
- Public support for the criminal justice system.
- New methods of measuring progress.

Characteristics of the Target Crimes

In 1971, more than 3 million violent crimes and burglaries were reported to the police in the United States (see Table 1). Since victimization surveys conducted by LEAA and the Crime Commission indicate that at least as many unreported violent crimes and burglaries occur as are reported,[7] it is highly probable that at least 6 million violent crimes and burglaries occurred in 1971.

---

[7] A preliminary national survey of several thousand households was conducted by LEAA to determine the extent and nature of victimization in 1970. The survey, a developmental step in preparation for a continuous national victimization survey, polled the population 16 years of age or older for forcible rape, robbery, aggravated and simple assault, burglary, larceny, and auto theft. Murder and nonnegligent manslaughter were not covered. The responses were for personal, not business, victimization. Hereinafter the survey will be referred to as LEAA 1970 Survey. For victimization data see also *Crime and Its Impact*, p. 17.

Table 1. Violent Crime and Burglary Reported to the Police, 1960 and 1971

	Murder and nonnegligent manslaughter	Forcible rape	Robbery	Aggravated assault	Burglary	Total
Number of Offenses:						
1960	9,030	17,030	107,340	152,580	900,400	1,186,380
1971	17,630	41,890	385,910	364,600	2,368,400	3,178,430
Percent Change 1960-1971	+95.2	+146.0	+259.5	+139.0	+163.0	+168.0
Rate per 100,000 Inhabitants:						
1960	5.0	9.5	59.9	85.1	502.1	661.6
1971	8.5	20.3	187.1	176.8	1,148.3	1,541.0
Percent Change 1960-1971	+70.0	+113.7	+212.4	+107.8	+128.7	+132.9

Source: Federal Bureau of Investigation, *Crime in the United States: Uniform Crime Reports—1971* (1972) p. 61. Publication referred to hereinafter as *UCR 1971*.

Trends in Crime Rates

From 1960 to 1971, numbers of reported offenses and crime rates increased greatly in all five target crime categories. Except for the rate for murder and nonnegligent manslaughter, which increased 70 percent from 1960 through 1971, the rates for all of the target crimes more than doubled over the 12-year period.

Studies of reported crimes show wide fluctuations in rate from decade to decade. If the period prior to 1960 is any guide, Americans do not necessarily have to expect ever-increasing crime rates.

Although it is difficult to assess the period prior to 1933, when the FBI first began to compile national statistics, the available evidence indicates that rises and declines in crime have occurred since the beginning of the Nation. Probable peaks of violent crime in the late 19th century and the early 20th century have been identified in earlier studies.[8]

At this point it is necessary to enter a caution about the data on which the Commission based its conclusions on the extent of crime. The only source of overall information on crime on a continuing basis is the FBI's Uniform Crime Reports (UCR), which tabulate and analyze the reports of local police departments about crime in their areas. Because the FBI has succeeded in securing better local reporting over the years, it is essential, in the words of the President's Crime Commission, to "distinguish better reporting from more crime."[9] In considering trends, it is also important to note changes in public attitudes toward reporting crime. Possibly some of the increase in the figures on forcible rape is due to the fact that women are not as reluctant as they once were to report rape.

Having said this much, the Commission points out what the UCR does show: that the number of crimes reported has risen much faster than the population. It may be assumed that the target crimes, which are widely regarded by the public as more serious, are better reported than many others. It therefore seems appropriate to make use of the UCR for basic data, with reference also to victimization surveys.

According to the UCR, the current "crime wave" did not get under way until the mid-1960's. From 1933 to 1940, the rate for one of the target crimes, forcible rape, rose 41 percent. Rates for all the others declined: criminal homicide by 14 percent, robbery by 51 percent, aggravated assault by 13 percent, burglary by 21 percent.[10] In view of the state of the early UCR figures, which have been

[8] Mulvihill and Tumin, *Crimes of Violence*, p. 52.
[9] President's Commission on Law Enforcement and Administration of Justice, *The Challenge of Crime in a Free Society* (1967), p. 3.
[10] Crime rates from 1933 furnished by the FBI.

FIGURE 1. MURDER AND NONNEGLIGENT MANSLAUGHTER KNOWN TO THE POLICE, 1933-1971

(Rates per 100,000 population)

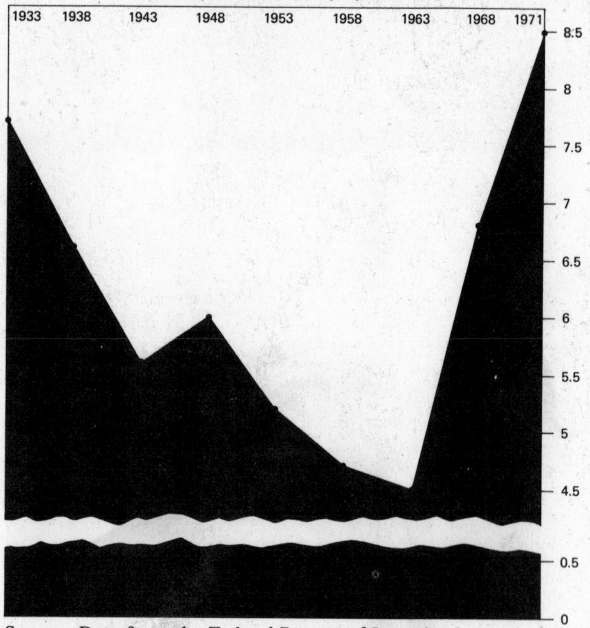

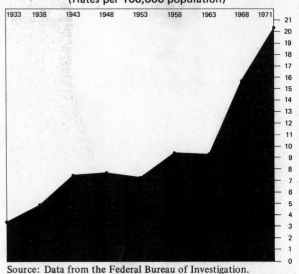

Source: Data from the Federal Bureau of Investigation.

FIGURE 2. FORCIBLE RAPE KNOWN TO THE POLICE, 1933-1971

(Rates per 100,000 population)

Source: Data from the Federal Bureau of Investigation.

questioned more vigorously than current statistics, no extensive conclusions can be drawn except that the crimes experiencing the greatest decreases in reported rates—robbery and burglary—probably did decrease.

FIGURE 3. ROBBERY
KNOWN TO THE POLICE, 1933-1971
(Rates per 100,000 population)

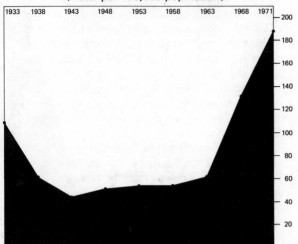

Source: Data from the Federal Bureau of Investigation.

FIGURE 4. AGGRAVATED ASSAULT
KNOWN TO THE POLICE, 1933-1971
(Rates per 100,000 population)

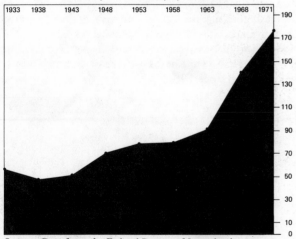

Source: Data from the Federal Bureau of Investigation.

From 1940 to 1963 the rates for rape, assault, and burglary rose gradually; the rate for robbery showed very little increase; and the rate for homicide declined appreciably. Beginning in the early 1960's, however, the rates for all five crimes rose steeply and continuously through 1971 (see Figures 1–5).

Preliminary data for 1972 released by the FBI indicate that violent crimes increased by only 1 percent over 1971. Robberies, which make up the largest number of crimes in the violent category, showed a 4 percent decrease. Murder was up 4

FIGURE 5. BURGLARY
KNOWN TO THE POLICE, 1933-1971
(Rates per 100,000 population)

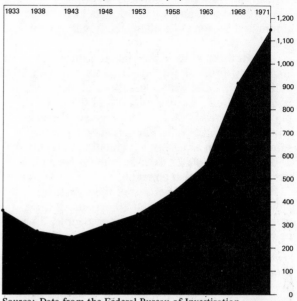

Source: Data from the Federal Bureau of Investigation.

percent, aggravated assault 6 percent, and forcible rape 11 percent. Burglary was down 2 percent.

It thus appears that the Nation might be reaching the peak of a crime cycle, but it is quite possible that crime rates will rise again. The past does not necessarily foreshadow the future.

Types of Offenders and Victims

In 1969, the Violence Commission noted several chief characteristics of violent crime, which, with one or two exceptions, are linked to burglary as well:

• Violent crime in the United States is primarily a phenomenon of large cities.
• Violent crime in the city is overwhelmingly committed by males.
• Violent crime in the city is concentrated especially among youths between the ages of 15 and 24.
• Violent crime in the city is committed primarily by individuals at the lower end of the occupational scale.
• Violent crime in the city stems disproportionately from the ghetto slums where most Negroes live.
• The victims of assaultive violence in the cities generally have the same characteristics as the offenders; victimization rates are generally highest for males, youths, poor persons, and blacks. Robbery victims, however, often are older whites.
• By far the greatest proportion of all serious violence is committed by repeaters." [11]

---

[11] *To Establish Justice, To Insure Domestic Tranquility,* pp. 20-24, 26. (The Violence Commission defined repeaters as persons with prior contacts with police.)

Current statistics on arrests and offenses reported in the 1971 UCR generally support the Violence Commission's findings on violent crime. They also indicate that burglary, which is a property crime, is less confined to central cities and less likely to be committed by nonwhite offenders than is violent crime.

Almost three-fifths of the violent crimes and almost two-fifths of the burglaries reported in 1971 took place in cities with populations of more than 250,000, where just over one-fifth of the U.S. population lived.[12] Since 1968, however, violent crime and burglary rates have risen faster in the suburbs than in cities with populations greater than 250,000 (see Table 2). Serious crime is becoming less a central city phenomenon.

In 1971, almost 60 percent of the arrests for violent crimes and more than 80 percent of the arrests for burglary involved young people, 24 years or younger.[13]

Table 2. Violent Crime and Burglary Known to the Police (Rates per 100,000 Population)

	Urban (cities over 250,000)	Suburban	Rural
Crime Rate 1968:			
Violent Crimes	773.2	145.5	108.4
Burglary	1,665.8	761.0	387.2
Crime Rate 1971:			
Violent Crimes	1,047.5	205.7	133.4
Burglary	2,026.1	974.5	484.9
Percentage Increase:			
Violent Crimes	+35	+41	+23
Burglary	+22	+28	+25

Sources: *UCR—1968-1971,* "Crime Rate by Area."

More than 90 percent of those arrested for violent crimes and burglaries in 1971 were males.[14] While there has been an overall increase since 1960 in the number and proportion of arrestees who are female, the percentage increase of males arrested for violent crimes has grown even faster. This has not been true of females under 18, where there was an increase of 229 percent. However, the priority crimes remain clearly the actions of males.

More than one-half of those arrested for violent crimes in 1971 were nonwhites, mostly blacks. One-third of those arrested for burglary in 1971 were nonwhites, again mostly blacks.[15]

Within a group of persons arrested in 1971 on

Federal charges of violent crime or burglary, from 65 percent to 77 percent had been arrested at least once before for violations of Federal or State law.[16] While FBI rearrest statistics include only those charged under Federal authority, available evidence indicates that similar high rearrest rates are the norm for States and localities as well. A reminder should be made here: arrest statistics show who has been arrested, not necessarily who committed an offense.

A national victimization survey made in 1970 by LEAA also shows that the persons most likely to be victims of violent crimes are males, youths, poor persons, and blacks.

The survey data do not indicate the sex or age characteristics of the heads of households victimized by burglary. They do show that the rate of victimization by burglary is more than one and one-half times as high for black families as for white ones. They also reveal no significant difference in the rate of victimization between households with incomes under $10,000 and those above $10,000.

This latter finding conflicts with the conclusion of the President's Crime Commission in 1967: "The risks of victimization from . . . burglary, are clearly concentrated in the lowest income groups and decrease steadily at higher income levels." [17] Because the President's Crime Commission also based its findings on a representative national survey, further research will have to be undertaken to resolve the inconsistency in the two sets of data. But it is likely that a shift in the pattern of victimization has occurred since 1966.

[12] *UCR—1971,* pp. 100-101.
[13] *UCR—1971,* pp. 122-123.
[14] *UCR—1971,* p. 126.
[15] *UCR—1971,* p. 127.

[16] *UCR—1971,* p. 38.
[17] *Crime and Its Impact,* p. 80.

Other Characteristics of Offenders and Victims

Additional characteristics of offenders, victims, and places of occurrence of the five priority crimes suggest important contrasts in factors associated with each offense.

Murders, assaults, and rapes tend to be "crimes of passion," a label that indicates the spontaneous and noneconomic elements of these crimes. It is known, too, that victims of criminal homicide and assaults frequently precipitate attacks by using insulting language or physical force in quarrels and disagreements.[18]

Studies of homicide and aggravated assault show that a substantial percentage of offenders and victims had been drinking before the event and one study of criminal homicides revealed that either the victim or the murderer had been drinking in almost two-thirds of the cases.[19]

Alcohol appears to be only a minimal factor in robbery, according to another study. When there was evidence of alcohol, at least as many victims as offenders were drinking. The study pointed out that "this somewhat reinforces the image of the robbery offender as an individual who rationally plans his act against an unsuspecting victim, in contrast to the offender in the other major violent crimes, who often acts more passionately and impulsively." [20] No comparable information on the role of alcohol in burglaries is available.

A popular explanation of the recent rise in reported crimes has been the use of drugs, especially heroin. There is considerable evidence that heroin-dependent persons frequently engage in theft, burglary, and robbery to support their habits. There is little evidence, however, that points to heroin as a significant factor in non-income-producing violent crime.[21] From an in-depth study of the relation between drug abuse and crime, the National Commission on Marihuana and Drug Abuse reported in 1973 that heroin-dependent persons usually commit crimes against property, principally shoplifting and burglary, though occasionally when desperate they will commit an assault, mugging, or robbery.[22]

Time and Place of Criminal Acts

The target crimes vary considerably as to where, when, and how they are committed.[23]

Victimization surveys and reported crime statistics answer many questions about where and when crimes are committed. Assaults occur about equally inside and outside buildings.[24] The home and various other inside locations are the likeliest locations for forcible rapes and homicides.[25] Sixty percent of reported burglaries occur in residences, as opposed to commercial establishments.[26] Possibly 60 percent of all burglaries and noncommercial robberies occur at night, as do two-thirds of the aggravated assaults and one-half of the rapes.[27]

Many persons are victimized more than once within relatively short time periods. About one in six robbery and assault victims during 1970 were victimized twice during the 12-month period, according to the LEAA victimization survey.

Eighteen percent of the households burglarized in 1970, according to the survey, were burglarized more than once in that year, 3 percent of them three times or more in the same year. About two in five of the burglaries reported in the survey in 1970 involved entries without force through unlocked doors, unlatched windows, or other means of access. These findings have particular relevance for crime prevention efforts by police and citizens.

Relationship Between Criminal and Victim

A critical factor differentiating the five target crimes is the relationship between the criminal and his victim. It has long been assumed that a majority of murders are committed by someone known to the victim, and the same theory has been held in regard to aggravated assault and forcible rape. However, victimization surveys are indicating that the

---

[18] Mulvihill and Tumin, *Crimes of Violence*, pp. 224-228. Precipitation was defined as first resort to insults or force.

[19] Data on the role of alcohol in violent crimes are summarized in Mulvihill and Tumin, *Crimes of Violence*, pp. 641-649. The homicide study is reported in Marvin E. Wolfgang, *Patterns in Criminal Homicide* (Wiley, 1966).

[20] Mulvihill and Tumin, *Crimes of Violence*, pp. 644-646.

[21] For a discussion of the relationship between drug abuse and crime, see Harwin Voss and Richard Stephens, "The Relationship between Drug Abuse and Crime," to be published in *Drug Abuse;* Richard Stephens and Stephen Levine, "Crime and Narcotic Addiction," to be published in Raymond Hardy and John Cull (eds.), *Applied Psychology in Law Enforcement and Corrections* (Thomas, 1973); and James A. Inciardi, "The Poly-Drug User: A New Situational Offender," in Freda Adler (ed.), *Politics, Crime, and the International Scene: An Inter-American Focus* (San Juan, P.R.: North-South Center Press, 1972), pp. 60-69.

[22] National Commission on Marihuana and Drug Abuse, *Drug Use in America: Problem in Perspective* (1973), p. 175.

[23] *UCR—1971*, p. 21.

[24] Mulvihill and Tumin, *Crimes of Violence*, p. 302.

[25] *Ibid.*

[26] *UCR—1971*, p. 21.

[27] Data on all burglaries, residential and commercial, are taken from *UCR—1971*, p. 21. Data on residential burglaries in LEAA 1970 Survey indicate that roughly 60 percent of these are committed at night. Data on noncommercial robbery, forcible rape, and aggravated assault are taken from LEAA 1970 Survey.

proportion of these crimes committed by strangers is increasing.

A special survey, conducted by the FBI in 1960 in cities where 38 percent of the U.S. population lived, reported that about one-third of all aggravated assaults were committed by strangers.[28] But the 1970 LEAA survey showed that nearly two-thirds of rapes and aggravated assaults were committed by strangers—i.e., the victim stated that the attacker was a stranger, or that he could not identify the attacker, or that the attacker was known by sight only (see Table 3). Almost all noncommercial robberies are committed by strangers.

Table 3. Offender-Victim Relationships

| Offense [1] | Status of Offenders | |
	Previously known to victim (percent)	Stranger [2] to victim (percent)
Forcible Rape	35	65
Aggravated Assault	34	66
Noncommercial Robberies	15	85

Source: LEAA
[1] Attempts and actual offenses.
[2] Stranger means that the victim stated that the attacker was a stranger, or that he could not identify the attacker, or that the attacker was known by sight only.

Accurate information on relationships between burglars and their victims is not available, principally because burglars are rarely confronted by the persons they victimize. Many burglaries—probably a majority—are committed by habitual offenders—individuals who are involved in dozens, and in some cases hundreds, of offenses. For example, interviews with Dallas County inmates held by the Texas Department of Corrections in 1972 found that 48 repeat offenders admitted to an average of 65 burglaries per inmate.[29] Obviously, such persons are unlikely to confine their activities to residences and establishments of persons with whom they are acquainted.

The relationship of the offender to the victim for the five target crimes has important implications in selecting crime reduction strategies. This relationship takes on additional meaning when put in the context of possible changes in general social and economic conditions.

[28] UCR—1960, p. 11.
[29] Dallas Police Department, Repeat Offender Study: Summary Report (July 1972), p. 5.

Socioeconomic Changes

Every serious study of crime has noted the association between fluctuations in crime rates and changes in population, social values, and economic conditions. Among the societal conditions most frequently linked with the problem of crime are the following:
• The proportion of young people in the population.
• Metropolitan area population growth.
• Population mobility.
• Family stability.
• Income distribution.

The Commission is sure that relationships exist between crime and social justice, technological progress, and political change, although the nature of such relationships remains exceedingly ill-defined. The long-term effect of greater personal and national affluence, for example, may well depend on what type of criminal behavior is being addressed. In setting crime reduction goals, therefore, the Commission considered these two questions:

1. What significant changes will occur in society during the next decade?

2. How will societal changes affect violent crime and burglary?

The following discussion covers the factors the Commission considered most pertinent in answering these two questions.

Proportion of Young People in the Population

One important crime-related factor is the changing age structure of the population. This is especially true for young males—the group noted above as most likely both to commit crime and to be victimized by crime. Calculations made by the Commission indicate that the proportion of the population aged 15 to 24 will decrease. (See Figure 6.)

Whereas young males increased as a percentage of the total population, and in absolute numbers, during the 1960's, their group will stop increasing—indeed will actually decline in both numbers and proportion of the population—by the late 1970's. The group increased by one-third—from 6.6 percent to 9.0 percent of the population—between 1960 and 1970. Its share of the population will peak around 1976 (9.5 percent) and decrease to about 8.5 percent in 1983.[30] This is about the same level as in 1968.

[30] Calculations derived from estimates and projections published by the Bureau of the Census. The projected percentages shown here for 1976 and 1983 are the medians of the calculated percentages of the four projections used by the Bureau of the Census. See Current Population Reports, Series P-25, No. 493, "Projections of the Population of the United States, by Age and Sex: 1972 to 2020" (1972); and P-24, No. 483, "Preliminary Estimates of the Population of the United States, by Age and Sex: April 1, 1960 to July 1, 1971" (1972).

16

FIGURE 6. PERCENTAGE OF MALES, 15-24, IN POPULATION, 1960-1985

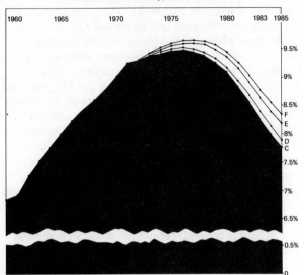

Source: Bureau of the Census.

Note: Lines F, E, D, and C are high, intermediate, and low projections of the percentage of males in the population. The median of the four projections for 1983 is about 8.5%.

A similar change will take place in the youth population as a whole, including both males and females. The 15–24 age group will stop increasing relative to the total population in about 1976 and will decline in absolute numbers beginning about 1980.

Thus, the pressures recently felt by the criminal justice system due to the unusually large numbers of youths resulting from the postwar "baby boom" will be substantially lessened during the 1970's and 1980's.

Metropolitan Area Population Growth

A quite different influence on crime may be expected from other changes in American demographic patterns in the decade ahead. Projections prepared by the National Commission on Population Growth and the American Future indicate that the United States will continue to become more urbanized over the next several decades. In 1970, about 71 percent of all Americans lived in metropolitan areas. By the year 2000, the Population Commission expects 85 percent of the population to be living in metropolitan areas. The increases in most metropolitan areas will be in suburbs rather than in central cities.[31]

While estimates of the magnitude of population changes may vary as projections are updated, the direction is clear. The population density of central cities will not change drastically, and parts of surrounding suburbs will become more dense. This is significant in light of the historical association between population density and crime rates. Robbery, burglary, and other property crime rates are considerably higher in central cities than in suburbs or rural areas. As shown in Table 2, however, violent crime and burglary rates have been rising faster in the suburbs than in central cities. It is probable that the suburbs already are beginning to feel criminogenic effects of steadily increasing urbanization.

Population Mobility

The move to urban areas will bring with it not only pressures and opportunities for antisocial behavior but also the loss of a sense of community that comes with widespread mobility.

The extent and impact of transiency in the population has been explored recently by Vance Packard, who estimates that "at least a fifth of all Americans move one or more times each year, and the pace of the movement of Americans is still increasing." He considers this widespread and constant movement to be a factor "contributing to the social fragmentation we are witnessing. . . ." [32] Pervasive movement produces rootlessness which in turn leads to a sense of anonymity that is felt by segments of large urban populations.

A lack of common experience in a crowded but transient populace makes the organization of citizen crime prevention efforts more difficult. It also hinders the development of close police-community relations.

Rootlessness or mobility may also be a factor leading to criminality. A longitudinal study of delinquent males in Philadelphia, Pa., found that one of the variables significantly associated with police contacts, especially repeated contacts, was degree of school and residential mobility—the more mobility, the more police contacts.[33] Although there may be

[31] Commission on Population Growth and the American Future, *Population and the American Future* (1972). The term "metropolitan area" refers to the Commission's definition: "Functionally integrated areas of 100,000 population or more, composed of an urbanized area or central cities of at least 50,000 people, and the surrounding counties." See also Patricia Leavey Hodge and Philip M. Hauser, *The Challenge of America's Metropolitan Population Outlook—1960-1985*, Research Report No. 3 for the National Commission on Urban Problems (1968), pp. 15-16.
[32] Vance Packard, *A Nation of Strangers* (McKay, 1972), pp. 6, 8.
[33] Marvin E. Wolfgang, Robert M. Figlio, and Thorsten Sellin, *Delinquency in a Birth Cohort* (University of Chicago Press, 1972), p. 246.

several explanations for this association, one of the most likely is that high mobility lessens ordinary community ties that restrain delinquency-prone youths from illegal acts.

In short, increasing population mobility is likely to contribute to America's crime problems during the next decade.

Family Stability

Society has long depended on the authority of the family as a major instrument of social control and thus of crime prevention. Whether it can continue to rely so strongly on the family is open to serious question. The next 10 years will probably witness declines in traditional family stability. Steeply rising trends in illegitimate births and divorces over the last 3 decades point to weaker family ties than in the past.

Income Distribution

Few developments will have greater influence on American life than changes in national income distribution. The proportion of the population in lower income brackets decreased throughout the sixties.[34] While increasing affluence is not assured, current projections are encouraging.

One analyst has estimated that by 1980 more than half of the Nation's households will have incomes of more than $10,000 a year, as against two-fifths in this

category in 1970.[35] (Estimates are in 1970 dollars.) At the same time, the proportion of households with incomes of $7,000 or below will decrease to less than one-third (see Figure 7). Thus the average will be rising and affluence will be spreading.

As these changes take place, the relationship of wealth, poverty, and crime becomes more difficult to assess. Greater affluence for the majority of the people means more valuable targets for burglary and robbery, possibly with less caution exerted by owners to protect possessions that can readily be replaced. Rising general affluence may mean that frustration and envy will in fact increase for persons in the lowest income brackets—one out of every nine families will have incomes below $3,000 a year, according to Linden's estimates—and this may lead to more attempts to supplement income by illegal acts.

On the other hand, greater affluence should mean that more citizens will have more of their basic wants

---

[34] The proportion of persons in the poverty bracket declined from 22.4 percent in 1959 to 12.6 percent in 1970, and total numbers also declined. (Bureau of the Census, *Statistical Abstract of the United States, 1972*), p. 329. There was a reversal in the trend in the year 1970 as compared with 1969. But most opinion and historical experience point to a return to the trend of declining numbers of persons living in poverty and their proportion of the population.

[35] Fabian Linden, "The Expanding Upper Income Brackets," *The Conference Board Record* (November 1971), p. 15.

FIGURE 7. THE CHANGING PYRAMID OF INCOME DISTRIBUTION
(Total households each year = 100%; based on 1970 dollars)

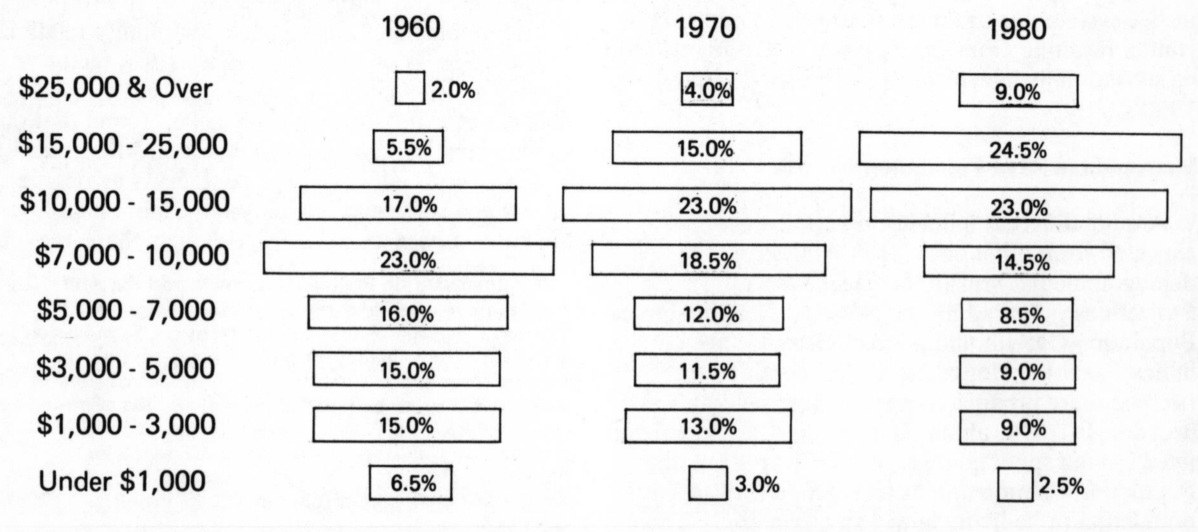

	1960	1970	1980
$25,000 & Over	2.0%	4.0%	9.0%
$15,000 - 25,000	5.5%	15.0%	24.5%
$10,000 - 15,000	17.0%	23.0%	23.0%
$7,000 - 10,000	23.0%	18.5%	14.5%
$5,000 - 7,000	16.0%	12.0%	8.5%
$3,000 - 5,000	15.0%	11.5%	9.0%
$1,000 - 3,000	15.0%	13.0%	9.0%
Under $1,000	6.5%	3.0%	2.5%

Source: Fabian Linden, "The Expanding Upper Income Brackets," The Conference Board Record (November 1971), p. 51.

satisfied than at any previous time in our Nation's history. The basic economic pressures that lead to stickups, break-ins, and violence may well be lessened.

Changes in Public Attitudes

Changes in attitudes now widely held by the American public may well affect crime in the decade ahead. How Americans feel about their lives, their jobs, their neighbors, and their government will ultimately shape society for better or worse. Two sets of attitudes—racism and lack of confidence in government—will be specifically treated here as they have been identified in other studies as critical variables in the recent rises in crime.

Frustration of Minority Aspirations

In 1969 a task force of the Violence Commission considered the paradoxical rise in crime rates in the late 1960's at the very time when inner city conditions were improving. Although substantial progress was being made toward overcoming the racial discrimination and lack of opportunity which appeared to be root causes of crime, the rates of violent crime rose faster than in the immediately

Preparing for employment day at a senior high school.

preceding years. The paradox could be ascribed, the Commission concluded, mainly to minority disappointments in the "revolution of rising expectations" and the loss of public confidence in social and political institutions.[36]

Today, 4 years after the publication of that report, there is little conclusive evidence that the country will quickly solve the problems of racial injustice and minority frustration. But neither is there evidence that the races are locked in irreconcilable conflict.

A national opinion survey on perceptions of racial discrimination conducted by the Harris organization in late 1972 showed that less than half the black respondents felt they had trouble getting into hotels and motels. About half felt their group was not discriminated against in getting quality education and entrance into labor unions. But in all the other aspects of personal and community life about which they were asked—decent housing, white-collar and skilled jobs, wages, treatment by police, and general treatment "like human beings"—considerable majorities of blacks reported feeling discrimination.[37]

Significantly, however, when compared with a survey on the same subject in 1969, fewer black respondents perceived discrimination on the job and in the community in 1972. In some areas the percentage drop was substantial. In 1969, for example, 83 percent of the black respondents felt discrimination in housing; the percentage in 1972 was 66. When two-thirds of the blacks still feel discriminated against in so important an area as housing, American society has a long way to go yet toward racial justice. But, at least in the opinion of some, progress is being made.

Another interesting point about the Harris surveys is that, in some key areas, the white residents in 1972 perceived more discrimination against blacks than they had in 1969. In the earlier year, for example, 19 percent of the whites thought blacks were discriminated against by the police; 25 percent of the whites thought so by 1972. Discrimination against blacks in housing and education was also more apparent to whites in 1972 than in 1969.

Finally, it should be mentioned that in another national survey taken in mid-1972 black respondents "were significantly *more* optimistic about their personal futures" (emphasis in original) than whites.[38]

These may appear to be small gains. But if disappointment of minorities in the revolution of

---

[36] *To Establish Justice, To Insure Domestic Tranquility*, pp. 38-43.
[37] The Harris Survey, January 15, 1973.
[38] William Watts and Lloyd A. Free (eds.), *State of the Nation* (Universe Books, 1973), p. 25.

rising expectations is a cause of violent crime, they have some importance for the future.

Whether they have permanent significance remains to be seen. The dismal heritage of years will not pass quickly. Bold and sustained government action is essential to progress.

Mistrust in Government

In contrast to the encouraging, though small, shifts in public opinion regarding racial problems, national surveys indicate that lack of public confidence in political institutions is reaching crisis proportions.

In 1970, the University of Michigan's Survey Research Center found that between one-third and one-half of those surveyed in a national sample responded affirmatively to questions asking whether they believed (1) that their government can be trusted only some of the time; (2) that the government is run for the benefit of a few big interests; and (3) that many officials are "a little crooked." [39] The percentages of respondents expressing these beliefs have increased significantly since the Center began periodic surveys in the late 1950's.

These findings are of great significance to the reduction of crime. In this society, citizens do not obey the law simply in response to threats by the authorities but because they acknowledge the right of the lawmaking institutions to lay down the rules and the right of the law enforcement agencies to enforce them. In other words, citizens recognize the legitimacy of the country's political institutions. As the Violence Commission put it, "what weakens the legitimacy of social and political institutions contributes to law-breaking, including violent crime." [40]

The findings are also discouraging in the light of the need for close cooperation between citizens and officials in crime-fighting efforts. Few citizens will long be willing to cooperate with officials whom they believe to have a hand in the till or to be "on the take" from illegal enterprise. Indeed, the impact of the Watergate problem and other aspects of the 1972 presidential election on the confidence of the people in this country in their government has yet to be assessed.

It cannot be said with certainty whether public cynicism about government is a deepening chronic malaise or whether it will abate along with the domestic turbulence of the 1960's and American military involvement in Southeast Asia. The Commission is hopeful, however, that public confidence will be restored by public leadership that is honest and fair.

Public Support for the Criminal Justice System

The fourth major factor that the Commission took into consideration in setting its goals for crime reduction in the decade ahead was public support for the criminal justice system.

In mid-1972 a national survey conducted by the Gallup organization showed that violence and crime were the domestic problems that most worried the respondents. And the respondents were willing to put their money where their worries were. A larger proportion of them were willing to approve government spending to combat crime than spending for any other activity, including air and water pollution, education, and mass transportation. [41]

As a matter of fact, the share of the Gross National Product (GNP) devoted to expenditures for the criminal justice system has been rising steadily for nearly 20 years. From 1955 to 1965, criminal justice expenditures rose from one-half to two-thirds of 1 percent of GNP, with an average annual increase of about one-hundredth of 1 percent. By 1971 criminal justice expenditures had risen to approximately 1 percent of GNP, with an estimated annual increase since 1966 of more than five times that shown in the 1955–65 period. [42] Although percentage increases have undoubtedly been influenced by expanded Federal spending, all levels of government have spent more for the criminal justice system. Preliminary estimates by the Law Enforcement Assistance Administration and the Bureau of the Census indicated total spending of $10,513,358,000 for 1971. [43]

The other major evidence of public support for the criminal justice system lies in the increasing participation of citizens in the operation of the system. No hard statistics are available, but, beginning in the late 1960's, there was an upsurge of citizen activity directly aimed at reducing crime. This took the form of working for better streetlighting, setting up neighborhood security programs, and other activities. Hundreds of local projects emerged

[39] "Election Time Series Analysis of Attitudes of Trust in Government" (Center for Political Studies, University of Michigan, 1971).

[40] *To Establish Justice, To Insure Domestic Tranquility,* p. 42.

[41] Discussed in Watts and Free (eds.), *State of the Nation,* pp. 35, 117-118. Interestingly, the means most favored to reduce crime was "to clean up the slums." Improvements in the criminal justice system received from one-third ("more police") to two-thirds ("improve jails") the number of mentions made of slum clean-up.

[42] Data from *Statistical Abstract of the United States* for appropriate years.

[43] "Expenditure and Employment Data for the Criminal Justice System, 1970-1971" (LEAA, unpublished).

in communities across the country. Citizen participation is one of the Commission's priorities for action, and it will be discussed in detail in this chapter. The reader should also refer to the chapters on community crime prevention and on corrections, as well as to the separate reports on these subjects.

NEW METHODS IN MEASURING PROGRESS

The establishment of crime-specific goals is a meaningless exercise if the rate of progress cannot be accurately assessed. One factor in the Commission's conclusions, therefore, was the ability to measure crime.

There are now two tools for measuring national crime rates: the UCR compiled annually by the FBI, and the national victimization survey developed by LEAA.

The UCR has the inherent limitation of being based on reports from police departments. Hence it includes only those crimes known to the police.

Victimization surveys made since 1966 in various cities indicate that at least half of all crimes against persons and property are not reported to the police. Moreover, there have been findings that police departments have not recorded fully the extent of crimes that are reported by citizens, or have not accurately classified and defined reported offenses.[44] Consequently, the victimization survey is widely believed to give a more precise estimate of the volume of crime and other dimensions of criminal activity, such as cost, than the UCR.

Automated police want/warrant system.

LEAA, in conjunction with the Bureau of the Census, is now conducting an annual victimization survey of a representative national sample of households and commercial establishments.[45] Local data will be provided by supplemental sample surveys in about 35 of the Nation's largest cities. These local surveys will be updated periodically. For the five largest cities—New York, Chicago, Los Angeles, Philadelphia, and Detroit—survey information will be provided biennially.

The surveys, which are expected to continue under Federal auspices, should provide a fairly reliable estimate of the true level of rape, aggravated and simple assault, robbery, burglary, larceny, and auto theft. Attempted crimes will be counted as well as crimes actually committed.

Homicide will not be included in the LEAA victimization survey. There is, however, probably little disparity between the actual incidence of homicide and that recorded by police.

In the case of rape, the resulting picture from victimization surveys may not be as clear as for other offenses, owing to the reluctance of victims to identify incidents. However, the interview technique may be more successful in eliciting information than the official reporting process. Discreet and indirect approaches to the incident are expected to overcome a good deal of the reporting problem. The fact that rapes are comparatively small in number will undoubtedly mean that it will take longer to establish a significantly reliable measure of change for this offense than for others which occur with far greater frequency.

The LEAA survey will ascertain the amount of property lost and recovered, attitudes toward police, fear, age and race characteristics of offenders, place of occurrence, and weapons used by assailants. Unlike UCR statistics, the LEAA survey will indicate offender-victim relationships. This will make it possible to measure progress towards reducing "high-fear" (stranger-related) crime which the Commission has set forth as a national goal.

In sum, the LEAA survey will make it possible to

[44] The usefulness of officially reported crime statistics has been widely debated. Doubts have been expressed as to how accurately UCR data can show the extent of and changes in crime. After careful study, a task force of the Violence Commission concluded, "For individual acts of violence covered by national police statistics, limitations on the accuracy of the data are apparent." Such limitations affect understanding of the levels, trends, incidence, and severity of crime. Mulvihill and Tumin, *Crimes of Violence,* pp. 16-38.

[45] The survey is described in detail in the Commission's *Report on the Criminal Justice System,* Appendix A. Information for the present brief description was also supplied by the National Criminal Justice Information and Statistics Service in LEAA.

achieve a more precise record of the volume and rate of crime. The first complete annual picture of victimization will emerge for 1973. Preliminary tabulations of annual survey results will be available approximately 8 months after the end of each year.

It should be noted that victimization surveys also present some problems. First, victimization surveys may be interpreted as showing an increase in crime. The data should show higher numbers and rates of crime than the public is accustomed to reading and hearing. This is attributable to greater accuracy, but citizens may find it difficult to distinguish between accuracy in reporting and actual increases in crime.

Second, victimization surveys are expensive. Therefore reliance on victimization surveys to assess national progress cannot mean discarding traditional police statistics. Surveys are too costly to be run on a continuous basis by LEAA in every jurisdiction.

Most States and localities will have to continue to rely on official police statistics to determine directions of change in their crime rates. Even those cities that are surveyed yearly by LEAA will need to use information on crimes known and reported to the police. Such data are essential to effective allocation of police manpower. They are an irreplaceable indicator of the extent to which citizens are willing to bring crimes to the attention of police. Unlike the LEAA victimization survey, most police departments do not collect statistics on offender-victim relationships. The Commission, however, urges that departments expand their statistical coverage to do so.

It is unrealistic to expect any measure of crime to be 100 percent accurate. Victimization surveys should be useful in evaluating reported crime statistics and vice versa. Not only will such cross-comparisons lead to more accurate data, but they should also encourage public confidence in official estimates of the crime problem. A lessening of public debate as to whether crime has gone up or down in the Nation and communities may be a byproduct of the development of victimization surveys.

A LOOK AHEAD WITH PRIORITIES FOR ACTION

The crime reduction goals proposed in the preceding pages are not the result of using some heretofore unknown formula. Nor were they the result of abstract or wishful thinking. They were decided upon after considering the nature of the target crimes and some of the social and governmental developments—past and future—that

will affect them. The Commission believes that reductions of the magnitude proposed are not unrealistic.

The Commission was led to this belief by the several signs discussed above, signs that point to the possibility of reducing the priority crimes. Among them are the probable reduction in the proportion of the population who are in the crime-prone 15-to-24 age bracket. Increasing national prosperity is an encouraging sign if it eliminates absolute poverty. Recent formation of citizen crime-prevention organizations and public willingness to approve increased government spending for the criminal justice system also augur well for progress toward the goal of reducing crime.

Among the priority crimes of murder, rape, assault, robbery, and burglary, the Commission has concluded that the greatest reduction is most likely to occur in the rates of the latter two. These differ in several key ways from the other priority offenses. Robbery and burglary are acquisitive crimes, committed for material gain, and often they are calculated and planned carefully. Usually, they are committed by persons who are strangers to the victims. They occur in environments that can be altered to reduce the opportunities open to the criminal. Large numbers of burglaries and robberies are vulnerable to relatively easily implemented deterrent strategies: police patrols, street lighting, citizen crime prevention activities, and speedy and effective court dispositions.

In addition, the Commission is convinced that society and the criminal justice system are capable of directing many delinquent youths and ex-offenders to lawful avenues of economic gain so that the attraction of the "easy money" of holdups and break-ins will be less important.

In short, there are solid grounds for optimism in deterring the acts themselves and in reducing the potential number of offenders.

The fact that the Commission has set lower percentage goals for reducing murder, assault, and rape does not mean that they are less important. Indeed, murder, rape, and assault are probably feared by the average citizen more than any other crimes.

The proposed percentage of reduction is lower for these so-called crimes of passion because they are less easily controlled than the other target crimes by conventional criminal justice methods. Many of these crimes are committed by acquaintances and are impervious to ordinary deterrent strategies. Victims of assault and homicide frequently show little inclination to avoid criminal attacks. Indeed, they often incite assailants by their own speech and actions. Alcohol—a drug that has proved consistently resistant to efforts to lessen its abuse—is an important catalyst in homicides, assaults, and, to a lesser extent, rapes. To reduce these crimes, a change in values is needed—an increased respect for others and a willingness to settle disputes by means other than violence.

The Commission proposes four priorities for action for reducing all of the target crimes. These are:
- Preventing juvenile delinquency.
- Improving delivery of social services.
- Reducing delays in the criminal justice process.
- Securing more citizen participation in the criminal justice system.

The Commission submits that many of the standards set forth in subsequent chapters are easily categorized within these priorities and lead to the accomplishment of the numerical goals established earlier in this chapter.

Priority: Preventing Juvenile Delinquency

The highest attention must be given to preventing juvenile delinquency, to minimizing the involvement of young offenders in the juvenile and criminal justice system, and to reintegrating delinquents and young offenders into the community. By 1983 the rate of delinquency cases coming before courts that would be crimes if committed by adults should be cut to half the 1973 rate.

Street crime is a young man's game. More than half the persons arrested for violent crime in 1971 were under 24 years of age, with one-fifth under 18. For burglary, over half of the 1971 arrests involved youths under 18.[46]

There is strong evidence that the bulk of ordinary crime against person and property is committed by youths and adults who have had previous contact with the criminal justice or juvenile justice system. Recent evidence in support of this assumption is a study of delinquency in all males born in 1945 who lived in Philadelphia from their 10th to their 18th birthdays. Specifically the study concluded that the more involvement a juvenile had with the police and juvenile justice authorities, the more likely he would be to be further involved.[47] Of the 9,945 subjects, 3,475 (35 percent) came in contact with police at least once. Of this delinquent group, about 54 percent had more than one contact with police. This 54 percent was responsible for 84 percent of all police contacts in the group. Eighteen percent of those having repeated contact with the police had

five or more contacts and were responsible for 52 percent of all police contacts in the delinquent group.

Increased efforts must be made to break this cycle of recidivism at the earliest possible point. One approach is to minimize the involvement of the offender in the criminal justice system. Minimized involvement is not a fancy phrase for "coddling criminals." It means simply that society should use that means of controlling and supervising the young offender which will best serve to keep him out of the recidivism cycle and at the same time protect the community. It is based on an easily justified assumption: the further an offender penetrates into the criminal justice process, the more difficult it becomes to divert him from a criminal career.

People tend to learn from those closest to them. It is small wonder that prisons and jails crowded with juveniles, first offenders, and hardened criminals have been labeled "schools of crime."

People also tend to become what they are told they are. The stigma of involvement with the criminal justice system, even if only in the informal processes of juvenile justice, isolates persons from lawful society and may make further training or employment difficult. A recent survey conducted for the Department of Labor revealed that an arrest record was an absolute bar to employment in almost 20 percent of the State and local agencies surveyed and was a definite consideration for not hiring in most of the remaining agencies.[48]

For many youths, as noted above, incarceration is not an effective tool of correction. Society will be better protected if certain individuals, particularly youths and first offenders, are diverted prior to formal conviction either to the care of families or relatives or to employment, mental health, and other social service programs. Thus a formal arrest is inappropriate if the person may be referred to the charge of a responsible parent, guardian, or agency. Formal adjudication may not be necessary if an offender can be safely diverted elsewhere, as to a youth services bureau for counseling or a drug abuse program for treatment. Offenders properly selected for pretrial diversion experience less recidivism than those with similar histories and social backgrounds who are formally adjudicated.

To assure progress toward the goal of minimizing the involvement of juveniles in the juvenile justice system, the Commission proposes that the 1973 rate of delinquency cases disposed of by juvenile or family courts for offenses that would be crimes if committed by adults be cut in half by 1983.

---

[46] UCR—1971, p. 121.

[47] Wolfgang, Figlio, and Sellin, *Delinquency in a Birth Cohort*, chs. 6, 14.

[48] Herbert S. Miller, *The Closed Door: The Effect of a Criminal Record on Employment with State and Local Public Agencies,* report prepared for the U.S. Department of Labor (February 1972), p. 100.

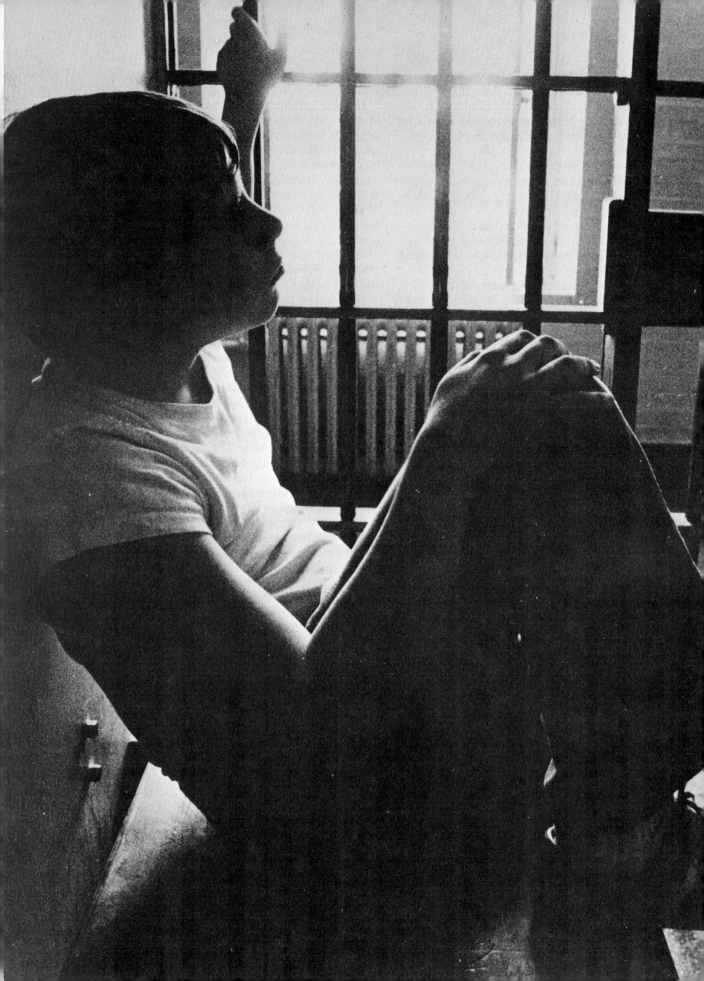

The Department of Health, Education, and Welfare, which collects information on juvenile courts, estimates that a little less than 40 percent of cases disposed of by courts are cases of running away, truancy, and other offenses that would not be crimes if committed by an adult.[49] These are the so-called juvenile status offenses.

The remaining 60-odd percent of cases estimated to be disposed of by juvenile or family courts are nonstatus crimes, those that would be crimes if committed by adults. It is the rate of these cases which the Commission would propose to cut in half.

Meeting the goal, the Commission believes, should result in significant decreases in crime through preventing recidivism and might also prove to be far less costly than dealing with delinquents under present methods. To process a youth through the juvenile justice system and keep him in a training school for a year costs almost $6,000.[50] There is no reason to believe that the cost of a diversionary program would exceed this figure, since most such programs are not residential. Indeed, diversion might prove to provide significant savings.

One final note should be added. Minimizing a youth's involvement with the criminal justice system does not mean abandoning the use of confinement for certain individuals. Until more effective means of treatment are found, chronic and dangerous delinquents and offenders should be incarcerated to protect society. But the juvenile justice system must search for the optimum programs outside institutions for juveniles who do not need confinement.

Priority: Improving Delivery of Social Services

Public agencies should improve the delivery of all social services to citizens, particularly to those groups that contribute higher than average proportions of their numbers to crime statistics.

There is abundant evidence that crime occurs with greater frequency where there are poverty, illiteracy, and unemployment, and where medical, recreational, and mental health resources are inadequate. When unemployment rates among youths in poverty areas of central cities are almost 40 percent and crime is prevalent, it is impossible not to draw conclusions about the relationship between jobs and crime. The Commission believes that effective and responsive delivery of public services that promote individual and economic well-being will contribute to a

---

[49] Estimates from U.S. Department of Health, Education, and Welfare.

[50] Derived from "Youth Service System: Diverting Youth from the Juvenile Justice System," paper prepared by the U.S. Department of Health, Education, and Welfare.

reduction in crime. The rationale for the value of a variety of services is well expressed in the Commission's *Report on Community Crime Prevention*. Having called for citizen action on such priorities as employment, education, and recreation, the report points out:

> This is not to say that if everyone were better educated or more fully employed that crime would be eliminated or even sharply reduced. What is meant is that unemployment, substandard education, and so on, form a complex, and admittedly little understood amalgam of social conditions that cements, or at least predisposes, many individuals to criminal activity.
>
> Thus a job, for example, is just one wedge to break this amalgam. Increased recreational opportunities represent another. Though one wedge may not have much effect on an individual's lifestyle, two or three might.

The Commission is aware that improvement of social services to a degree necessary to have an impact on crime will take time. Building career education programs into elementary and secondary school curriculums, for example, cannot be accomplished in the next 2 or 3 years. But it must begin now if society is to realize benefits at the end of 10 years and beyond.

The Commission particularly wishes to call attention to the provision of drug and alcohol abuse treatment. Communities must recognize the diversity of drug abuse and alcohol problems and the need for a number of alternative treatment approaches. Citizens must be willing to make the investment that such treatment requires, not merely because it will reduce crime but because adequate treatment is essential to deal with an increasingly serious national health problem.

Priority: Reducing Delays in the Criminal Justice Process

Delays in the adjudication and disposition of cases must be greatly reduced and the period between arrest and trial must be reduced to the shortest possible time.

In recent years, backlogs in the courts have become a well-publicized symbol of inefficiency in the entire system. In large cities, many cases have been subject to delays of 300 to 1,000 days from arrest to trial and final disposition. Legislatures and other parts of the criminal justice system, as well as judges, defense attorneys, and prosecutors, must bear some of the responsibility for the problem. Delay in the criminal justice process frustrates law enforcement efforts and develops a sense of injustice in offender, victim, and citizen alike.

The negative byproducts of judicial delay are many. The number of defendants incarcerated and

awaiting trial is reaching alarming proportions in many large cities, and detention facilities are dangerously overcrowded. The LEAA National Jail Census in 1970 revealed that 52 percent of the jail inmates were awaiting trial.[51] Pretrial incarceration is costly to the individual, for it denies him income and, in fact, may cause him to lose his job. Extended incarceration resulting from judicial delay is also costly to the public, since pretrial detainees must be fed and supervised.

Alternatives to incarceration such as bail and release on recognizance present another set of problems in cases of long delays between arrest and trial. A 1968 survey in the District of Columbia found ". . . an increased propensity to be rearrested where the release period extends more than 280 days." [52]

The pressures of heavy backlogs contribute to the notorious practice of plea bargaining. Faced with an overwhelming caseload, prosecutors seek to avoid time-consuming trials by disposing of felony indictments through negotiated guilty pleas to less serious felonies and misdemeanors. Whether viewed from a rehabilitation or deterrence perspective, workload-motivated plea bargaining is an undesirable practice that can be gradually eliminated if accompanied by less burdensome court backlogs.

Speeding up the criminal justice process may not reduce crime by itself, but when coupled with effective treatment alternatives and intelligent correctional decisions, it should have a significant impact. Additional judges will undoubtedly be needed in many jurisdictions, but much can be done to improve the adjudicatory process by streamlining court procedures.

Priority: Increasing Citizen Participation

Citizens should actively participate in activities to control crime in their community, and criminal justice agencies should actively encourage citizen participation.

The criminal justice system depends on citizen participation. Most crimes do not come directly to the attention of police; they are reported by citizens. Without active cooperation of citizen jurors and witnesses, the judicial process cannot function. Institutional education and training programs will not be useful to the offender if he cannot find

employment in the community in which he is released. The best-trained and equipped police force will fare poorly in the battle against crime if the citizens it serves do not take basic precautionary measures to protect themselves and reduce criminal opportunities.

Citizens in many communities are organizing to form block crime prevention associations and court-watching groups, and to furnish volunteers to work in the criminal justice system. One striking example is a nationwide program that began with the involvement of a few citizens in Royal Oak, Mich. The Volunteers in Probation program grew from eight citizens in 1959 to an estimated quarter of a million nationwide in 1972.

The Royal Oak concept utilized volunteers and professionals together and statistics indicate that volunteers and professionals working together can provide intensive probation services that are three times more effective than those provided by a probation officer working alone.[53]

Citizen cooperation with police also has great potential, but it is largely unrealized. In 1970, 18 percent of the households in America took some form of home protection—special locks, lights, alarms, watch dogs, and/or weapons.[54] Whether the measures adopted were the most effective that could have been chosen is another matter. Certainly every police department could perform a useful service by actively disseminating its crime-prevention knowledge to citizens. It is not necessary to sell self-protection to many persons, certainly not to those who have been victimized before. Yet, in many jurisdictions, aggressive outreach programs for crime prevention are nonexistent. The Police chapter of this report identifies in greater detail what some departments have done in this area.

All criminal justice agencies can do much in their operations to encourage citizens' involvement. They first must organize their operations to increase acceptability to the citizens they serve and to encourage these citizens to support their activities. This means, for example, that police must process complaints efficiently and courteously; that courts must minimize the time lost by jurors and witnesses; that corrections must run its institutions to permit the community reasonable access to those incarcerated. These are minimums. Criminal justice agencies can do much more, if they actively seek to explain their role to citizens' groups and show how citizens themselves may participate in

[51] Law Enforcement Assistance Administration, *1970 National Jail Census* (1971) p. 1.

[52] J. W. Locke and others, *Compilation and Use of Criminal Court Data in Relation to Pre-Trial Release of Defendant: Pilot Study Report* (National Bureau of Standards, 1970), p. v.

Youth learning welding at a Job Corps center.

[53] Information from project director, Judge Keith Leenhouts, Sept. 11, 1972. For details on the Royal Oak project, see the Commission's *Report on Community Crime Prevention*, chapter on Citizen Action.

[54] Data from LEAA 1970 Survey.

community crime prevention. Above all, criminal justice agencies must understand and know the communities they serve. Active personnel recruitment from all facets of the community is essential if citizens and the criminal justice system are to work together as a team.

CONCLUSION

This chapter has dealt with the Commission's research and findings involving the factors affecting the reduction of crime.

In succeeding chapters of this book, the Commission proposes its broad outline for action by State and local units of government and by citizens to reduce crime.

In addition, the complete standards and recommendations of the Commission are set out in its volumes on *Criminal Justice System, Police, Courts, Corrections,* and *Community Crime Prevention.*

Chapter 3

Toward A System Of Criminal Justice

"Fragmented," "divided," "splintered," and "decentralized" are the adjectives most commonly used to describe the American system of criminal justice.

The sheer number of independent agencies is the most visible evidence of fragmentation. According to a 1970 survey, there are 46,197 public agencies in the criminal justice system that are administered at the State or local government level in towns of over 1,000 population. Most States have hundreds of criminal justice agencies. For example, in Wisconsin, a medium-sized State whose criminal justice structure is typical of other States, there are 1,075 separate criminal justice agencies. These include 458 law enforcement agencies, 221 courts, 197 prosecution offices, five defenders' offices, 98 adult and juvenile corrections departments, 72 probation offices, and 24 other criminal-justice-related agencies.[1]

Words such as fragmented and divided, however, refer not only to demarcations in authority, but to differences in states of mind, and not only to physical distances, but to distances in philosophy and outlook.

In a recent study of conflict within a large urban criminal justice system, police, courts, and

[1] Law Enforcement Assistance Administration, *Criminal Justice Agencies in Wisconsin* (1972), pp. 1, 10.

Communications center in a large city police department.

corrections personnel were asked what problems were caused for them by other criminal justice agencies. A sample of the responses reveals the different perspectives of those interviewed.

• Criticisms of law enforcement: "Police are disrespectful and tend to harass parolees." "Most of them believe in a police state and if one doesn't agree with their values, etc., they classify that person as the enemy."

• Criticisms of the public defender: "Excessive use of technical legal points to free an obviously guilty person." "Oftentimes this agency will attempt to stall a case by using questionable techniques in court."

• Criticisms of city and district attorneys: "Tend to overcharge by filing too many charges of greater severity than offense calls for." "Go it alone attitude —entire division created for juvenile justice work with no discussion or involvement of probation people."

• Criticisms of municipal and superior courts: "The sentences have little or no relation to the crimes charged." "Entirely too many cases dismissed due to minor technicalities."

• Criticisms of departments of corrections and probation: "They take a soft approach to criminals." "Has no real rehabilitation—sends problems back to the community."

These perceptions are not surprising. Criminal justice agencies are highly dependent upon one another. What particular law enforcement, courts, and corrections agencies do in handling offenders and processing information affects all the rest. Yet attorneys, patrolmen, and corrections officers frequently have quite different on-the-job experiences, constitutional responsibilities, educational backgrounds, professional objectives, and social class origins.

In addition, crime is an emotional issue. Its causes and solutions are the subject of intense disagreement among police, courts, and correctional personnel. General consensus among professionals can rarely be reached on basic questions such as:
• Which crime problems should receive greater criminal justice attention? Which ones should receive less?
• Which criminal offenses should be removed from the books? Which ones should be added?
• Which arrestees should be diverted before trial? Which ones should not?
• Which offenders should be channeled into community-based corrections? Which ones should not?
• Which aspects of the criminal justice process need to be improved immediately? Which ones can afford deferred action?

Lack of agreement on answers to these basic questions presents criminal justice with its most difficult dilemma. If criminal justice professionals cannot reach a consensus on what to do about crime and criminals, it is unrealistic to expect the public and political leaders to do so. The most enduring problems facing the criminal justice system are not technical or financial—they are political. The consequences of lack of professional agreement are deadlock, inaction, and confusion in making public policy.

MAJOR RECOMMENDATIONS

Discussed in this chapter are three concerns common to the total criminal justice system: criminal justice planning, criminal justice information systems, and criminal justice education. Major recommendations call for:
• Development by States of a general system of multiyear criminal justice planning.
• Establishment of criminal justice coordinating councils by all major cities and counties.
• Creation by each State of an organizational structure for coordinating the development of criminal justice information systems.
• Establishment by each State of a Security and

Privacy Council to oversee security and privacy of information contained in criminal justice information systems.
• Establishment of strict security and privacy procedures to protect the integrity of criminal history files.
• Establishment by agencies of higher education of criminal justice system curriculums and programs to prepare persons to work in the criminal justice systems.

Action on the Commission's standards in each of these areas should bring greater consensus on common goals and priorities. Another byproduct should be more meaningful relations in the day-to-day contact among police officers, judges, defense attorneys, prosecutors, and corrections officers.

The areas of planning, information systems, and education are crossroads at which the various components of the criminal justice system come together. They present joint endeavors that can assist professionals in overcoming the unnecessary friction that currently characterizes the system.

CRIMINAL JUSTICE PLANNING

A community has received $250,000 in additional funds for law enforcement and crime prevention purposes. How should this money be spent?

In an urban city, it will pay for 10 policemen for 1 year, including salaries, uniforms, training, equipment, overhead, and fringe benefits. The same money would pay for eight new prosecutors together with their necessary support services. It might also pay for 3 months of special training in prerelease centers for each of 120 offenders or pay for an entire year of noninstitutional aftercare for 70 people in the system. The same money might greatly aid narcotics treatment centers, or maintain for 1 year two or three youth services bureaus that provide help for delinquent and troubled youth.

With such highly diverse alternatives as those discussed above, it is exceedingly difficult for executives, budget chiefs, and legislators to make intelligent choices.

The decisionmaking process, however, can be made more rational by improved planning techniques. The Commission recommends:
• Multiyear planning in each State, taking into account all available Federal, State, and local resources.
• Metropolitan area coordinating councils to plan across county and city boundaries.
• Expanded membership from non-criminal-justice sources on criminal justice planning councils.

Chief Justice Warren E. Burger speaks at the National Conference on the Judiciary in 1971.

• Formalized exchanges of ideas and personnel between planning and operating agencies.

State Planning Under the Law Enforcement Assistance Program

In the past 4 years, a beginning has been made toward establishing a network of institutions that will define appropriate goals and crime control strategies for State and local criminal justice activities. The Omnibus Crime Control and Safe Streets Act of 1968 requires each State wishing to receive Federal law enforcement assistance funds to create a State Criminal Justice Planning Agency (SPA) and to develop an annual State comprehensive plan.

Upon approval of the comprehensive plan by the Law Enforcement Assistance Administration, a block action grant is awarded. The grants are called block action because they are awarded as a lump sum rather than on a categorical program-by-program basis, and because they provide direct support to State and local police, courts, corrections, and other criminal justice programs. Smaller "block planning" grants also are awarded to support the planning and grant administration efforts of the SPA's and whatever regional planning councils the SPA's establish.

Since the passage of the Safe Streets Act, all 50 States, American Samoa, Guam, the District of Columbia, Puerto Rico, and the Virgin Islands have established SPA's. Overseeing the policymaking of the SPA's are supervisory boards whose members represent State and local criminal justice offices, citizen groups, and non-criminal-justice public agencies. Although an SPA director is administratively responsible to his Governor, the comprehensive plan that he and his staff have designed usually must be approved by the SPA supervisory board. In most cases the Governor formally appoints members of the SPA supervisory board and the boards of any regional planning councils the State might establish.

The States have been receiving planning and action grants in increasingly larger amounts. In 1969, $43.65 million was made available to the States. In 1972, this had increased to $497.44 million in planning and action grants.[2]

Criminal justice is still an activity funded primarily through State and local sources.[3] The Federal block grant contribution is far less than 10 percent of the combined State and local criminal justice expenditures, which in 1971 totaled $9,302.23 million.

The actual funds received from the Federal Government under the Safe Streets Act may be less important in the long run than the stimulus the Act provided to criminal justice planning. For the first time, State governments have a staff arm for closely examining criminal justice problems from a systemwide perspective. In a number of States, SPA's are becoming useful instruments for policy analysis and comprehensive reform.

In Nebraska, for example, the legislature's Judiciary Committee and the Nebraska Crime Commission (SPA) in 1971 cooperated in the examination of such problems as court reform, law enforcement consolidation, changes in bail practices, and prison and parole reform. In Kentucky, in 1972, the SPA recommended to the General Assembly a 12-point legislative package that included: revision of the criminal laws, State support of police educational and training incentives, authorization of work and educational release for misdemeanants and felons, and establishment of a public defender system. Much of the recommended legislation subsequently was passed.

While SPA activities such as those described above are signs of emerging planning capabilities, the role of SPA's as conduits for Federal funds has received the most attention in the press and in the halls of Congress. Faced with the need in the late 1960's and early 1970's to provide operating agencies with the resources to deal with crime, many SPA's became preoccupied with funding.

[2] Source: LEAA.
[3] Source: Bureau of the Census and LEAA.

Due to a variety of intergovernmental problems, in the first 3 years of the Safe Streets Act program SPA's experienced great difficulty in disbursing their action grants to State and local police, courts, corrections, and other criminal justice agencies. Data released in 1972 indicate time lags of more than a year between congressional appropriation and SPA disbursement of funds in some instances. At the end of fiscal year 1972, for example, 10.2 percent and 47.9 percent of the block action funds appropriated during fiscal years 1970 and 1971, respectively, still had not been disbursed.[4]

SPA's were attacked by critics of the Safe Streets Act program for disbursing funds too slowly. They also were criticized for not establishing adequate fiscal controls for the awarding of subgrants. Specific instances of mismanagement of funds by SPA's led to congressional charges of inefficiency and waste. In more than one SPA, fiscal control personnel replaced planners, as executive directors acted to insure the financial integrity of their programs.

As attention to the funding role of the SPA's increased, the concept of total criminal justice planning was given a low priority by both LEAA, which required plans for Safe Streets funds, and by the States that produced them. Within guidelines furnished by LEAA, SPA's produced weighty and lengthy volumes that often had questionable information value for the executive, legislator, administrator, technician, and concerned citizen. A major deficiency of the plans to date is their frequent inability to address the question of State and local agency priorities for reducing crime. States have just begun to define their crime problems and make decisions about the patterns of criminal activity in their jurisdiction. A Commission staff survey of the 1972 plans revealed that:

• Four States did not cite any crime statistics in their plans.
• Only 19 States cited data in their plans on the nature and extent of juvenile delinquency. These data usually were based on either police arrests or referrals to juvenile court.
• Many States did not cite common criminal justice performance statistics that relate to crime control; e.g., apprehension rates, recidivism rates, and court processing rates.

The absence of basic crime-oriented statistics in formal planning documents raises questions as to whether many SPA's see themselves as planners or simply grant administrators. A quantitative assessment of State crime problems and criminal justice system response is an obvious first step in even the most basic planning process.

---

[4] Source: LEAA.

A second deficiency of the plans is that they generally attempt only to specify what use will be made of the funds available from LEAA and other Federal sources. In its 1972 planning grant application to LEAA, the Wisconsin Council on Criminal Justice succinctly stated the problem:

A reality that the Safe Streets planning concept does not take into account . . . is that Safe Streets funds represent only a small fraction of local government moneys available for law enforcement improvement. Regional plans [and state plans] cannot be realistic until the improvement strategy takes into account revenue for law enforcement improvement from all sources inclusive of local and state moneys.

If criminal justice planning is to have full impact upon the system, the scope of planning needs to be broadened to include the entire budgetary picture for criminal justice at the State and local levels.

The Commission recommends that SPA's develop by 1978 a general system of multiyear planning that takes into account all funds directed to crime control activities within the State.

This system would include all sources of Federal funds as well as State general and capital funds; State subsidy funds to local governments; local government funds; and private donations, endowments, and contributions.

Under a broadened planning process, proposed statewide changes in criminal justice programs would be analyzed and set forth by SPA's for Governors, legislators, budget directors, agency heads, local officials, and the public. Priority problems calling for significant changes in State policy would receive special staff attention. Consideration of funding sources would not be limited to Safe Streets money.

Such a planning process would have several benefits. A truly comprehensive multiyear plan for criminal justice would make planning, programing, and budgeting more visible. It would encourage much needed question-asking by legislators and the press. It would provide a statement of crime-oriented goals and standards to which the public could hold elected leaders accountable. A multiyear plan would provide a reference point for budget and appropriations decisions.

Presently, the Michigan Council on Criminal Justice (SPA) is developing an expanded formal planning process. While it may take several annual cycles to define it, the Michigan objective is to develop a multiyear plan for the prevention, control, and reduction of crime and delinquency in the State to be carried out through the allocation of resources at the Federal, State, and local levels as well as through private resources. The experience in Michigan may provide a useful case study for other States.

Metropolitan and Regional Planning

The systemwide perspective that SPA's can provide at the State level must also be provided at the local level. Large cities and counties in most States now are receiving direct planning money either from the State or from regional planning councils. A movement toward local criminal justice coordinating councils (CJCC's) has taken place in large metropolitan areas. A main objective of these CJCC's is to plan and coordinate local criminal justice activities. Many CJCC's receive Safe Streets assistance. At the end of 1971, 33 of 50 of the Nation's largest cities had CJCC's.

CJCC's are creations of local government. They may derive formal authority from a resolution or ordinance adopted by the city council and/or county board of supervisors, or from an executive order by the mayor and/or the county chief executive. On the other hand, CJCC's may operate informally at the request of the mayor and/or the county chief executive and by the agreement of the various participating agencies.[5]

Usually headed by local chief executives, CJCC's are more than mere funnels of Safe Streets funds. With broad-based representation of various elements of the criminal justice system and competent staffs, they can suggest and plan for programs that have nothing to do with Federal funding.

The oldest and one of the most successful CJCC's is that of New York, N.Y. Planning is accomplished through a 74-member council comprised of representatives of the criminal justice system, other public agencies, and citizens, and a 16-member executive committee headed by the mayor. A staff of 20 professionals supports the council's activities. The NYCJCC has been designated by the State as the regional planning council for New York City, and administers State and Federal subgrants and grants. It also submits proposed legislation to the State legislators. It engages in program development with every agency in the city that bears directly upon criminal justice and the levels of crime. Acting as an occasional mediator in interagency conflicts, it permits police, prosecutors, and corrections officials to plan for the effects of one part of the system upon another.

The primary purpose of CJCC's is to coordinate local criminal justice planning efforts, and to serve as a staff for local authorities by exploring alternatives for crime control programing. In New York City, for example, the local jail was overcrowded. The

---

[5] National League of Cities and United States Conference of Mayors, *Criminal Justice Coordinating Councils* (1971), p. 3.

CJCC analyzed the costs and benefits of various alternatives including construction of a new facility, release-on-recognizance projects, diversion projects, and speed-up of court processing. The research done by the CJCC and the consideration given to this research by the mayor and city council were critical in making an informed decision.

CJCC's may assume additional responsibilities such as reviewing and planning for Safe Streets funds from the State and the Federal Government. As with any local agency they would be subject to statewide regulations and legislation. CJCC's are no longer experimental institutions, but essential parts of the criminal justice system.

The Commission recommends that all major cities and counties establish criminal justice coordinating councils under the leadership of local chief executives.

Metropolitan cities and counties should be encouraged to consolidate criminal justice planning and coordinating operations. In metropolitan areas with a population of more than 250,000, a criminal justice planning office should be established with a minimum of one full-time position for a professional planner to aid chief executives and the CJCC in developing priorities and programs.

Participation in the Planning Process

Criminal justice planning must reach beyond traditional police, courts, and corrections processes. Crime control requires participation by persons who are not criminal justice practitioners. It is important to have the involvement of locally elected officials, non-criminal-justice public agencies, labor unions, business associations, and citizen groups.

The participation of minority members on planning agency supervisory boards and councils is also critical. Boards that wish to concentrate efforts on urban street crime cannot afford noninvolvement or mere token involvement of minority populations, since these groups contribute disproportionately to both offender and victim statistics.

Criminal justice planning agencies and councils should seek the participation of criminal justice operating agencies, government departments, and private citizens and groups in the planning process.

The Commission recommends that at least one-third of the membership of State and local planning agency supervisory boards and councils be from officials of non-criminal-justice agencies and from private citizens.

Many boards of SPA's already reflect a

non-criminal-justice emphasis. A 1971 internal LEAA survey indicated that 22 States had more than one-third of their board membership from non-criminal-justice sources.

The concept of participation should also be extended to operating agencies. It serves no purpose to establish a superstructure of State and local criminal justice planners if police departments, prosecutors, public defender offices, courts, and corrections systems do not themselves take part in planning. Planning must begin from the ground up. Setting goals and priorities, developing programs, and defining performance measures must be undertaken in the greatest detail at the agency level.

In a number of States, law enforcement, courts, and corrections agencies are invited by the SPA to submit their positions on the development of needs and priorities for the State plan. The agency submissions are reviewed by the SPA and, where appropriate, are incorporated into the plan.

To avoid being insulated from concerns of other parts of the criminal justice system, operating agencies and planning agencies have initiated temporary staff exchanges. Exchanged personnel contribute to the spread of new ideas and innovation throughout the system. The NYCJCC, for example, has drawn upon various criminal justice agencies in developing its plans and programs.

The Commission recommends that criminal justice planning agencies request direct written communications from operating agencies to assist them in defining the jurisdiction's objectives, needs, problems, and priorities. Temporary exchanges of personnel between criminal justice planning agencies and operating agencies should be undertaken on a regular basis.

The criminal justice planning standards suggested by the Commission are not radical, nor entirely novel. Planning is so basic an activity that a person not aware of the chaos of large urban criminal justice systems would scarcely think it need be mentioned. Unfortunately, it must be. In the United States a monolithic criminal justice system is unthinkable. The judiciary is staunchly independent; Federal, State, and local legislators and other elected officials jealously guard their independence as well. If the imbalances and conflicts of the present system are to be reduced, a comprehensive and participatory planning effort of the type described in this chapter is essential.

CRIMINAL JUSTICE INFORMATION SYSTEMS

Organizing the Nation's criminal justice information into a useful body of knowledge was

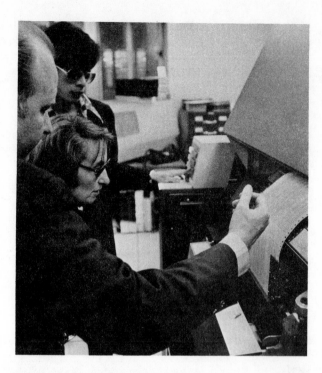

Printout of jury selection list.

talked about for decades but little was done. Recently, however, the urgency of the Nation's crime problem, and the availability of computers and data processing equipment, have made integrated State and national information systems a possibility.

Along with many other disciplines, criminal justice has been experiencing an "information explosion" since the late 1960's. Its characteristics are steadily increasing demands for more capability in gathering, processing, and transmitting information, and steadily increasing information needs.

More frequent use of the computer and other automated technology is a national trend. In 1968, according to LEAA, only 10 States in the Nation had automated State-level criminal justice information systems. By 1972, 47 States had operational automated information systems serving at least one component of the system.

The uses of information and computers vary from jury selection to police manpower allocation to correctional program placement. A recent survey of States by LEAA identified 39 different police functions, 23 different court functions, and 13 different corrections functions performed by automated information systems in one or more States or cities (see Table 3.1).

Criminal justice agencies—like most public and private agencies—are voracious consumers of information. As the pace and complexity of change

Table 3.1.   Criminal Justice Functions Performed by Automated Information Systems

POLICE:
  FUNCTION

Activity Reporting
Administration/Finance
Alphabetic Index
Arrests
Command and Control
Communications—Message
  Switching
Communications—On-Line
  Inquiry
Communications—Other
Computer-Assisted Dispatch
Crime Lab
Crime Trend Analysis
Criminal Associates
Criminal History
Evidence Control
Field Contact Reporting
Fingerprint Processing
Juvenile Index
Licensing/Registration
Missing Persons
Modus Operandi
Narcotics Control
Organized Crime
Performance Evaluation
Planning
Police Personnel
Research Statistics
Resource/Allocation
Simulation/Modeling
Stolen Licenses
Stolen Property—Guns
Stolen Property—Vehicles
Stolen Property—Other
Subjects-in-Process
Training
Uniform Crime Reporting
Vehicle Maintenance
Warrants/Wanted Persons
White Collar Crime
Workload Analysis

COURTS:
  FUNCTION

Administration/Finance
Assignment—Attorneys
Assignment—Courtroom
Assignment—Judges
Calendaring/Scheduling
Case Control
Case Disposition Reports
Citation Control
Courts Personnel
Criminal History
Defendant Control
Docketing
Evidence Control
Fines, Collateral, Bail
Jury Management
Juvenile Records
Probation Control
Process Service Control
Research/Statistics
Simulation/Modeling
Summons Control
Warrant Control
Witness Control

CORRECTIONS:
  FUNCTION

Administration/Finance
Corrections Personnel
Inmate Accounting
Inmate Records
Menu Planning
Performance Evaluation
Physical Goods Inventory
Planning
Prison Industries
Prisoner Behavior Models
Rehabilitation
Research/Statistics
Trust Fund Accounting

Source: United States Department of Justice, LEAA, *Computer Summaries from the Directory of Automated Criminal Justice Information Systems (1973),* pp. 37, 45, 53.

in the criminal justice system quickens, police, courts, and corrections agencies will seek more information and a faster response in its delivery.

To avoid duplication of effort and to facilitate effective collection and proper dissemination of information during this period of rapid expansion, the Commission recommends that:

• State offices coordinate development of information systems.
• High priority be given to development of criminal history and offender-based transaction statistics systems.
• Each State establish a Security and Privacy Council to prevent improper use of information.

Development of Information Systems

Decisions must be made as to which information systems deserve priority attention and which ones are less important. Choosing the right jurisdictional level at which to apply and use the developing criminal justice information systems technology is also a critical decision.

At the present time, local, State, and Federal agencies are spending considerable moneys for the hardware and impedimenta of incompatible and duplicative information systems. Money is being wasted and the human resources, technical talents, and skills available for development of a criminal justice information system are being diffused in many redundant development efforts.

The availability of Federal funds has contributed to the diffusion of effort. Most State criminal justice planning agencies have been faced with decisions on a project-by-project basis where all projects appear to be reasonable and no setting of priorities is possible. As funding expands, the demand increases. Nearly every State is in the position of having a plethora of information systems which cannot be integrated into a usable network. The price of neglected planning is often high; millions of dollars are spent by State and local governments in large urban States without obtaining the necessary information in its most usable form.

The Commission recommends that each State create an organizational structure for coordinating the development of criminal justice information systems.

Such a structure would: (1) prepare a master plan for the development of an integrated network of criminal justice information systems; (2) provide technical assistance and training to all jurisdictions in data collection methods, system concept development, and related areas; and (3) arrange for audit and inspection of State and local information systems.

Proper jurisdictional responsibilities in an integrated network of criminal justice information systems are set forth in the Commission's *Report on the Criminal Justice System*. Standards define State, local, and component system roles based on several principles of system integration.

The most important principle of system integration is that identical records should not be contained within two separate repositories unless there are strongly overriding considerations of total system efficiency to be gained thereby. In practice, this means that there should not be, for example, criminal histories kept at the local level unless the State is temporarily unable to provide this service. In a time of rapid automated information technology, duplicative systems are usually unnecessary and wasteful.

In 1971, the FBI's National Crime Information Center (NCIC) began operating a nationwide system for the exchange of criminal histories among States. This system is the result of an LEAA-funded program of intergovernmental cooperation on information systems among Federal, State, and local governments called Project SEARCH. Since the Commission's work is confined to State and local governments, it set no standards for the FBI, LEAA, or any other Federal agency. However, because State and local governments are primary data sources for the NCIC, implementing the Commission's report would affect the national level as well.

Various other operational and management needs of criminal justice agencies are discussed in the Commission's *Report on the Criminal Justice System*. Standards, for example, are set for improving the collection and processing of local police crime statistics. In addition, the Commission identified two information needs that merit the highest priority attention—criminal histories and offender-based transaction statistics (OBTS).

Criminal Histories and OBTS

The criminal history record is a major thread in tying the criminal justice system together. It shows, as no other document or record does, the actions of the total system on individuals. It describes the official actions of police agencies, judicial and supportive agencies, and all correctional components.

The uses of criminal histories are varied. A police detective may use a criminal history to indicate whether a suspect is likely to have committed the crime under investigation and also the suspect's possible whereabouts. A district attorney may find an arrestee's criminal history invaluable in making recommendations on the question of bail and its amount. Most judges who face the choice of placing a convicted defendant on probation or sending him to prison realize that a criminal history is vital to intelligent sentencing.

Closely allied to the need for criminal history data on a given offender is the need for aggregate data on offenders processed through the system, namely, offender-based transaction statistics (OBTS). OBTS data have come to be thought of as "derivative" from individual criminal histories since many data elements are the same. Statistics on what happens to offenders at each significant step in the criminal justice process can provide answers to questions such as these:

What percentage of those arrested are prosecuted?

What percentage of those prosecuted are acquitted or dismissed?

What is the average length of time between arrest and final disposition?

What percentage of arrestees wait more than 1 year before the final disposition of their cases?

What percentage of offenders in institutions and community-based corrections programs are rearrested and reconvicted upon release?

The evaluation of whether a part of the system is meeting its basic objectives must have its roots in the statistics describing the passage of offenders through the system. Without OBTS data, planners and legislators frequently find themselves relying on the uncertain grounds of good intentions and the often ill-founded assumptions of conventional wisdom.

In spite of need for particular and statistical data derived from individual criminal histories, most criminal justice systems find it difficult to produce, rapidly and easily, complete criminal history information. Local police department files are still the most important sources of criminal history information. Known as "rap sheets," summary criminal history records are kept by police and commonly shared with other criminal justice agencies. In most jurisdictions there is no immediately available substitute to the rap sheet; indeed they are vital to the functioning of urban criminal justice systems.

Nevertheless, there are major difficulties in relying totally on local information. Rap sheets are often not complete; followup on the disposition of the offender after he has been arrested is frequently spotty. Offenders may be arrested for offenses in other cities and counties without the arrests ever showing up on the records of the original jurisdiction. Some offenders are highly mobile. For instance, a New York study of 869 persons arrested in a 2-month period revealed that one in five had been arrested at least once before in another jurisdiction.[6]

In most localities criminal history information is in manual files, impeding fast retrieval. Yet, police conducting investigations and judges setting bail cannot tolerate long delays. Retention of criminal history data in many files makes the compilation of offender-based transaction statistics on a continual basis all but impossible.

The need for States to become repositories for criminal history information is clear; this need coincides with other needs requiring statewide attention, such as on-line files on wanted persons, stolen autos, and other identifiable stolen items.

---

[6] New York State Identification and Intelligence System, *System Development Plan* (1967), p. 58.

The Commission recommends that all State criminal justice information systems provide computerized criminal history files and collection and storage of additional data elements to permit collection of offender-based transaction statistics.

Advisory committees representing information users from all parts of the criminal justice system should be established to assure compatibility of systems designs. National requirements such as the FBI's National Crime Information Center (NCIC) specifications must be considered in the design of information systems.

Privacy

The permanent storage, rapid retrieval, and national coverage of a computer-based criminal justice information system can deprive a citizen of his "right to privacy"—his right to be free from unwarranted intrusion in his affairs.

The problem in establishing a criminal justice information system is to determine who should have access to the files or computer terminals, who should be eligible to receive information from these files, and under what circumstances.

For these reasons, the collection and dissemination of criminal history information and other criminal justice information should be carefully supervised.

The Commission recommends that each State adopt legislation to establish a Security and Privacy Council which is vested with sufficient authority to adopt and administer security and privacy standards for criminal justice information systems.

Fifty percent of each Council's members should be private citizens.

In its *Report on the Criminal Justice System* the Commission establishes a number of standards that it recommends should be enacted into legislation and enforced by Privacy and Security Councils. Among those adopted were key standards on the purging, access, and dissemination of criminal history information and the individual's right to review official records.

Criminal justice files contain information that may be useful to a wide range of agencies outside the criminal justice system, for background investigations of potential employees of public agencies and private firms, for determining eligibility for occupational licenses, for credit evaluation, and for general public information supplied by news media.

The potential damage to privacy is increased when the information in criminal justice files is inaccurate, incomplete, misleading, and unnecessarily disseminated to persons outside the criminal justice system.

In view of the sensitivity and content of criminal history files, the Commission recommends that strict security and privacy procedures be established to insure that there be no dissemination outside the government.

Credit bureaus, news media, employers, employment agencies, and other seekers of information should be denied access to criminal histories. Although items in a criminal history file are for the most part matters of public record, the government should not compile the items and turn the composite over to persons outside of government. This recommendation may appear to be an exception in freedom of information laws and practices, but the Commission believes the protection of individual privacy to be of paramount concern in this instance.

Files should be reviewed periodically to eliminate inaccurate, incomplete, misleading, unverified, and unverifiable information. Individuals should be accorded the right to inspect criminal history files pertaining to them and to challenge the validity of inaccurate or misleading entries. In addition, information that, because of its age, is no longer a reliable guide to the subject's present attitudes or behavior should be purged from the files.

Information concerning individuals convicted of serious crimes should be purged from active files 10 years after the date of release from supervision by the criminal justice system. For less serious crimes, the period should be 5 years. Exceptions to this purging rule should be made in the case of wanted persons, persons under indictment, and multiple offenders.

The principle of purging should also apply to simple arrest records. The economic and personal damage resulting from an arrest that does not lead to conviction is unnecessary yet often substantial. Although the existence of an arrest record is neither an indication of guilt nor a reliable guide to a person's character, it may become an automatic disqualification for employment.

The Commission recommends that all copies of information filed as a result of an arrest that is legally terminated in favor of the individual should be returned to that individual within 60 days of final disposition, upon order of a court, or if requested by the agency that disposed of the case. Exceptions should be made in the case of persons against whom a criminal action or proceeding is pending or who have previously been convicted of a crime.

In its *Report on the Criminal Justice System,* the Commission acknowledges that purged information may be removed from active files and still retained for internal recordkeeping and bona fide research purposes. Information that is purged, but not returned or destroyed, should be held in confidence, in separate files, and not disseminated except under several narrowly defined cases specified in the Commission's report.

Legislation should be enacted that limits questions about arrests on applications for public and private employment and licenses, and that specifies other civil rights and privileges applicable to those arrests. (See the chapter in this report on Community Crime Prevention for a further discussion of removing employment barriers resulting from arrests and convictions.)

Few persons doubt the necessity for the criminal justice system to be aware of community conditions and potential criminal activity. Controversy occurs, however, on what information should be gathered, how it should be obtained, and who should have access to it. The threat to individual rights from unrestricted intelligence operations is direct. Leaks occur. Details that should be strictly private become public news. Reputations may be destroyed and careers ruined. The Commission wishes to discourage the retention of demonstrably inaccurate and unnecessary intelligence information and to prevent its dissemination.

In no instance should criminal history files be linked with intelligence files. To minimize the threat to privacy, criminal history files must contain only information concerning formal contacts with the criminal justice system such as arrest, charge, and release information. Unproven allegations, rumors of illicit associations, and subjective opinions have no place in criminal history files which of necessity will be used by the entire criminal justice system and possibly by other government agencies.

All of the privacy standards discussed above and others specified in the Commission report would be promulgated and enforced by the State Privacy and Security Councils in the absence of controlling national legislation.

Developing adequate information systems that safeguard basic rights is not a police problem or a courts problem or a corrections problem, it is a criminal justice problem. Issues surrounding such areas as criminal history exchanges, offender-based transaction statistics, and privacy and security requirements must be decided on a multiagency basis. The Commission information systems standards present a suggested course of action that will unify the criminal justice community in this critical area.

Police officers attending college.

CRIMINAL JUSTICE EDUCATION

Higher education in criminal justice has been stimulated by a number of trends in recent years: increasing monetary support for criminal justice education through LEAA, increasing emphasis on career preparation in higher education, and rising pay scales making criminal justice attractive as a career. An indication of the rapid advances that have been made is that, in 1972, 515 institutions of higher education offered full-time degree programs in law enforcement, compared to only 65 a decade earlier.[7]

A characteristic of contemporary higher education in criminal justice is that, like the criminal justice system itself, its roots lie in a number of different disciplines and programs: law, criminology, sociology, public administration, political science, police science, and social work. A serious disadvantage of the present educational structure is that it does not provide common approaches to the problems of crime and justice that currently divide the system.

Legal education historically has deemphasized criminal justice. In many law schools a single course in criminal law is sufficient for graduation. Outside of law schools, most professionally oriented higher education programs have dealt with police only, neglecting a core curriculum that could apply equally to police, courts, and corrections agencies. Law enforcement programs have focused on training-type courses that can be more effectively provided outside of universities and colleges. Some colleges and universities, for example, have courses in such obvious training areas as officers' notebook procedures, first aid, defensive tactics, and weapons instruction.

Only a few colleges and institutions of higher education offer useful graduate programs in criminal justice to middle and upper management personnel who wish to upgrade their professional skills. College catalogs have scarcely acknowledged the emerging discipline of criminal justice planning in their course offerings in spite of the serious need for skilled planners in the hundreds of jurisdictions throughout the country.

By failing to treat criminal justice as a whole, many institutions of higher education have overlooked an opportunity to help unify a frequently divided and unnecessarily competitive system.

The Commission recommends that criminal justice system curriculums and programs be established by agencies of higher education to unify the body of

[7] International Association of Chiefs of Police, *1972-73 Directory of Law Enforcement and Criminal Justice Education* (1972), p. 2.

knowledge in law enforcement, criminology, social science, criminal law, public administration, and corrections, and to serve as a basis for preparing persons to work in the criminal justice system.

Possible models for criminal justice education programs are presently available from the community college to the graduate level. In California, core curriculums have been developed for criminal justice education in the community college system. The State University of New York and the University of Southern California have pioneered in the development of graduate curriculums in criminal justice. Classes in subjects of common interest to police, courts, and corrections personnel, such as the prevention and control of crime and the administration of justice, reflect the systemwide perspective of such schools.

One of the reasons that criminal justice education is in such an unsettled state is that practitioners and academicians have not tried to define jointly what role higher education is to play in career development. A national survey of law enforcement programs by LEAA found that most curriculum development has proceeded independent of systematic analysis of the roles police, courts, and corrections personnel are expected to perform.

The Commission urges that criminal justice education programs be developed with the active contribution of practitioners. If criminal justice education is to be effective, practitioners must understand the purpose of new programs and education must be familiar with the everyday concerns of practitioners. The Commission standards provide for the systematic development of both education and training curriculums according to a general statewide policy. State planning agencies, standards and training councils, criminal justice agencies, and agencies of higher education would all participate in the formation of the State's policy.

In proposing its standards, the Commission realizes that education alone cannot mold behavior. However, when combined with exposure to different interests in the criminal justice system and the community, it can be an important catalyst for change.

CONCLUSION

At the conclusion of this chapter, a judgment made at its beginning bears repeating: "The most enduring problems facing the criminal justice system are not technical or financial—they are political."

No one agency alone has been given the societal responsibility of reducing crime. Questions of major policy in criminal justice require agreement among police, courts, corrections, and other public and private agencies. The Commission's standards on criminal justice planning, criminal justice information systems, and criminal justice education present avenues for reaching agreement. Planning agency supervisory boards and college classrooms are forums where various parts of the system and the non-criminal-justice community may come together to discuss particular concerns and ultimate objectives. Criminal justice information systems that are centrally planned and organized can provide data badly needed in understanding the problems of the criminal justice process.

The standards proposed in this chapter will take time to implement. Their impact will not easily be measured by immediate decreases in crime. Yet they are among our most important recommendations. They provide for a rational future for crime control.

Chapter 4

Community Crime Prevention

The term "community crime prevention" can mean citizens patroling their neighborhoods or conducting campaigns to improve streetlighting and reduce auto thefts. The term also can mean the renovation of slums, the improvement of schools, jobs for the unemployed, and the counseling of troubled young people.

These and many other activities are part of community crime prevention. Any public or private activity outside the conventional criminal justice system which is directed toward reducing crime is, in fact, community crime prevention.

MAJOR RECOMMENDATIONS

The Commission's standards and recommendations regarding community crime prevention cover such diverse but critical areas as:
• Citizen volunteers in criminal justice.
• Expanded public employment programs in areas of high unemployment.
• Career education in elementary and secondary schools.
• Individualized community drug abuse treatment services.
• Physical design of buildings, parks, and

Volunteer counseling a youth referred by juvenile court.

thoroughfares to reduce criminal opportunities.
• Ethical codes of conduct for governmental officials.

These varied approaches to community crime prevention are based on the assumption that there is no single solution to the crime problem. Indeed, actions designed to combat one type of crime may have no impact on another. A methadone maintenance program, as an example, might be useful in preventing shoplifting by addicts but may have no significant effect on the murder rate. A streetlighting campaign may prevent auto theft and vandalism but may not reduce aggravated assault.

Similarly, one type of program may not be beneficial to all offenders. Alternative strategies must be designed to deal with particular cases—treatment programs for the addict and the alcoholic; special counseling for the young offender; and job training and placement for the unemployed offender.

The following synopsis of the Commission's *Report on Community Crime Prevention* focuses on three areas of activity outside the traditional criminal justice system that can contribute significantly to reducing serious, high-fear crime. These areas are citizen action, the delivery of public services, and the reduction of criminal opportunities. In a fourth and final area, integrity in government, the Commission presents recommendations for reducing another serious crime problem—official corruption.

45

Citizen action project.

CITIZEN ACTION

Action by private citizens is at the heart of community crime prevention.

Citizens can improve education, employment, and recreation; citizens can devise programs to reduce criminal opportunities by designing safer buildings; citizens can insure the integrity of elected and appointed officials.

In recent months, citizens in many communities have contributed directly to the prevention and reduction of crime by:
• Conducting campaigns to improve streetlighting.
• Serving as volunteers in probation departments or corrections institutions.
• Providing employment and training for ex-offenders, disadvantaged young people, or ex-addicts.
• Counseling young people on such diverse problems as drug abuse, alcohol, and family disputes.
• Reporting crime to the police and serving as volunteers in neighborhood security programs.

No national inventory exists of the time and effort Americans freely give to others and to their communities. The Commission's staff, however, reviewed hundreds of accounts of successful citizen action projects reported in daily newspapers, magazines, professional newsletters, and scholarly journals. It followed up the most promising projects with hundreds of discussions with people who have knowledge and experience in these areas, and, in the case of several, with on-site visits. The staff also interviewed dozens of community leaders, some heading local efforts and others affiliated with national organizations such as the U.S. Chamber of Commerce, the National Council on Crime and Delinquency, the Junior Chamber of Commerce, and the National Alliance for Safer Streets.

The Commission drew two important conclusions from its investigation. First, private group activity specifically directed at preventing crime is increasing. Although no hard statistics are available, during the late 1960's and early 1970's hundreds of local projects emerged in communities across the country. Second, most citizen efforts are designed to complement, not supplant the existing operation of the criminal justice system. Although occasionally given wide publicity, extralegal vigilante efforts are not characteristic of most citizen crime prevention activity.

The benefits of responsible citizen action appear to be many. A community spirit often develops when neighbors join together to solve common problems. Volunteers frequently can provide more personal attention and care to a particular problem or individual than can a harried professional. Citizen involvement also can plug many holes in the delivery of needed community services that otherwise would be unavailable because of lack of funds, personnel, or other resources.

Citizen action crime prevention efforts often fall into three general areas: neighborhood security, volunteers in criminal justice, and multipurpose community improvement activities. Each of these types will be discussed below.

Neighborhood Security

In many communities the only response to crime has been a retreat behind locks, bars, alarms, and guards. Although these prophylactic measures may be steps in self-protection, they can lead to a lessening of the bonds of mutual assistance and neighborliness.

Other communities, however, have developed collective means of protection in addition to traditional self-protection measures. The principle behind neighborhood security efforts is group action to make blocks, apartments, streets, and parks safer from and less vulnerable to crime.

In some areas, citizens have banded together to report crimes in progress or suspicious activities in their neighborhoods. Organizations offer rewards to those reporting criminal activity or hold special crime prevention clinics to reduce robbery and burglary. Citizens have initiated campaigns to educate people to the seriousness of shoplifting or to give tips on preventing auto theft.

In Roxbury, Mass., residents joined a self-help program by signing house-watch contracts under which they agree to be alert to and report to police suspicious behavior in the neighborhood. To combat increased burglaries, thefts, and robberies in the area, they refused to buy or even tolerate the sale of stolen goods. They also marked belongings with social security numbers, so that stolen goods could be identified and returned. This evolving sense of community was in evidence in early 1972 when the planned opening of a bar by alleged organized crime elements was successfully opposed by the neighborhood.

Often the byproduct of group action is a heightened sense of security. Tenants in a New York City apartment building, for example, called a meeting in response to a series of burglaries. They not only resolved to watch out for each other but found that getting to know each other had enhanced their safety. As one tenant remarked, ". . . we now have friends to run to, not just faceless, nameless neighbors. . . . I now know when to be suspicious of people I pass in the halls and when to smile and say hello." [1]

Volunteer Programs in Courts and Corrections

While some citizen efforts are designed to increase the safety of persons and property or to prevent certain crimes, other efforts are aimed at strengthening agencies in the criminal justice system.

Perhaps the largest group of citizens assisting the system are volunteers who work in the courts or in corrections institutions. In the early 1960's, a few pioneer courts began to use volunteers to provide desperately needed probation services. The idea spread quickly and the national director of Volunteers in Probation estimates that today there are about 250,000 volunteers working in courts, prisons, and juvenile institutions. These volunteers, most of whom work individually with offenders, provide services and counseling not otherwise available.

Volunteers in San Diego County, Calif., contributed more than 30,000 hours of service to probationers in 1971; in Royal Oak, Mich., some 500 individuals furnished more than $250,000 a year in services on a $17,000 budget from the city. When probationers from Royal Oak were compared with probationers from a nonvolunteer court, it was found that Royal Oak probationers were less hostile and had substantially lower recidivism rates: approximately 15 percent of the Royal Oak probationers committed subsequent offenses, compared with nearly 50 percent of the other group.[2] Massachusetts, noting the success of these programs, has passed a law that requires the commissioner of probation in that State to initiate and develop volunteer programs.

Studying the court system is another effective citizen action approach. Groups of housewives, professionals, and businessmen have undertaken court-watching programs, studies of the pretrial process, or surveys of courtroom efficiency. Based on these studies, citizens have recommended more efficient methods of selecting judges, reducing court backlog, and improving juvenile care procedures.

The Washington, D. C., Pretrial Justice Program, for example, is concerned with practical alternatives to pretrial detention. Studies and reforms have been suggested to minimize the use of pretrial detention consistent with public safety. The group has helped those detained in jail by reporting and attempting to resolve cases of error and delay, and by securing the admission of some defendants into community programs. Other citizen groups have implemented projects to divert defendants from the criminal justice system at a point between arrest and trial, thereby reducing caseloads.

Citizens now are also a part of a substantial movement for correctional reform. Many citizen groups such as the National Council on Crime and Delinquency (NCCD) are concerned with educating the public and legislators to the potential benefits of work release programs, community-based corrections, and other diversion measures.

Citizen organizations are promoting correctional reforms by conducting jail studies, by informing others about the problems faced by offenders while in prison and after release, by encouraging the construction of halfway houses and community-based facilities, and by supporting reform legislation.

In one project, citizen volunteers inspect jails in Jefferson City, Mo., and report their findings to the county court. As a result, 12 antiquated jails have been closed; the citizens' group has recommended that they be replaced with new regional facilities.

Community Improvement

Successful citizen programs have been directed against the building blocks of

[1] "The Cities Lock Up," *Life Magazine* (November 19, 1971), p. 32.

[2] National Institute of Mental Health, "Royal Oak, Michigan, Municipal Court Research Study," p. 3.

crime—unemployment, substandard education, drug abuse, and inadequate or nonexistent recreational opportunities. Programs include encouraging dropouts to stay in school, tutoring students with learning problems, and offering alternative educational experiences such as street academies or vocational programs.

In Philadelphia, Pa., for example, the Urban Coalition has developed a vocational program for inner city youth. In this program, the business community and the school system cooperate to train a youth for a specific job in a specific industry. Other citizens counsel youths, establish scholarship funds, or work to familiarize students with the law.

Many businessmen have assumed responsibility for crime prevention by hiring disadvantaged youths and by employing ex-offenders. Some businesses have agreed to fill a certain percentage of their openings with the hard core unemployed. The JOBS program of the National Alliance of Businessmen has placed almost 1 million disadvantaged youths in businesses, unions, and industry.

The religious community, with its concern for human dignity and justice, has much to offer in crime prevention resources. Some congregations have contributed their buildings, facilities, and equipment for community programs, especially those for children and youth.

In Chicago, Ill., for example, an inner city parish has become over a period of years a service center to the entire community. A child care center and Head Start program in the church have helped neighborhood children through their preschool and school years, while also allowing mothers to obtain job training and employment in lieu of welfare assistance. A drug awareness center has been opened in the basement of the rectory, and sports and social activities are supervised in the parish community center.

There are also multipurpose citizen groups that become engaged in a wide variety of neighborhood security, criminal justice volunteer, and general community improvement activities.

In one example of effective citizen mobilization, the Indianapolis Crime Crusade has organized 80,000 women who have been instrumental in the return of more than 1,000 dropouts to school, formed a court-watching program, supported increases in police salaries, and, with the Jaycees, initiated a campaign for improved streetlighting.

In the area of government reform, the Better Government Association in Chicago, Ill., has investigated instances of waste and inefficiency, as well as corruption, in government. The group estimates that up to 60 percent of their investigations are effective and result in the passage of new laws,

changes in regulations, or indictments of corrupt officials. Group representatives claim that these investigations saved taxpayers up to $50 million in 1970.

The importance of citizen involvement at the neighborhood level is reflected in the 1974 New York City budget, which carries a $5 million proposal for a block security plan. Under the program, block associations and tenant groups would develop their own crime prevention plans and the city would provide the funds to implement them. Such support might involve direct funding, as in New York City, or it might mean making public facilities available for group meetings or providing public recognition for outstanding service to the community.

The Commission recommends that every citizen contribute to local community crime prevention efforts. Government agencies should encourage and support citizen action programs to prevent and reduce crime. Existing community organizations should explore ways they can relate their activities to crime prevention.

GOVERNMENT RESPONSIVENESS

Some of the problems faced by the criminal justice system can be alleviated to some degree by responsive action on the part of other segments of government.

Open, responsive governments can encourage citizen involvement in crime prevention. When citizens find government complex, confusing, and uninviting, a chasm can develop between city hall and the community. The burden of cutting through the red tape of an impersonal bureaucracy falls primarily on those most dependent on its services and least equipped to deal with its complexity—the elderly, the poor, the uneducated, those with language barriers, and minority and ethnic populations unfamiliar with governmental structures.

To maximize government responsiveness, the Commission recommends that government units open neighborhood offices and that local governments develop complaint centers. These programs, together with a greater flow of information, can bring the community together.

City governments should establish neighborhood facilities, such as multiservice centers and "little city halls," to aid in dispensing government services and to improve communication between citizens and government agencies.

In this way citizens can receive effective services

close to their homes with a minimum of bureaucratic red tape. A neighborhood center can help to convince citizens that government is concerned about their needs. The objectives of decentralization are a more citizen-oriented service delivery system and increased citizen participation in government.

The concept of decentralized municipal services is not new. Since the late 1920's, branch city halls that provide most city services have been operating in Los Angeles, Calif., to reach more conveniently more than 40 subcommunities in the city.

Before community involvement in governmental processes can become a reality, community members must be able to obtain information on which government decisions and programs are based. Informing citizens about the activities of the local government will help assure the public that the government is working in its best interest.

The Commission believes that local governments should provide access to such information by:
• Enacting "right to know" laws that provide citizens with open and easy access to agency regulations, audits, minutes, and other pertinent information.
• Permitting local radio and television stations to cover official and public meetings on a regular basis.
• Holding public hearings to acquire an understanding of the real concerns of the community.

An orderly and effective mechanism for general redress of citizen grievances will also bring local government closer to its citizens. Individual agencies often do not have the time or personnel to respond to complaints. In addition, citizens sometimes find bureaucracy so confusing they are unable to locate or identify the department that could help them. Citizens' attitudes toward government are adversely affected when local governments rely solely on haphazard procedures to respond to citizen complaints, and when there is no regular monitoring to insure the public is served adequately.

Municipal governments should establish a central office of complaint and information to improve government effectiveness and to permit citizens to obtain information and direction on any problem with a minimum of "red tape."

The Commission also proposes the establishment of mass media action line programs that will assist government officials to respond to citizen requests and complaints. Direct exchange can allow the public to become familiar with city officials and to gain insight into the complexities of governmental processes. It also will help insure greater accountability to the public of elected and appointed officials.

The remoteness of government and a declining sense of community have been noted as two significant characteristics of urban America. They are undoubtedly linked, but they need not become permanent conditions. There are signs of a renewed interest among citizens in the problems—including crime—of their cities and towns. A responsive government can help sustain this interest.

DELIVERY OF PUBLIC SERVICES

The need to deliver all public services in a comprehensive fashion is becoming increasingly apparent in urban areas. Education, employment, health, sanitation, and criminal justice agencies frequently have found themselves addressing mere segments of larger problems. An illustration of the fact that social ills rarely occur in isolation comes from the Model Cities Program of the Department of Housing and Urban Development. What follows is a profile of a 1970 neighborhood typical of many depressed areas in cities and towns across the country.

Unemployment in the low-income model neighborhood (MN) is 6.2 percent, compared with 3.4 percent for the entire city. Ten of the 11 schools in the target area have mental maturity, reading, and arithmetic norms one and two grades below the national average. The high school dropout rate is 16 percent, compared with 9 percent for the school system as a whole. Only 4 percent of the model area housing is "standard." Existence of outside toilets attests to primitive conditions.

Overcrowding is characteristic in the model neighborhood. Since 1960, the population has increased but the number of housing units has decreased. The target area has only three supervised playgrounds with a combined area of 2.6 acres. Thus 5.9 percent of the total city-supervised playground area serves 15 percent of the city's population. There are 8 miles of unpaved streets and sidewalks in the MN, in sharp contrast to the historic section of the city, with its beautiful old buildings and well-kept parks and gardens.

Health conditions in the MN are below the city and county rates. In 1968, infant mortality rates per 100,000 persons were 42.5 in the county and 60 in the MN; tuberculosis rates were 42 in the county and 105 in the MN; infectious syphilis rates were 27.6 in the county and 115 in the MN.

Dependence on public welfare is heavy, yet few social service agencies are located within the MN or have outreach services there. Residents complain of inadequate coordination between the public and private agencies that provide social services.

Finally, life in the target area is threatened by a high incidence of crime. With only 15 percent of the

31 32 33 34 35 36 37 38 39 40 41 42 43 44 45 46 47 48 49 50 51 52 53 54 55
tiles are cold-blooded,
scales, and breathe
lungs.
reptiles son d
tienen escamas,
an con pulmo
FEBRUARY
SUN MON TUES WED THURS FRI SAT
69 70
HEL
Pledge
Paper

population, the MN experiences 33 percent of the homicides and rapes and 27 percent of the felonious assaults. Juvenile delinquency, as represented by the number of arrests, is also high. The arrest rate of persons under 18 years of age in the target area is 48.2 per 1,000, compared with 33.8 per 1,000 for the whole city.

As the Model City example suggests, public services are not always adequate to meet the pressing needs of many individuals. Those in need of public services are likely to have multiple problems: youths involved in crime are often dropouts and unemployed; a drug-dependent person may require not only medical treatment, but employment counseling and skill training as well.

In some neighborhoods important services are simply not available or are severely deficient. Low income areas often suffer while middle- and upper-class neighborhoods receive a high level of service.

The Commission believes municipal services should be allocated to neighborhoods on the basis of need.

Achieving this end will require the expenditure of sufficient funds to maintain equally effective services in all areas of the city or jurisdiction. Also needed is a means of coordinating existing social, medical, and rehabilitative services so that persons may be treated comprehensively.

Social Service Delivery Mechanisms: Youth Services Bureaus

In addition to the equitable delivery of services, there is a need for coordinating existing social, medical, and rehabilitative services. Efforts must be made to develop comprehensive service delivery systems that avoid wasteful duplication, open lines of communication to the community, and better assist individual clients through a coordinated delivery of services to arrive at their best functioning level. One of the most important examples of comprehensive services delivery is the youth services bureau.

These bureaus in large part were the result of a recommendation by the 1967 President's Commission on Law Enforcement and Administration of Justice, which urged communities to establish them to serve both delinquent and nondelinquent youth referred by police, juvenile courts, schools, and other sources. The bureaus were to act as central coordinating units for all community services for young people.

Bilingual instruction in an elementary school.

A national census in 1972 identified 150 youth services bureaus in operation in many States and territories. In the absence of national standards, local youth services bureaus have developed according to the needs and pressures of each community.[3]

In most localities, however, the youth services bureau, at a minimum, is a link between available resources and youth in need. It first identifies services and resources in the community and then refers clients to an agency that can provide the required services. Social services made available might include employment, job training, education, housing, medical care, family counseling, psychiatric care, or welfare.

Once a young person has been directed to another agency, the youth services bureau follows up to assure that adequate services are being provided. The bureau acts as a services broker, matching the young person with the service he or she needs. When services are not available through governmental or volunteer sources, they may be purchased from private agencies or independent professionals.

In Worcester, Mass., for example, coordination of services for individual youths is taking place through case conferences. Representatives of all agencies involved with a young person meet to gain a complete view of the youth's problems and to develop a comprehensive plan to meet his needs. In some instances, the youth or the youth and his parent attend the case conference. In order to strengthen the youth's responsibility, he is encouraged to contribute to the decisions that will affect him. After the youth is referred to another agency, the bureau systematically follows up to assure that services are being provided.

Specialized services often are needed to help a child and to keep him out of trouble with the law. A child might need services that are not available in the community, such as an alternative educational experience, career training, drug treatment, a group residence, or psychiatric services. It is frequently the responsibility of the youth services bureau to identify these gaps in service and to promote the development of needed resources.

The Youth Development Service in Billings, Mont., as an example, provides little direct service to youth. Instead, it brings agencies together to develop community priorities, to eliminate service duplication, and to redirect resources when current projects are inappropriate. The Youth Advocacy Program in South Bend, Ind., attempts to influence

[3] William Underwood, *A National Study of Youth Service Bureaus,* U. S. Department of Health, Education, and Welfare, Youth Development and Delinquency Prevention Administration (December 1972).

Youth Services Bureau

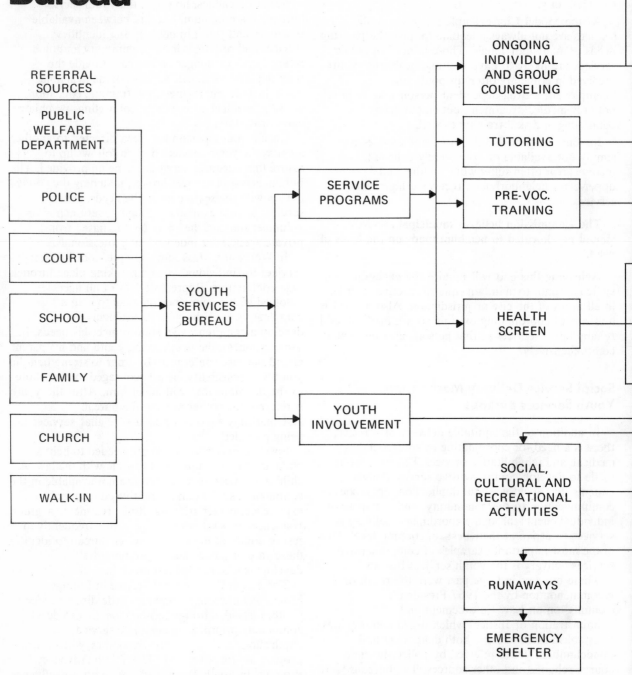

REFERRAL SOURCES

PUBLIC WELFARE DEPARTMENT

POLICE

COURT

SCHOOL

FAMILY

CHURCH

WALK-IN

YOUTH SERVICES BUREAU

SERVICE PROGRAMS

YOUTH INVOLVEMENT

ONGOING INDIVIDUAL AND GROUP COUNSELING

TUTORING

PRE-VOC. TRAINING

HEALTH SCREEN

SOCIAL, CULTURAL AND RECREATIONAL ACTIVITIES

RUNAWAYS

EMERGENCY SHELTER

Source: Derived from material developed by the
Youth Development and Delinquency Prevention
Administration, U.S. Department of Health, Education, and Welfare

YOUTH SERVICES SYSTEM

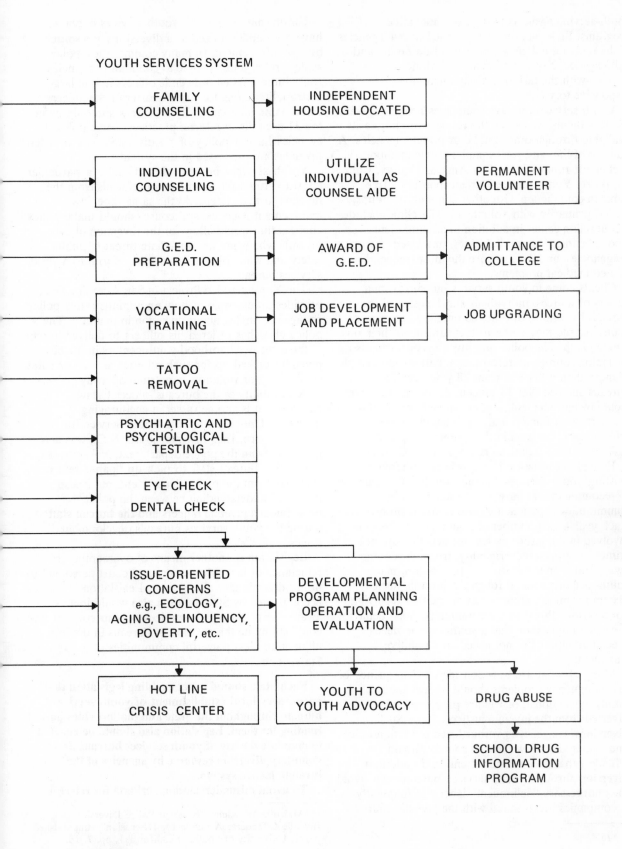

youth-serving agencies to develop innovative programs. Field workers are assigned to five agencies —the recreation department, schools, a family and child agency, city government, and Model Cities—with the task of making them more responsive to youth.

Youth services bureaus sometimes provide specific services themselves when the services are not easily available through other public or private agencies. A number of bureaus, for example, provide temporary shelter for runaways. In Los Angeles County, Calif., the Basset Youth Service Bureau sponsors a free clinic in conjunction with other community groups, staffed primarily with volunteers. The clinic includes a counseling center in addition to an outpatient medical clinic. Venereal diseases, unwanted pregnancies, and drug use are the most frequently treated medical problems.

Clients come to youth services bureaus from a variety of sources. Individuals may be referred to bureaus by schools or other community agencies, or young people may come to the bureau on their own seeking help. The police and juvenile court can also be major sources of referrals. A nationwide sample of more than 400 cases from 28 youth services bureaus showed that 13 percent of the referrals were from law enforcement; 30 percent were referred by self, friend, or family; and the remainder were referred by schools and other public and private agencies.[4] (See Youth Services Bureau Chart.)

Enough information has now been gathered on existing youth services bureaus for the Commission to recommend that bureaus be established in communities experiencing serious youth problems. Each year a vast number of young people become involved in the justice system for acts that are not crimes for adults: incorrigibility, truancy, running away, and even stubbornness. In addition, many youths are processed through the juvenile justice system for minor offenses that are neither recurring nor a serious threat to the community. Such behavior is often an indication that a young person needs special attention, but not necessarily punitive treatment.

Many of what are now considered delinquency or predelinquency problems should be redefined as family, educational, or welfare problems and diverted from the juvenile justice system. Such diversions can relieve overburdened probation offices and courts and allow them to concentrate on offenders that need serious attention. In addition, diversion through youth services bureaus can avoid the unnecessary "delinquent" label that frequently accompanies involvement with the juvenile court.

Unfortunately, existing youth services bureaus have been underutilized as a diversionary resource by law enforcement. In many communities, police seldom refer young people to community agencies. In 31 interviews with juvenile officers in one large metropolitan area, fully one quarter of the officers could name no community resources and only two of the 31 used direct referral practices. Some police agencies have a policy of no diversion—all arrested juveniles are processed in the system.[5]

Youth services bureaus should make a particular effort to attract the diversionary referrals from the juvenile justice system. At the same time, law enforcement agencies and courts should make policy changes that would allow for the diversion of every juvenile who is not an immediate threat to public safety and who voluntarily accepts referral to a youth services bureau.

The Youth Service Project in San Antonio, Tex., provides an example of how an administrative policy change is bringing about diversion in that city. The police chief has ordered his officers to deliver to one of the three neighborhood youth centers in the city juveniles picked up for such offenses as glue or paint sniffing, liquor violations, and running away.

Accessibility of the bureaus' offices to law enforcement is another asset in encouraging diversion. Until recently, the Youth Service Bureau of Greensboro, Inc., in Greensboro, N.C., was across the street from the police department. Not only did this enable bureau staff to pick up "paper referrals" each day from the police department, but it also increased understanding between the police department's juvenile officers and the bureau staff during the youth services bureau's developmental stages.

Legislation is another means of overcoming the reluctance of law enforcement and court personnel to utilize diversionary alternatives. Legislation accompanied by State funding also would increase awareness of the youth services bureau concept and could stimulate the creation of bureaus in the less affluent and less powerful communities of each State.

Each State should enact enabling legislation that encourages local establishment of youth services bureaus throughout the State and that provides partial funding for them. Legislation also should be enacted to mandate the use of youth services bureaus as a voluntary diversion resource by agencies of the juvenile justice system.

To avoid misunderstanding, criteria for referrals

---

[4] *Ibid.*

[5] Malcolm W. Klein, "Issues in Police Diversion of Juvenile Offenders: A Guide for Discussion" (unpublished paper, University of Southern California), pp. 7, 16.

should be developed jointly and specified in writing by law enforcement, courts, and youth services bureau personnel.

Diversion can take place only if there is cooperation and communication between concerned parties.

In California, some of the criteria presently considered by juvenile justice agencies in diverting youth to youth services bureaus include: nonprobation status, first offense, age, minor offense that does not threaten the public safety, residence in the project area, cooperative attitude toward voluntary referral, and the need for additional services the bureau can provide.

In a few communities, what masquerades as a youth services bureau is actually a field office for probation surveillance. Where probation services are particularly limited, court referrals ordering youths to participate in the bureau's programs may seem to be an expeditious alternative. But such action negates the role of the bureau as a program in which young people participate by choice. The bureau becomes part of the traditional enforcement machinery by deciding, in effect, whether or not a youth must be returned to juvenile court. Thus, the stigma of a coercive officially mandated service remains, without the legal safeguards currently emerging in the justice system itself.

Referrals to the youth services bureau should be completed only if they are voluntarily accepted by the youth. Youths should not be forced to choose between bureau referral and further justice system processing.

In making this recommendation, the Commission departs from the original recommendation of the President's Crime Commission. In its report, that Commission said that the youth services bureau could be vested with the authority to refer back to court within 30 to 60 days "those with whom it cannot deal effectively."

Such a practice can result in an extension of control over the youth by community institutions, without providing the legal safeguards of the justice system. Sherwood Norman, writing in *The Youth Service Bureau: A Key to Delinquency Prevention,* stated that to refer to court upon a young person's failure to cooperate ". . . would be a clear indication to him that the youth services bureau was not a voluntary agency but rather part of the justice system and therefore coercive."

The essence of any social service delivery system is the marshaling of resources in a coordinated way to bring clients to the best functioning level. As stated earlier, the youth services bureau provides a

Job-training program center.

useful model for delivery of service systems which should be applied to adults as well as young persons.

Employment

There is a definite association between unemployment or underemployment, and crime. Some individuals who cannot find satisfactory jobs or who are discriminated against in the labor market will turn to illegal activity as a source of income. The President's Commission on Crime in the District of Columbia in 1965 found that of adult offenders surveyed, 60 percent had no history of regular employment at the time of arrest and the majority, whether employed or not, were in unskilled occupations. Among the offenders about whom income information was available, 69 percent earned less than $3,000 annually and 90 percent earned less than $5,000.[6]

A 1972 study comparing national youth arrest rates, unemployment rates, and labor-force participation rates over 2 decades concluded that lack of employment opportunities among white and black youths was a key factor in generating property crime.[7]

Assisting those with severe employment problems is, in the Commission's judgment, an important way

[6] *Report of the President's Commission on Crime in the District of Columbia* (1966), pp. 127, 130.
[7] Llad Phillips, Harold L. Votey, Jr., and Darold Maxwell, "Crime, Youth and the Labor Market," *Journal of Political Economy* (May/June 1972), pp. 491-504.

to prevent crime. As in other areas, particular attention must be given to programs for young persons. Unemployment among young people became gradually more serious during the 1960's. In 1960, the unemployment rate for teenagers aged 16 to 19 was three and one-third times the adult rate; in 1971, it was more than four times the adult rate.[8] The problem is even more critical among minority youths in cities. In 1971 the unemployment rate among nonwhite teenagers aged 16 to 19 in low income urban areas was 38 percent compared with an overall unemployment rate for all teenagers of 16.9 percent.[9]

Ex-offenders are another group that has traditionally experienced difficulties in the labor market, particularly in periods of rising unemployment. Evidence from manpower programs suggests that in slack labor markets, training, placement, and job development tend to be less effective than when there are many unfilled jobs. In the Manhattan Court Employment Project, which has continued up to the present time, placements have dropped from 270 in the first year to 135 in the third, even though, judging by placements per referral, efforts have apparently improved. The problem is that fewer employers are willing to talk to or hire ex-offenders as long as qualified candidates without criminal records are available.

It is increasingly doubtful that the private sector alone can provide enough jobs to produce satisfactory changes in unemployment rates among urban youths and ex-offenders. Even in the best of times, meaningful public employment will be needed if the chronically unemployed are to be put to work.

The Commission urges expanded public employment programs in areas of high unemployment. Programs should offer full-time, part-time, and summer employment.

Most likely, these programs will require joint cooperation and funding from two or more levels of government. There are a number of different public employment strategies whose adoption depends upon community priorities: transitional jobs that would serve as stepping stones to permanent jobs in the public sector; permanent jobs that would provide a program of education, experience, and training needed for advancement; temporary job slots for offenders immediately after their release from confinement; and jobs that would serve as an alternative to incarceration for misdemeanants.

In the private sector, the Commission urges employers and unions to institute or accelerate efforts to expand job or membership opportunities to the economically and educationally disadvantaged. Various employment approaches could include work-study programs, summer and after-school employment, and job training and development for out-of-school youths.

In its *Report on Community Crime Prevention,* the Commission notes outstanding examples of private initiative. One of the most successful summer programs was developed by the Philadelphia Urban Coalition's High School Academy in 1970 and repeated in the summer of 1971. This effort provided work for students under 17 who were too young to get regular summer jobs. Under the auspices of the Urban Coalition and with the assistance of Junior Achievement, the students formed their own company, the Edison Electric Shop. The youths earned $1.75 an hour, and functioned under their own management with the help of a teacher-director, whose salary was paid by the Coalition.

Youth for Service in San Francisco, Calif., developed jobs for inner city youth by contracting with urban development and community action programs to build, repair, and maintain mini-parks in the blighted areas of the city. A similar group in Chicago, Ill., is running a food store, a boutique, a paper recycling program, and a restaurant.

The success of public and private efforts to expand employment opportunities depends to a large extent on general economic conditions. The close relationship between poverty area unemployment and national economic conditions suggests that a high national employment rate is essential if inner city unemployment is to be reduced. From 1968 through 1971 unemployment rates in urban poverty areas dipped below 5.5 percent only twice,[10] a level that most economists and politicians decry as unacceptable. At both times the national unemployment rate was around 3.5 percent.[11] The increase from 3.5 percent total unemployment at the end of 1969 to 5.9 percent in 1971 was accompanied by a rise in urban poverty area unemployment from 5.5 to 9.7 percent.[12]

[8] *Manpower Report of the President,* U. S. Department of Labor (March 1972), p. 79.

[9] *Manpower Report of the President,* U. S. Department of Labor (March 1972), Table 1, p. 78, and U. S. Department of Commerce, Bureau of the Census, *Statistical Abstract of the United States,* 93rd edition (1972), Table 356, p. 223.

[10] Bureau of Labor Statistics, U.S. Department of Labor, *Handbook of Labor Statistics—1971,* p. 104, and *Handbook of Labor Statistics—1972,* p. 113. The poverty neighborhood classification used is based on a ranking of census facts according to 1960 data on income, education, skills, housing, and a proportion of broken homes. The poorest one-fifth of these tracts are considered poverty neighborhoods.

[11] *Handbook of Labor Statistics—1970,* p. 125.

[12] *Handbook of Labor Statistics—1972,* pp. 113, 129.

The Commission recommends that economic policy be concentrated on maintaining aggregate employment at a high level. The Commission believes that the ultimate goal of such policy should be to assure that the unemployment rate in poverty areas is no greater than the national rate.

Consideration must also be given to changing credit, taxation, and expenditure policies that may have an impact on unemployment.

Criminal Records and Employment

Surveys estimate that approximately 25 percent of the national population may have nontraffic arrest records. The chances that a black male from an urban area will be arrested have been estimated at from 50 to 90 percent.[13]

There is little doubt that arrest records are a barrier to employment. In the private sector, few firms exclude former offenders as a blanket policy, but often selection criteria tend to have this effect in practice.

In a survey in New York City, 75 percent of the employment agencies contacted said they would not recommend an individual with an arrest record, regardless of the disposition of the charges against him.[14]

Barriers to employment are at least as forbidding in the public sector as they are in the private sector. Most States, counties, and cities ask questions about prior arrest records when hiring. Few of the applications state that a record does not automatically bar the applicant. Civil service statutes that govern hiring often use language that could be and apparently is grounds to exclude large numbers of individuals with mere arrest records.[15]

Responses from employers indicate that employees with criminal records are not different from other employees. Agencies in a national survey were asked whether employees with criminal records were better than, the same as, or worse than other employees in each of eight categories: punctuality, attendance, honesty, judgment, initiative, cooperativeness, accuracy, and industriousness. There was little difference between employees with criminal records and other employees. What little difference there was in the reports was favorable toward employees with records.[16]

The Commission's standards on information systems (see Chapter 3) prohibit the dissemination of criminal records to private employers, provide for the return of arrest records of individuals not convicted of a crime, and direct the purging of criminal records after certain periods of time.

To eliminate arbitrary barriers to employment, legislation should be enacted prohibiting employers from inquiring about an applicant's criminal history after records have been purged or returned.

Government civil service regulations, moreover, should specify that no person can be barred automatically from taking a civil service test because of a criminal record.

Education

Schools are the first public agencies that most children contact. For this reason, the schools inevitably have been proposed as vehicles for the solution of a host of public problems including the problem of crime. In making its recommendations, the Commission is well aware of crushing demands already placed upon local schoolteachers, principals, and school boards.

Nevertheless, individuals sometimes come to the attention of the criminal justice system because the educational system has not met their personal needs. The fact that the public schools have not helped a large portion of young people is reflected in high youth unemployment rates and high dropout rates. Twenty percent of those who now enter grade five leave before high school graduation, and only 28.7 percent of 1971 high school graduates went on to college. Yet 80 percent of the effort in schools is structured to meet college entry requirements.[17] Too often classroom instruction is not related to life outside. Undoubtedly many of the 850,000 students who left elementary and secondary schools in 1970 and 1971 did so because they felt their educational experiences were irrelevant.[18]

The Commission believes that the primary goal of American education should be to prepare and interest people in satisfying and useful careers.

Schools should plan programs that will guarantee

---

[13] Herbert S. Miller, *The Closed Door* (prepared for the U. S. Department of Labor, February 1972), p. 147.

[14] Albert G. Hess and F. Le Poole, "Abuse of the Record of Arrest Not Leading to Conviction," *Journal of Research on Crime and Delinquency* (1967).

[15] Miller, *The Closed Door*, pp. 4, 6, 7.

[16] *Ibid.*, pp. 100-101.

[17] Statistical data abstracted from: (1) Kenneth B. Hoyt, R. Evans, Edward Mackin, and Garth Mangum, *Career Education: What It Is and How to Do It* (Olympus Publishing Co., 1972); (2) U.S. Department of Health, Education, and Welfare—Office of Education Materials; and (3) U.S. Bureau of Census, *Statistical Abstract of the United States—1972.*

[18] National School Public Relations Association, "Dropouts: Prevention and Rehabilitation" (Washington: NSPRA, 1972), p. 3.

that every child leaving school can obtain either a job or acceptance to an advanced program of studies, regardless of the time he leaves the formal school setting.

The San Mateo, Calif., school district, for example, formally accepts responsibility for insuring that students are employable whenever they choose to leave school—whether as dropouts from the 10th grade or with advanced degrees.

If schools are going to make guarantees of this kind there must be a shift to career education. In career education programs, instruction is related to the world of work and opportunities are provided to explore or receive training in a career. Career education may begin in first grade or earlier and continue beyond high school graduation. It should bring an awareness to students of the wide range of jobs in American society and the roles and requirements involved.

The Seattle, Wash., public school system has a prototype career education program that offers occupational information to students at all grade levels, from kindergarten to grade 12, and integrates materials into every subject of the curriculum. Another program inverts the curriculum. Students choose preparatory trade areas as electives, staying in each long enough to become oriented to the occupation, explore it, or be trained in it. A core of general education courses—communications and humanities—accompanies the program.

A significant approach to career education is a cooperative education program, Project 70,001, operating since 1969 in Wilmington, Del. The program provides on-the-job work experience and related classroom instruction to students unable to participate in or benefit from regular programs of education and training. Similar programs have been started in Dover, Del.; Harrisburg, Pa.; Kansas City, Mo.; and Hartford, Conn. The Wilmington project combines the efforts and resources of a large shoe manufacturer, the Distributive Education Clubs of America, the Delaware Department of Public Instruction, and the Wilmington Public Schools.

In the Education chapter of the Commission's *Report on Community Crime Prevention,* additional approaches designed to make school systems more responsive to the individual student are recommended.

Varied alternative educational experiences should be provided to students who cannot benefit from classroom instruction. School counseling and other supportive services should be available. There should be bilingual programs for young people who are not fluent in English. There should be a guarantee of functional literacy to every student who

does not have serious emotional, physical, or mental problems.

Aside from fulfilling the primary objective of preparing young people for adult life, school systems may also contribute to community crime prevention by serving as centers for community activities. The traditional school operating 5 days a week for 39 weeks a year is an unaffordable luxury. Schools can become total community opportunity centers for the young and the old, operating virtually around the clock, 365 days a year.

In Flint, Mich., schools are used for a wide variety of community services: adult education and retraining; recreation and counseling; civic meetings; health clinics; YMCA, YWCA, Boy and Girl Scouts, Big and Little Brother activities; job counseling and placement; senior citizen activities; and parent aid in developing curriculums. Members of the community are represented by a neighborhood council that advises the school and expresses the desires of the residents. There are 92,000 people per week using schools after hours; 80,000 adults enroll in classes each year. The accessibility of the school and the wide variety of programs offered there have greatly increased citizen involvement in the community. Special programs for men and women in trouble with the law have been tremendously successful in Flint schools. Among the total population, there are indications of decreasing rates of juvenile crime, dropping out of high school, and parole recidivism.

The Flint experience and others like it provide positive examples of the multipurpose use of educational facilities. The Commission urges authorities to make schools available to all citizens as centers for community involvement and adult education.

Drug Abuse Treatment and Prevention

During the past decade, the nonmedical use of drugs by increasing numbers of people has become an urgent problem. In addition to the familiar alcohol and nicotine, doctors, researchers, and criminal justice professionals have had to become better acquainted with other types of drugs—amphetamines, heroin and other narcotics, barbiturates, hallucinogens, and antidepressants.

A link between some drugs, particularly heroin, and criminal behavior does exist, although many myths and inaccuracies surround that link. Drug abuse does not automatically cause crime. Many heroin or multidrug users were involved with crime before drug use and would continue their illegal activities whether addicted or not. Many recent heroin-dependent persons have grown up in a subculture in which both criminal and addict lifestyles are common. Crime and addiction can be two sides of the same coin.

The National Commission on Marihuana and Drug Abuse in 1973 reported that recent estimates on the daily cost of supporting a heroin habit range from $20 to $100, fluctuating accordingly to availability and location. Assuming that a heroin-dependent person had a daily habit of $20, the cost of his habit could amount to $7,300 per year.

It seems relatively safe to assume that most addicts cannot support their habits without supplementing their income through illegal means since judging from available evidence, cited by the National Commission on Marihuana and Drug Abuse, a majority of heroin-dependent persons have below-average incomes.

This illegal activity usually takes the form of property crime—primarily burglary and shoplifting —rather than crimes against persons. Pimping, prostitution, and drug dealing are also major sources of income for heroin-dependent individuals.

To combat drug-related criminal activity, communities must take steps to prevent further drug abuse or addiction and to offer treatment to those individuals already involved with drugs.

The Commission urges the establishment of multimodality drug treatment systems that would provide a comprehensive range of services in communities with a significant number of drug abusers.

Nonmedical drug use involves different kinds of people who are drug-dependent in varying degrees and ways, who live in a variety of cultural settings, and who use drugs for different reasons. A multimodality approach enables the drug abuser or user to be treated in a program suited to his individual needs so that he may regain his position as a functioning member of society. Some of the recommended elements of multimodality treatment systems include crisis intervention and drug emergency centers, methadone treatment programs, therapeutic communities, and narcotics antagonist programs.

The Commission does not recommend the inclusion of heroin maintenance in a multimodality treatment system. After careful consideration, the Commission has concluded that heroin maintenance is a potentially harmful method of treatment both to the individual and to society as a whole.

Modality: Crisis Intervention Centers

Basic to any system of care are the lifesaving,

hospital-based emergency room forms of service designed to treat overdoses, toxic drug reactions, transient psychotic episodes, and severe withdrawal illness. These centers, located in a hospital or community clinic, should offer both medical aid and psychological services, such as hotline telephone help and various types of counseling.

Modality: Methadone Treatment Programs

Methadone is a synthetic narcotic that is being distributed to an estimated 80,000 of this country's several hundred thousand heroin addicts. When administered in maintenance doses, methadone permits some chronic compulsive heroin users to become law-abiding, productive members of society. Opportunities can be provided to addicts to withdraw completely from methadone maintenance when they have made a satisfactory adjustment to a heroin-free existence and when they express a desire to end all involvement with drugs.

Methadone treatment has passed through a phase during which many observers felt it represented the solution to the heroin problem. However, a more moderate position seems to be indicated at present. The rate of those retained in treatment was once thought to be as high as 80 percent or more, but studies over a period of time indicate it actually approaches 50 percent.

High-dose methadone maintenance, nevertheless, is viewed today as an important treatment method for heroin addicts. It retains in treatment, on a voluntary basis, a much larger percentage of patients than other approaches. Evaluations performed on individuals undergoing methadone maintenance indicate that their rearrest record is low and that, in time, significant numbers find their way back to employment, school, or training.

Modality: Therapeutic Communities Staffed in Part with Ex-addicts

Therapeutic communities are drug-free environments in which the drug user is treated as an underdeveloped, immature personality. The existence of a community prepared to accept or reject the individual is at the core of the process. Banishment from this "family" group is a severe punishment.

Therapeutic community treatment is generally a less successful approach than methadone maintenance but one that may be effective for certain individuals. The treatment is wholly free of drugs and is often demanding and difficult. Few individuals "graduate" into self-sufficiency outside the therapeutic community. Residents are expected to remain in the community for extended periods of

It is better
to understand than
to be understood

time ranging from 18 months to 2 years or more. In many program settings, there are no nonaddict representatives establishing limits or rules of conduct. Rather, participants are confronted by ex-addicts who themselves abstained from further drug use. In cases in which primary responsibility for operating the program does rest with ex-addicts and paraprofessional staff, the Commission believes that backup services of psychiatrists, teachers, and employment specialists should also be readily available.

Modality: Narcotics Antagonist Programs

When taken in adequate amounts, narcotics antagonists such as cyclazocine and naloxone block the effects of heroin and other narcotic drugs. Although some success with narcotics antagonists has been achieved, it has been with relatively small numbers of patients. Many of the drugs used as antagonists produce undesirable side effects. Cyclazocine, a long-acting antagonist first used in 1966, is not well received by many narcotics addicts who complain they feel uncomfortable while taking the drug. In addition, patients are able to interrupt its use for a day in order to experience the euphoric effects of heroin. Naloxone, another drug utilized, has few side effects, but its short duration of action has limited its usefulness.

A major effort is now underway to find a safe long-acting antagonist. Should such research be successful, a much more extensive use of antagonists in treatment will be possible than now is the case. The Commission does not necessarily endorse the narcotics antagonist concept, but only recommends that this concept be considered and carefully evaluated as one more potential element of a multimodality approach.

Modality: Variations in Treatment Approach

Communities might also consider variations in the four treatment approaches discussed above. For example, they might consider low-dosage methadone programs, or closed or open residential centers and halfway houses. A closed facility provides a therapeutic environment in which addicts can live free of their drug use with the help of constraints while an open facility operates without physical and other restraints.

Compulsory Drug Treatment

Many drug-dependent individuals live from day to day, experience one crisis after another, and are

Methadone dispensary.

unable to relate to any kind of treatment on a voluntary basis. Probation, deferred prosecution, and civil commitment all can and are used to structure compulsory treatment for such individuals. When compulsory treatment is indicated, individuals should be assigned to a coordinating body that is capable of making appropriate treatment decisions. Courts should be encouraged to rely on these coordinating committees through statutory action or through procedural means. Due process should always be assured. Compulsory treatment by deferred prosecution, probation, or civil commitment need not be equated with institutional confinement. Rather, all possible treatment options should remain open and existing public and community resources, including private treatment agencies, should be brought to bear on the treatment process.

Drug Abuse Prevention

In addition to treatment modalities, the Commission also recognizes the importance of drug abuse prevention. Past prevention efforts, however, often have been misdirected. Scare tactics have been used to stress the dangers of drug use. These efforts were discredited by many young people who had tried one or more drugs, and who find antidrug representations not substantiated by their own experiences. Prevention programs frequently failed to point out that each individual will respond to a drug in a different way, depending on such factors as the amount taken and the frequency of use.

The Commission believes that each community should implement a carefully designed program to prevent drug abuse. When information on drugs is misrepresented to young people, it can often discredit an entire prevention effort.

Drug education should begin in the home before the child enters school. Teachers in the school should receive special training in drug education and prevention. Programs also should concentrate on helping the individual solve the problems that led him to drug use and should provide him with constructive alternatives.

The Commission urges that effective drug abuse prevention programs be established. Such programs should present information objectively on drugs and drug abuse.

Coordinating Prevention and Treatment Efforts

Both prevention and treatment activities should be coordinated through a central State agency and local coordinating agencies.

These agencies should assume responsibility for

61

setting priorities for delivery of services, avoiding duplication, and determining the extent to which funded programs are effective. Basic standards on training, staffing, administration, and programing also should be adopted by such agencies.

Coordinating agencies should work closely with the Special Action Office for Drug Abuse Prevention, the Federal agency charged with overall responsibility for Federal drug abuse prevention programs.

REDUCING CRIMINAL OPPORTUNITY

An important assumption throughout the delivery of services section is that the provision of lawful alternatives to crime—satisfying employment and drug abuse treatment, for example—will persuade some persons to abandon or avoid criminal careers. But as this chapter emphasized at the outset, it is unrealistic to expect an improved delivery of service strategy to be effective in all cases. The Commission believes that protective measures taken by public authorities, commercial establishments, and private homeowners can also play an important role in deterring criminals.

Of all the things a citizen or community can do to reduce crime, the most immediate and most direct approach is to eliminate obvious opportunities for criminals. Locked cars, well-lighted streets, alarm systems, and properly designed and secure housing make crime, particularly acquisitive crimes such as larceny, burglary, auto theft, and robbery, more difficult to commit.

The following section contains the Commission's general recommendations for security precautions that can be taken by both individuals and public officials.

Building Design

The physical design of residential complexes and housing can increase or decrease the probability that crime will occur. A housing complex designed so that all areas may be easily and frequently observed by tenants, passers-by, and police patrols can discourage criminal behavior. On the other hand, elevators, fire stairs, and underground parking garages that are hidden from public view easily mask the activities of unlawful intruders.

In *Death and Life of Great American Cities,* Jane Jacobs describes the loneliness and apprehension that large, anonymous housing projects evoke in many city dwellers:

The corridors of the usual high rise low income housing buildings are like corridors in a bad dream: creepily lit, narrow, smelly, blind. They feel like traps and they are. These traps are what people mean when they say, time and again, "Where can we go? Not to a project! I have children, I have young daughters . . ." [19]

In a recent book, partially funded by LEAA and entitled, *Defensible Space,* Oscar Newman has identified spatial arrangements that improve the security of buildings by opening certain areas to public view. He recommends that: (1) semipublic areas such as stairways and halls be visible to residents and passers-by; (2) front entrances be positioned along the street; (3) lobbies be well lit and designed so that all activity is visible from the street; (4) semiprivate areas such as paths and hallways be easily seen by tenants from apartment windows; and (5) elevators be monitored with electronic surveillance devices.

Newman's findings confirm the beliefs of those who fear massive housing complexes. Public housing projects with more than 1,000 units and seven or more stories were found to have crime rates almost one and one-half times higher than similar projects with less than 1,000 units and fewer than seven stories.[20] Newman also found that feelings of anonymity and lack of community pervade many large projects.

There are, however, positive actions that can be taken to make even the largest projects safe. By subdividing the interiors of these buildings (so that certain stairways and halls serve only small groups of families), small social groups are formed whose members jointly maintain and survey this shared area. Small walkup or garden apartments that are subdivided this way have lower crime rates.

Unfortunately, most public housing is planned and designed without considering the security system that should be built in. The placement of elevators, doors, or windows, or the installation of locks and burglar-resistant glass can be costly once a building is constructed. Many architects and physical planners are not aware of crime prevention construction techniques, and the information and experiences available through law enforcement agencies are rarely utilized.

Law enforcement agencies, criminal justice planners, and professions involved in architectural

[19] Jane Jacobs, *The Death and Life of Great American Cities,* as quoted in the Rand Institute, *Improving Public Safety in Urban Apartment Dwellings: Security Concepts and Experimental Design for New York City Housing Authority Buildings* (Rand: 1971), p. 105.

[20] Oscar Newman, *Defensible Space* (Macmillan, 1972), p. 28.

A civilian reserve police officer marking a television set with the owner's Social Security number.

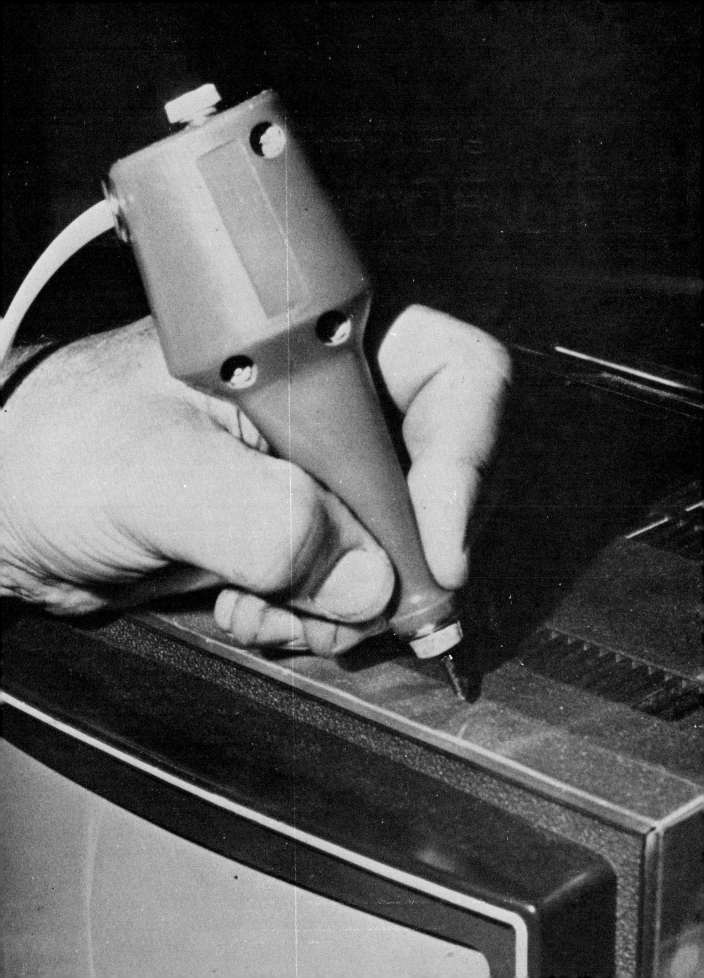

design and physical planning should coordinate their efforts to reduce criminal opportunity through improved design of buildings, thoroughfares, parks, and other public places.

Security Codes

Many communities are attempting to reduce residential and commercial burglaries by adopting security codes or by revising building codes to include security measures. The usual approach is to set specification standards for security devices and hardware in terms of specific styles and materials to be used. Thus a code might prescribe the thickness of a door or the type and design of locks. The materials and devices specified by such standards frequently become obsolete as better products are developed. Such codes also provide little incentive to manufacturers to develop better products. They divert attention from what security devices can accomplish to how they are made.

Security requirements should be included in building codes and stated in terms of effectiveness, not design.

The test of lock systems, for example, would not be their construction, but the degree of force and the length of time needed to overcome particular systems.

The formulation of these requirements or standards should be primarily the task of building, fire, and public safety departments. There should also be consultation with community criminal justice planners, transportation and sanitation departments, architectural firms, and proprietors.

At this writing, California is considering statewide standards for buildings. The standards would be based on performance and effectiveness of security hardware rather than design.[21]

Lighting

Reports from a number of urban cities and counties generally support the use of lighting as one means of achieving safe streets.

In St. Louis, Mo., as an example, a program of improved streetlighting was initiated in 1964. The first area completed involved the downtown business district, which consists of large department stores, brokerage firms, investment companies, and comparable business establishments.

In a comparison of crime in 1963, the last full year before improvements, and in 1965, the first full year after improvements, it was found that crimes against persons in the improved lighting area decreased by 40.8 percent. Auto thefts decreased by 28.6 percent and business burglaries decreased by 12.8 percent.[22]

Other reports of crime reductions associated with improved streetlighting have come from New York City, Detroit, Mich., and Washington, D. C. Proponents of streetlighting argue that it deters would-be criminals and increases the chances that actual offenders will be seen, recognized, and apprehended. Streetlighting also reportedly encourages nighttime use of the streets, itself an important deterrent to street crime.

Even the most enthusiastic advocates of streetlighting, however, admit a need for further evaluation and research. Factors such as police patrol levels, displacement of criminal activity, and seasonal change must be taken into account in rigorous studies so that the advantages and disadvantages of lighting will be more completely known.

On the basis of available evidence, the Commission recommends that units of local government consider the establishment of improved streetlighting programs in high crime areas.

The wishes of the residents and property owners should be considered at the outset of such programs and the experiences of comparable jurisdictions should be reviewed before such programs are begun.

Other Considerations

In addition to security measures already mentioned in this chapter, other measures such as alarms and intruder detection devices, legislation to aid police in tracing stolen cars, anti-shoplifting programs, and multimedia campaigns to encourage motorists to lock their cars must be considered.

One problem common to many measures designed to reduce criminal opportunities is that of the displacement of crime or the "mercury effect." Simply put, this term refers to the shifting of criminal activity from relatively secure high-risk areas to unprotected low-risk areas. Skeptics of the usefulness of security measures argue that they merely move criminals around, rather than reduce crime. There are two responses to such arguments. First, many crimes are crimes of opportunity; locking cars and removing keys can prevent spontaneous joyriding;

---

[21] State of California, Office of the Attorney General, Attorney General's Building Security Commission, "Preliminary Report to the California Legislature: Building Security Standards" (1973).

[22] J. Parker Heck, "Light Up for Safety" (prepared for the Street and Highway Safety Lighting Bureau, Cleveland, Ohio), pp. 9-10.

secure doors and windows will discourage the casual burglar. Second, criminals are not infinitely mobile; their area of operations can extend just so far before robberies, thefts, and burglaries become less profitable and not worth the trouble or risk.

The Commission is persuaded that systematic programs to reduce criminal opportunity will reduce crime if they are implemented with the joint cooperation of public agencies, citizens, and police.

INTEGRITY IN GOVERNMENT

Although many of the recommendations in this report are directed toward reducing street crime, the Commission also considers official corruption to be one of the most damaging forms of criminal activity in society.

The Commission recognizes that most people in public service are honest and dedicated. Official corruption, nevertheless, does exist, and in some jurisdictions has involved the highest elected and appointed officials.

Charges of corruption, some of which have led to convictions, have been brought against officials throughout the United States. Since 1969, more than 60 elected or appointed officials in a large Eastern State have been indicted or convicted on Federal or State criminal charges. In another, smaller State, similar charges have been brought against at least 24 officials, including a former Governor, two State senators, a State attorney general, and several other State and local officers or employees.

Corruption, as defined in this report, is not limited to its most egregious and sensational form—cash purchase of official favor. Corruption includes all of the circumstances in which the public officeholder sacrifices or sells all or part of his judgment on matters within his official purview in return for personal gain. Corruption thus defined includes a direct or tacit agreement between the official and the person requesting action that would benefit the official (cash, securities, a share in a business venture, or the promise of a future job on the outside) in exchange for official action or inaction.

Conflict of Interest

Certain types of activity are clearly incompatible with the responsibility of public employment. A conflict of interest exists when an official intentionally disregards the public's interest in return for personal gain, or when, because of financial interest or outside pressures, he is unable or unwilling to perform his duties impartially.

The Temporary Commission of Investigation of

Display of literature on organized crime.

the State of New York included in its report to the 1971 State Legislature the story of a resident engineer in the city of Yonkers Engineering Department. In that position, the man (Mr. S.) was responsible for verifying compliance with his department's specifications for all contractors doing business with the city.

In the course of the commission's investigations, testimony revealed that Mr. S. and at least two construction inspectors also employed by the city were privately employed by the contractors whose work they were charged with inspecting. The three city employees were moonlighting in the largest sewer project ever handled by Yonkers, a contract totaling $916,431; at the same time they were acting in their official capacity to insure the project's compliance with city regulations.[23]

Conflicts of interest can be a problem whenever public officials exercise power and discretion over decisions that affect many citizens. Because of the enormous impact such measures can have on special interest groups and individuals, public officials are approached continually by people who want to influence official action.

A proper system of conflicts regulation and a code of ethical principles to guide officials are needed. Present conflict of interest regulations are inadequate at the State and local levels. As of 1969, only 26 States had any laws on this subject, and none of these States included local government employees within the scope of the law's coverage.[24] Among the

[23] *Thirteenth Annual Report of the Temporary Commission of Investigation of the State of New York* (March 1971), pp. 96-109.

[24] All statistics are taken from *Assembly of the State of California, Ethical Conduct and Governmental Integrity: The Conflict of Interest Issue* (1970).

States that have enacted laws, only a few approach the requirements of an adequate safeguard.

Another failing of current legislation is that it often does not deal with borderline or minor cases of official misconduct that do not warrant criminal prosecution. The purchasing agent who accepts a dinner invitation or a small gift from a supplier should be subjected to a reprimand rather than criminal prosecution. The Commission believes that no single law or type of law is sufficient to deal with the gamut of ethical problems that underlie an official's conduct. A system of various types of provisions—criminal laws, ethical guidelines, and an enforcement body—is essential to assure the public that officials will act with integrity.

The Commission recommends that States, in addition to criminal sanctions, adopt provisions for an ethics code and an ethics board to enforce and interpret the provisions of the code and to apply administrative sanctions.

This code should require that public officials disqualify themselves from taking official actions when a conflict of interest might exist; should prohibit acceptance of gifts, favors, services, or promises of future employment that might influence their performance of official duties; and should prohibit acceptance of positions of employment that might involve conflicting duties.

States also should adopt provisions requiring public officials to disclose fully and openly their financial and professional interests.

This is perhaps the most effective method of conflict of interest regulation; it seeks to deter wrongful conduct by giving the public access to information on areas of an official's professional and private life that offer the greatest potential for conflict.

Political Campaign Financing

A potential for corruption or conflict of interest exists when a candidate for political office is forced to rely on large contributions from special interest groups. Such contributions might be made as an attempt to purchase goodwill and influence future decisions or they might be payment for favors or preferred treatment already received. These practices are certainly widespread. Various studies have estimated that 15 percent of the money for State and local campaigns comes from persons engaged in illegal gambling and racketeering who seek

protection for their illegal activities.[25] If correct, this would mean that well over $15 million might have come from criminal elements in the 1972 State and local elections.

In order to reduce opportunities for corruption in campaign financing, the Commission recommends that States impose and enforce realistic campaign spending limitations, require full disclosure of financial contributions to all parties and candidates for local and State office, and prohibit contributions from significant government contractors, labor unions, trade associations, and corporations.

Government Procurement, Zoning, Licensing, and Tax Assessment

Government procurement, zoning, licensing, and tax assessment are functions of State and local governments often known for inefficiency, mismanagement, and corruption. Commercial enterprises and individuals dealing with government have a tremendous stake in these areas and the opportunity for graft exists when explicit and precise standards are not adhered to.

In the competitive area of governmental purchasing, the unethical vendor needs only a slight edge to beat the competition on a given contract. With the cooperation of the corrupt government employee, the vendor can utilize various devices to maximize his profits at the expense of the purchaser. The losers in such transactions are the government and ultimately the taxpayer, who will pay more than the goods or services are worth or who will purchase materials that cannot be used.

Most States have taken steps to upgrade the integrity of the government procurement function by creating centralized State purchasing agencies. Centralization has encouraged efficiency and economy in purchasing as well as the professionalization of purchasing agents.

---

[25] According to Alexander Heard, this estimate "embraces funds given in small towns and rural areas by individuals operating on the borders of the law who want a sympathetic sheriff and prosecutor, but who are not linked to crime syndicates. This estimate applies chiefly to persons engaged in illegal gambling and racketeering. It does not extend, for example, to otherwise reputable businessmen who hope for understanding treatment from building inspectors and tax assessors." Alexander Heard, *The Costs of Democracy* (University of North Carolina Press, 1960), p. 165, fn. 73, also pp. 154-168; see also Harold D. Laswell and Arnold Rogow, *Power Corruption and Rectitude,* (Prentice Hall, 1963), pp. 79-80; and Donald R. Cressy, *Theft of the Nation: The Structure and Operations of Organized Crime in America* (Harper and Row, 1969), **p. 253.**

States snould adopt formal procedures for setting and disseminating commodity specifications, handling complaints, encouraging competition, and insuring timely delivery of goods and services. A State purchasing agency should be established with an advisory board composed of the heads of the finance committees of the legislature, the purchasing director, and the heads of the various sections of the purchasing agency.

Some of the corruption in zoning, licensing, and tax assessment occurs because otherwise honest citizens become so frustrated with government bureaucracy and red tape that they are willing to offer bribes and kickbacks just to get action in governmental decisions. In New York City, there are at least 40 different licenses or permits required to construct a new building. A construction delay of several days resulting from a pending permit would cost contractors substantially more than they lose in payoffs to officials to speed up permit processing. According to one estimate, as much as 5 percent of the total construction costs in the city are attributable to graft paid to city employees.[26] Five percent of the estimated $1.5 billion annual construction bill amounts to $75 million.

Cash payments for zoning changes are not uncommon in some communities. A favorable zoning decision can boost the value of certain pieces of land and may mean substantial profits. Corruption in tax assessments also involves large sums. For example, when the assessor of a large metropolitan area discovered he was being investigated by a local citizen group for "arbitrary and manipulative" operation of his office, he "reassessed" nine high rise properties in the city. The reassessment of those nine buildings added $34 million to the city's tax base.[27]

The Commission believes that the greatest single cause of corruption in these three areas of government operation is the availability of excessive discretion involving significant sums of money. Vague and improperly stated decision guidelines invite attempts at manipulation and fraud and are, at a minimum, indicative of sloppy management.

Each jurisdiction should develop explicit criteria for use by officials in making decisions in zoning, licensing, and tax assessment.

---

[26] "5 Percent of Building Costs Are Laid to New York Graft," *Washington Post* (October 20, 1971).

[27] *Moore et al.* v. *Cullerton*, 72-c-680 filed in U.S. District Court for the Northern District of Illinois. See also "A $16 Million U. S. Steel 'Tax Break' Charged," *Chicago Daily News* (May 18, 1971), and "Charge Loop Bank Gets Big Tax Break," *Chicago Today* (July 13, 1971).

Investigation and Prosecution of Corrupt Officials

An essential part of eliminating corruption and the influence of organized crime in government is a firm commitment on the part of State and local government to seek out and prosecute vigorously all types of corrupt practices in which the government is involved.

The first step is for State and local units of government to assess the nature and extent of their corruption problems. Because each jurisdiction has different statutory powers, administrative organizations, and social and political makeup, the Commission was unable to propose a single set of standards for investigation and prosecution of corruption cases. However, it has set out broad, general guidelines that State and local governments can use in developing their anticorruption approaches.

The Commission strongly believes that the first line of defense against illegal conduct by government officials is a local prosecutor's office staffed by well-compensated and adequately trained personnel. It is recognized, however, that there are cases where local authorities are technically not prepared or are unwilling to handle corruption problems.

States having a history of public corruption at State and local levels should establish an ongoing statewide capability for investigation and prosecution of governmental corruption and organized crime.

This capability might take the form of a corruption investigation unit under the State attorney general, a special grand jury convened when needed by legislative act or executive order, or a State investigation commission created by constitutional amendment. The experiences of New York and New Jersey with investigation commissions provide useful models for other States.

One of the most vital attributes of an anticorruption unit (and one that currently is absent in all existing State investigation commissions) is its power to prosecute the case as it develops. The Commission recommends that this power be granted to the anticorruption unit.

IMPLEMENTING COMMUNITY CRIME PREVENTION ACTIVITIES

Many of the programs and activities discussed in this chapter will require financial underwriting. In many instances, sufficient funds should be available at the State or local level, or in the case of many citizen activities, from private sources.

Under certain circumstances, some crime prevention programs might qualify for support from funds provided by LEAA. LEAA makes its funds available to States, which in turn fund projects at the operational level.

In other circumstances, funds might be available from other Federal agencies, including the Department of Health, Education, and Welfare (HEW). Aid in the form of information, speakers, films, and expert assistance might be available from such agencies as the Special Action Office for Drug Abuse Prevention and the Bureau of Narcotics and Dangerous Drugs, to name only two.

Citizens, groups, and organizations should inform themselves fully about the availability of funds for the particular kind of program they have in mind. Congress has directed how the funds can and cannot be used. In some cases, there may be uncertainty about the propriety of using funds for certain projects.

CONCLUSION

The local community is one of the Nation's most underdeveloped and underutilized crime fighting resources. It is a resource that needs to be utilized by everyone concerned about the incidence of crime in his community.

A community may translate its concern about crime into action through the individual and group efforts of its citizens, through its local institutions such as schools, youth services bureaus, and religious organizations, and through the responsible and responsive efforts of its governing bodies.

Neither in this chapter, nor in its *Report on Community Crime Prevention,* has the Commission exhausted the possible approaches that a community may take to reduce and prevent crime. Indeed, there are as many viable approaches to community crime prevention as there are citizens who deplore the conditions that are known to cause crime. What is needed is a positive commitment to action.

Chapter 5

Police

In the decade that just passed, the American people witnessed massive riots and demonstrations and experienced widespread fear of crime and personal violence. The people sought answers and demanded solutions.

The police were at the center of controversy and the pressure to change was immense. Fortunately, this pressure was accompanied by support never before experienced by American law enforcement practitioners. One chief of a large city termed 1968 the "year of the policeman." Others looked to the seventies and predicted that it would be the "decade of the policeman."

The police have responded to the call for change. Progress in many areas is evident. Law enforcement agencies throughout the land have taken steps, some small and unsteady, others large and bold, to come to grips with their problems and to assume roles previously shunned by police administrators. These efforts portend more effective police service.

MAJOR RECOMMENDATIONS

In this chapter the Commission highlights some of the more important changes taking place in law enforcement and calls on every police agency to work toward their implementation. In its *Report on Police,* the Commission sets forth in even greater detail specific standards for improving the effectiveness of the police function.

The Commission's recommendations are directed toward increasing the effectiveness of the police in reducing crime. The recommendations and standards recognize the patrolman as the primary force in reducing and preventing crime. They seek to enhance his role. Major recommendations call for:
• Active crime prevention efforts by the police working with the community.
• Diversion of juveniles, drunks, and mental patients from the criminal justice system.
• Use of the patrolman as the primary investigator for crimes which come to his attention.
• Consolidation or elimination of police departments with fewer than 10 full-time police officers.
• Increased use of civilians.
• College education entrance requirements for employment of police officers.
• Legislation authorizing police officers to obtain search warrants by telephone.
• Continuing analysis of crime trends and deployment of special units to react to developing crime trends.
• Establishment of different classifications and pay levels within the basic patrolman category.

• Development of units within police departments to work with prosecutors, courts, and corrections officials and to follow specific cases and individuals through the criminal justice system.

THE POLICE ROLE

Maintenance of order and enforcement of law are the two traditional missions of the police. As society has become more complex, many and varied demands have been put upon the police because of their unique authority. In developing its recommendations the Commission recognized the many functions which police agencies perform, including:
• Prevention of criminal activity.
• Detection of criminal activity.
• Apprehension of criminal offenders.
• Participation in court proceedings.
• Protection of constitutional guarantees.
• Assistance to those who cannot care for themselves or who are in danger of physical harm.
• Control of traffic.
• Resolution of day-to-day conflicts among family, friends, and neighbors.
• Creation and maintenance of a feeling of security in the community.
• Promotion and preservation of civil order.

These functions represent the core elements in the contemporary role of police. However, controversy exists as to the emphasis which should be placed on each of these functions. The Commission has recognized that local governments and citizens are in the best position to determine their needs, and the ultimate definition of the police role and the degree of emphasis to be placed on each function should be consistent with the laws and needs of the community that is being served.

It also is crucial that the police role be defined within the legal limits of authority. There are numerous laws that set out the authority under which the police must operate. In addition to and in accord with the pertinent law, guidelines should be developed for handling such problems as the resolution of family disputes and neighborhood altercations; the taking into custody of adults and juveniles, alcoholics, drug offenders, and the mentally ill; and the control of civil disorders.

Every police agency should write out a detailed statement of its role. The statement should be consistent with the United States Constitution and the laws of its State or city and the policies of the government the agency serves. The statement should identify the absolute limitations on the use of force by police and should establish guidelines for the use of discretion in making arrests and maintaining order.

WORKING WITH THE COMMUNITY

The communities of this Nation are torn by racial strife, economic chasms, and struggles between the values of the old and the viewpoints of the young. These circumstances have made it difficult for the policeman to identify with and be identified as part of a community of citizens. As communities have divided within themselves, there has been a breakdown in cooperation between the police and the citizens.

The problem is particularly acute in large urban population centers. Here, the fibers of mutual assistance and neighborliness that bind citizens together have grown precariously thin.

Yet it is a fact that cooperation between the police and the community is the first step in effective crime control. As an essential ingredient to cooperation, every police agency should formally recognize the importance of communication with the public and constantly seek to improve its ability to determine the needs and expectations of the public, to act upon these needs and expectations, and to inform the people of the resulting policies developed to improve the delivery of police services.

The police must obtain information from the community as to its needs, and the public also must be informed of the police agency's roles so that it can better support the police in their efforts to reduce crime. Toward this end, the Commission recommends that:
• Police agencies should participate in educational efforts at the elementary, secondary, and college levels, and in youth programs aimed at improving the community's cooperation with and understanding of the police.
• Agencies should encourage public speaking engagements by police officers and should hold open houses and tours of police facilities.
• Police agencies should publish annual reports and periodic bulletins on significant crime trends and developments in police operations.

Many police agencies have used the schools to increase public understanding of the police role. "Officer Friendly" programs at the elementary school level have been particularly effective. The programs teach children traffic and bicycle safety and encourage them to accept policemen as their friends.

Programs at the secondary level require more careful structuring to be effective. They must delineate between the officer's enforcement role and his educational role. The Commission's examination

of these programs indicates that an officer's primary assignment should include teaching classes on the role of the police and serving as a counselor. The assignment should not include law enforcement duties except as related to counseling.

In one program instituted by a major metropolitan police department, officers were assigned to selected schools with full-time faculty status and limited law enforcement duties. During 1970–71, approximately 2,000 students were given attitude tests that showed that the program created favorable changes in student attitudes toward the law and the police.

Programs of adult education and college education involving personnel from local police agencies also have been implemented effectively.

In addition to school activities, many agencies have found that police-supported recreational programs aid development of better relationships between the officers and young people of the community. Some departments, for example, have provided funds from their budgets to send children to summer camp. Other departments have established and supplied equipment for Police Athletic Leagues and Police Boards for Youth. These programs are all established on the principle that they are an effective force in crime prevention because they encourage youths to view police as a positive force and help them to understand their own responsibilities toward the law.

Community Relations

The Commission recommends that police agencies in major metropolitan areas establish a specialized unit responsible for maintaining communication with the community. In smaller agencies, the police chief executive should assume direct responsibility for maintaining communication.

The unit should be no more than one step removed from the chief executive in the chain of command. It should identify impediments to communication within the community and devise methods of overcoming these impediments, including the use of public opinion polls, neighborhood meetings, and radio and television to elicit public opinion.

Reducing Criminal Opportunity

The vital role the police can play in educating the public to take self-protective measures and reduce criminal opportunity must be recognized by police departments. Direct police crime prevention efforts include the security profile program conducted by the Michigan State Police, in which residences and commercial establishments are compared and rated against a comprehensive checklist of security measures by the police. Insurance companies are then encouraged to give discounts in burglary and robbery insurance premiums to those who get a high rating by the police.

The California Criminal Justice Council has funded a series of burglary prevention programs which reduced burglary by significant amounts in 1973 in the affected areas. These programs include publicity campaigns on how to prevent burglary, voluntary door-to-door inspection of residences and commercial establishments by specially trained police officers, encouragement of the establishment of neighborhood security programs in which people in the community work with the police to report crime and alert their neighbors to developing crime trends, and establishment of special telephone numbers for citizens to report anonymously crimes in progress or crimes about to be committed.

The single most successful crime prevention program instituted in recent years is the Operation Identification program established originally by the Monterey Park, Calif., police department and implemented since by a number of police departments and citizen groups across the country. In this program citizens use engraving tools to put an indelible marking, such as a social security number, on their personal belongings. A list of marked property is then filed with a central agency such as the police department and warning stickers are placed on the outside of residences. Participating residences are rarely, if ever, burglarized.

Yet another example of neighborhood self-protection and police cooperation is provided by the tenant patrols of the New York City Housing Authority, in which more than 11,000 volunteers in more than 600 apartment buildings act as the eyes and ears of the police department, reporting suspicious persons or circumstances to the police.

Every police agency should establish programs that assist and encourage members of the public to take an active role in preventing crime. Police agencies should assist actively in the establishment of volunteer neighborhood security programs, and police agencies in major metropolitan areas should establish crime prevention units to work with the community in reducing criminal opportunities.

Police and the News Media

The relationship between the police and the news media in a democratic society is characterized by complementary interests. The news media have a legitimate need for information about police activities and they offer an excellent channel for informing the public about the nature of police tasks and problems.

As long as individual freedom is protected in all cases, agency policy should give the media the right to receive information upon request. There should be a basic presumption that information will be supplied upon request unless the released information would be improper due to court order. Policy should express respect for the news media, their role in a democratic society, and their value to effective police service.

In addition to responding to requests for information, police agencies should establish policy and procedures that provide for notifying the media about newsworthy events. In one metropolitan area, departments use special police radio broadcast channels to inform newspapers and broadcasting organizations of significant or unusual occurrences. In another area, police departments have established a newswire teletype circuit over which subscribing news media agencies routinely receive notification of serious or unusual events in which the police agency is involved.

Every police agency should acknowledge the important role of the news media in reporting on police activities and the need for the police agency to be open in its relations with the media.

Agencies should:
• Establish policies which protect and foster the right of the press to obtain information for dissemination to the public.
• Establish a regular news liaison function for responding to inquiries from the media and for disseminating information on police activities.

Minority Community Needs

A critically important community problem confronts the police in urban areas with significant minority populations. A disproportionate amount of crime often occurs in these areas. Inhabitants of these areas frequently feel that they have less influence on police enforcement policies and practices than do other community residents. They are not convinced that the police serve them or respect them as citizens.

Some police departments, therefore, have established programs that seek the views of the minority community on police service. Other departments have provided training for their officers in race relations, community awareness, and ethnic history.

For example, the Dayton, Ohio, police department developed a training program in which new recruits

Police officers meeting with school class.

were assigned as professional assistants to 14 different social action agencies during the first 4 weeks of training. This was followed by a training and service program that combined community awareness and role identification.

In Kansas City, Mo., recruits trained in role identification and social awareness were the subject of substantially fewer complaints during the first 6 months of service than were their associates who had not received this training.

The most encouraging development has been the efforts of some major city departments, working with organizations such as the Urban Coalition, to recruit minority citizens as police officers. These efforts have produced encouraging results and the police chief of Washington, D.C., in response to a question from a reporter on how his department had reduced crime in Washington, cited the increase in minority officers on the police force as a major factor.

The Commission recommends that every police agency that has racial or minority groups of significant size in its jurisdiction insure that the needs of minorities are actively considered in the establishment of police policy and the delivery of police service. Affirmative action should be taken to achieve a proportion of minority group employees that approximates their proportion in the population of the area.

Recruit and inservice police training programs should provide explicit instruction in community culture. The training should be general as to the whole community and specific as to significant minority or ethnic groups in the community. Training programs should stress interpersonal

75

communications and should rest on a single standard of fair and equal treatment for all persons.

Further, every police agency should insure that recruitment, hiring, assignment, and promotion policies do not discriminate against minority groups. Every police agency should engage in positive efforts to employ ethnic or minority group members.

Citizen Grievances

All efforts to establish effective relations with the community will fail if the police agency is not responsive to complaints from the community about general police services and about individual officers. Accordingly, it is imperative that police agencies establish procedures for insuring that complaints about police service are handled in an expeditious and fair manner. The procedures should insure that every police agency inform the public on a continuing basis of its complaint reception and investigation procedures. Complaint forms should be developed and made available to the public.

The procedures should insure that the making of the complaint is not accompanied by fear of reprisal or harassment. Complete records of complaint reception, investigation, and adjudication should be maintained in a central record and statistical center. Complaints should be chronologically recorded. Information based on these records should be published regularly and made available to the public.

Every police agency should insure that all allegations of service misconduct and all complaints are investigated by a specialized unit or individual in the agency.

The Commission recommends that every police agency establish procedures to facilitate full and fair processing of complaints about general police services and about individual officer's conduct. Every person making a complaint should receive written verification that his complaint is being processed by the police agency. Every person who files a complaint should be notified of its disposition and personal discussion regarding this disposition should be encouraged.

Patrol and Crime Prevention

Of all the functions performed by the police, there is none more important than the day-to-day job of the patrol officer. The patrol officer is the community's first line of defense against crime.

In its simplest terms, patrol is the deployment of police officers in a given community to prevent and

deter criminal activity and to provide day-to-day police services to the community.

Every police chief executive should insure that all elements within the agency provide maximum assistance and cooperation to the patrol officer and patrol officers should be relieved of minor tasks in order to increase their capability to reduce crime.

A survey done for the 1967 President's Crime Commission found that almost 48 percent of all arrests are made within 2 hours of the commission of the crime and 36 percent of all arrests are made within an hour. The Commission then went on to conclude that "ways should be found of getting persons with investigative experience to crime scenes with the greatest possible rapidity—before crimes, in police terms, are cold."

In the view of the National Advisory Commission an important way is to enlarge the patrol officer's investigative role. Too often the patrol officer's involvement in a criminal investigation is limited to taking reports. He is expected to interview witnesses and victims, conduct a preliminary investigation, formulate a report, and return to service, all within 30 minutes. The result is usually a hastily prepared report, a cursory preliminary investigation, and an unsolved crime.

Patrolmen should receive training in conducting investigations and in gathering evidence. Patrol officers should be utilized to conduct the complete investigation of crimes which do not require extensive followup investigation and patrol officers should be utilized to follow up and close out investigations of these crimes.

Geographic Policing

The Commission has been encouraged by the efforts of police departments in recent years in developing policing programs that insure stability of assignment of individual patrol officers within a given neighborhood and community. Under these programs, police agencies require patrol officers so assigned to meet on a regular basis with persons who live and work in the area to discuss and identify crime problems and the proper solution to these problems.

The "Basic Car Plan" initiated by the Los Angeles City Police Department and followed by other departments utilizes the geographic policing concept. It has been successful in involving thousands of citizens in a direct effort to make their neighborhood safe and is built on two major premises. The first premise of the program is that an officer assigned to

77

a given area and given primary responsibility for reducing crime in that area can prove more effective than an officer randomly assigned to an area and given no specific crime reduction responsibility. This can be even more true when the patrolman's investigative role is expanded as recommended earlier.

The second premise is that support of citizens living and working in the community is essential for successful policing and is the best method of reducing crime; this support can best be obtained through long-term assignment of officers to a neighborhood and through police efforts to communicate with citizens.

In many respects, the program is an update of the concept of the police "walking the beat," which was generally abandoned in the late 1940's and early 1950's because reformers were concerned that the officer on the foot beat could be corrupted by his familiarity with local residents and was slow to respond to the scene of an emergency. To solve the latter problem, they put him in a radio car; to solve the former, they transferred him frequently so that he would not have a chance to become corrupt.

There are better means available to police departments to control corruption, including departmental audits of police arrests and the use of internal discipline investigative units. Police need to return to patrol programs that establish stronger ties to the community while maintaining the flexibility and speed of response provided by the patrol car.

The Commission recommends that every police agency adopt policing programs that insure stability of assignment in a given geographic area for

Police officers with civilian auxiliary patrolman.

individual patrol officers who are operationally deployed.

Every police agency should insure that officers assigned to geographic policing programs meet regularly with persons who live or work in their area. Every patrol officer assigned to the program should be responsible for control of crime in his area and should, within the framework of the agency's objectives and policy, be granted authority to determine the means he will use to fulfill that responsibility.

Team Policing

Team policing incorporates the concept of geographic policing and carries it even further. First experiments in team policing took place in Europe and certain aspects of it were recommended in the President's Commission on Law Enforcement and Administration of Justice. Since the issuance of that Commission's report, team policing has become one of the most popular forms of police reorganization and innovation. It has been practiced in different ways in different agencies and has received considerable publicity. However, no definitive study has yet been made of its effectiveness and the changes to be achieved. Total team policing can be defined as:

1. Combining all line operations of patrol, traffic, and investigation into a single group under common supervision;

2. Forming teams with a mixture of patrolmen, investigators, and specialists in such areas as juvenile delinquency and drug abuse;

3. Permanently assigning teams to geographic areas; and

4. Charging the teams with total responsibility for all police services within their respective areas.

Most team policing systems have not taken this total approach, but from the experience of cities that have implemented various aspects of team policing programs, the Commission is satisfied that these programs have a significant potential for crime control.

The Commission recommends that every police agency examine and test the team policing concept to determine its value in improving the agency's efforts to reduce crime, improve the quality of police service, and enhance police-community cooperation.

Police Community Reserves

Many police agencies in this country utilize citizen reserve officers to supplement the regular force of officers. Many reserves are authorized to make arrests and perform all of the routine police functions. Reserves operate on a part-time basis and can be used to provide backup manpower, increase police-community cooperation, and perform many valuable volunteer services.

Utilization of reserves is an extension of a tradition that precedes the existence of structured police forces. The early use of reserves in this country is a sordid history of the misuse of police power beginning with deputized posses and vigilantes in the West in the 19th century, and carrying through to the American Protective League that was established as a citizens' auxiliary to the United States Department of Justice in 1917. The league, operating without legal authority, conducted mass roundups of suspected draft dodgers, enemy aliens, and deserters.

This history has produced many opponents to the police reserve concept. However, it is the opinion of the Commission, based on an analysis of modern-day programs, that properly structured and standardized civilian reserve programs can make a valuable addition to a police force.

One excellent modern-day use of reserves is the Reserve Deputy Sheriff's Program conducted in Los Angeles County, Calif., which uses reserve patrolmen and reserve specialists who are specially trained and selected.

Reserve personnel donated 374,867 man-hours of police service to the County of Los Angeles during fiscal year 1970–71, resulting in a total cost savings to the county in police salaries of over $2 million.

If reserve officers are used, there must be clear standards for their training and use. Police agencies should furnish the reserve officer with the uniform and equipment of a regular sworn officer upon completion of all training requirements. Until the reserve has completed training requirements, his uniform should readily identify him as a reserve officer, and he should perform his duties under the direct supervision of a regular sworn officer. The Florida State Police Standards Board has developed a set of standards that could provide a sound basis for utilization of police reserves.

Every police department should consider employment of police reserve officers to supplement the regular force of officers and increase community involvement in local police service.

Diversion

It is becoming increasingly clear that every suspect need not be arrested and that every suspect should not be processed through the courts and correction processes. Juveniles, alcoholics, the elderly, the mentally ill, drug users, the physically sick or handicapped frequently need help outside the criminal justice system. The police can and should assist in bringing to light community resources, in opening new avenues of help to people coming to their attention, and in diverting these people out of the criminal justice system.

These efforts have two main advantages: by relieving the burdens both on courts and on corrections of processing individuals who could be more appropriately handled outside the criminal justice system, they free valuable criminal justice resources and provide more effective help to the individual. In the case of juveniles, counseling and informal referral are often more effective than formal procedures. Detoxification treatment, therapy, and counseling are clearly more appropriate for alcoholics than traditional confinement and release.

Some police agencies are reluctant to engage in diversion, particularly diversion with referral to welfare agencies. As an example, the vast majority of juveniles taken into custody in 1971 (over 1.2 million) were either referred to juvenile court or handled within the police department and released. Less than 2 percent were referred to welfare agencies.[1]

Diversion does not take place in many departments because police are either not familiar with private and public resources or such resources are simply not available. These problems can and should be corrected by cooperation among police, criminal justice planners, and community officials.

Some agencies eschew diversion in the belief that they will be accused of selective and unequal law enforcement. This difficulty can be avoided, however, if police agencies will develop written criteria specifying who can be diverted and under what circumstances.

Every police agency should establish formal criteria for diverting from the criminal and juvenile justice system all individuals coming to their attention for whom processing into the justice system would be inappropriate or for whom the use of resources outside the criminal and juvenile justice system would be more appropriate.

These guidelines are to be developed after consultation with prosecutors, judges, and other criminal justice personnel. States and units of local government should enact legislation and ordinances authorizing diversion and authorizing and funding alcohol detoxification, drug treatment, youth services

---

[1] Federal Bureau of Investigation, *Uniform Crime Reports—1971* (1972), p. 112.

bureaus, and other appropriate diversion-oriented programs.

PLANNING AND ORGANIZING FOR MORE EFFECTIVE LAW ENFORCEMENT

Proper planning for effective use of resources necessarily begins with the collection and analysis of data that reflect the community's needs for police services, and the type of activities performed by the police. Reported crimes, arrests, and calls for service must be analyzed by type, date, time, and location. The amount of police time expended on these functions, on preventive patrol, on traffic enforcement, and on nonemergency and noncriminal matters must be analyzed.

The extent of the analysis required should be consistent with the volume and nature of the local demands for police services and the size and resources of the agency.

Every police agency should conduct workload studies on a regular basis; information obtained from the workload studies should form the basis for establishing patrol and investigation operational objectives and priorities.

Deployment

Crime and workload data may indicate the advisability of special task forces to deal with particular crimes or series of crimes.

In one city, for example, reported crime and arrest data are collected by each precinct on each shift. These data are transmitted to the headquarters crime analysis unit, which records and analyzes them. When the unit detects significant trends, it dispatches officers from a special headquarters tactical squad to selected areas of the city to provide increased patrol investigative capability. The tactical squad includes uniformed officers, plainclothes officers, and officers in disguise. The department credits this technique with having a substantial impact on the reductions in reported crime it has recorded in recent years and similar experiences have been reported in other departments.

The Commission recommends that police departments in major cities establish tactical squads for flexible, highly mobile, and rapid deployment against special crime problems. The tactical squad should be deployed on the basis of current crime pattern analysis and projected criminal activity. A full-time tactical force should include an analytical staff element.

Responsibility for Police Service

Almost all local governments can benefit from some form of combined police service. At one extreme, local government can get out of the police business entirely by contracting for all police services from another government or agency, or State and local police agencies may simply develop ways to assist and reinforce each other.

Consolidation can frequently upgrade police service and lower its costs. Because it is larger, the consolidated agency usually has superior resources. Because it eliminates much duplication, citizens get more for their money.

Local governments should analyze the various methods of combining police services, compare the cost effectiveness of each to that of its own operations, and develop applications to its own operations.

The most comprehensive combined service is total consolidation of local government. One type of total consolidation took place in 1965 when personnel of the North Sacramento, Calif., police department were absorbed into the Sacramento police department.

A second type of total consolidation is the merger of a city government with a county government. In 1968 in Florida the 474-man Jacksonville police department merged with the 260-man Duval County sheriff's office under the office of the sheriff. In January 1973, the city of Lexington and Fayette County, Ky., merged under a charter establishing the Lexington-Fayette Urban County Government with a single police department.

A further method of providing consolidated police services includes contracting for police service. The most frequent type of contract is the city-county contract. In Los Angeles County, approximately 29 cities ranging in population from 1,000 to 100,000 contract with the county to provide total police services. Each jurisdiction contracting with the county can, through the contract process, establish the amount of police service to be provided.

There are also advantageous arrangements between States and local jurisdictions. In New Jersey and Kentucky, State police departments provide contract services to certain jurisdictions in their respective States.

A number of agencies have also undertaken to provide consolidated support and operative services in selected areas. In the Kansas City, Mo., metropolitan area, a metro squad composed of personnel assigned by the various participating agencies in the metropolitan area assists in investigating major cases (primarily homicides) deemed likely to constitute a metropolitan threat.

Arrests have been made in more than 70 percent of the cases investigated by the metro squad. Additionally, numerous arrests for offenses other than those being investigated have been made by the metro squad. The squad functions throughout the multijurisdictional geographic area, even transcending the Missouri-Kansas State line.

In 1972, the Jefferson County and Louisville, Ky., police departments merged seven major functional areas: training, records, information systems, fingerprinting and identification, photo laboratories, planning and research, and communication systems. This has resulted in greater efficiency and effectiveness of these services and the operations of the two police departments.

Total Consolidation of Small Police Departments

It is the view of the Commission that 10 police officers should be considered the minimum level required for an agency to operate as an independent entity.

The facts are as follows: approximately 80 percent of the 25,000 police agencies in the United States have fewer than 10 full-time commissioned officers, yet they account for less than 10 percent of the total full-time police officers in the United States.

Small agencies often are not able to serve their communities efficiently. The Advisory Commission on Intergovernmental Relations in its 1971 report on *State-Local Relations in the Criminal Justice System* noted:

Small police departments, particularly those of ten or less men, are unable to provide a wide range of patrol and investigative services to local citizens. Moreover, the existence of these small agencies may work a hardship on nearby jurisdictions. Small police departments do not have adequate full-time control in preliminary and investigative services and may require the aid of larger agencies in many facets of their police work. Moreover, lack of adequate basic police services in one locality can make it a haven for criminals and thus impose social and economic costs on the remainder of the metropolitan community.

Other studies show that five sworn police officers are required to provide one sworn police officer on a full-time, around-the-block basis, allowing for days off, vacation and sick time, and other variables. To provide for the full-time employment of two policemen, a local government would ideally need to hire 10 police officers. If fewer than 10 sworn personnel are employed, the employment is usually not cost effective and often results in inadequate services.

The Commission recommends that any police agency employing fewer than 10 sworn officers combine with one or more other agencies to improve efficiency in delivering police services. In remote areas where there is no nearby local agency, combined or contract programs with county or State agencies should be established.

MAXIMUM USE OF HUMAN RESOURCES

Of all the resources committed to the law enforcement process, manpower is at once the costliest and the most important. Nationally, more than 80 percent of all police budgets is committed to salaries.[2] It is imperative that police obtain maximum productivity from available manpower.

Recruitment

The first step in obtaining an effective police force is the recruitment and selection of competent personnel. It is imperative that police agencies engage in forceful, active recruiting to bring their departments to authorized strength.

The Commission recommends that every police agency aggressively recruit applicants when qualified candidates are not readily available. In recruiting applicants, a variety of techniques should be implemented, including use of professional recruiters and central government personnel agencies, development of cooperative personnel systems with other police agencies, and utilization of all agency personnel in the recruitment process.

Police recruitment efforts should concentrate on college-educated applicants. Recruitment resources should be applied according to the agency's needs for personnel with varied ethnic and minority characteristics. Residency should be eliminated as a prerequisite for employment and decentralized application procedures should be utilized.

Education

More than half of the Nation's young people now go on to college. In terms of education norms, an undergraduate degree today is equivalent in prestige to a high school diploma at the turn of the century. Yet most police agencies have failed to take notice of this change and for many agencies the minimum required education level is the same as it was 40 years ago, a high school education.

Police agencies have lost ground in the race for

[2] Kansas City Police Department, "1970 Survey of Municipal Police Departments," (1970).

highly qualified employees. College graduates look elsewhere for employment, and police work has often come to be regarded by the public as a second-class occupation. It is ironic that this is taking place when studies are showing that police officers with a college background perform at a significantly higher level than police officers without a college degree.

A 1972 study by the Rand Institute in New York, N.Y., revealed that men who had college degrees demonstrated better on-the-job performance than the average policeman and had a low incidence of misconduct.[3] These findings are similar to the results of a 1968 Chicago study, which revealed that the highest rated group of tenure officers were those with significantly high levels of education.[4] Upgrading the educational level of police officers is one of the more important challenges facing the police service in the 1970's.

The Commission recommends that every police agency require immediately, as a condition of initial employment, completion of at least 1 year of education at an accredited college or university and that by 1983, every police agency require, as a condition of initial employment, completion of at least 4 years of college-level education or a baccalaureate degree at an accredited college or university.

It is imperative that police agencies upgrade the educational levels of their present officers as well as their recruits, since many of these officers will be performing police services for some years to come. Police agencies therefore should establish incentives to encourage police officers to achieve a college-level education. Officers' assignments should be made, where possible, to accommodate attendance at local colleges, and financial assistance to defray educational expenses should be provided. Increased pay should be provided for the attainment of specified levels of academic achievement.

Training

There is a serious flaw in the police profession—the insufficiency of initial and inservice training given to most policemen. Perhaps no other profession has such lax standards, or is allowed to operate without firm controls and without licensing.

The average barber receives 4,000 hours of training. The average policeman receives less than 200 hours.

---

[3] Bernard Cohen and Jan M. Chaihen, *Police Background Characteristics and Performance Summary* (Rand Institute, May 1972).

[4] Melany E. Baehr, *Psychological Assessment of Patrolman Qualifications in Relation to Field Performance* (Government Printing Office, November 1968).

In 1931, the National Commission on Law Observance and Enforcement (Wickersham Commission), impressed by what it saw taking place in larger police agencies, predicted that the time for thorough police training had come and that within 15 years high quality police training would be all but universal in the United States. What that Commission perhaps failed to see is that only large agencies have the resources to provide adequate police training. Smaller agencies cannot develop the needed programs.

Yet this training must be made available to all policemen in all agencies. The people have a right to expect high quality police professionalism everywhere.

Every State should enact legislation that establishes mandatory minimum basic training of 400 hours for police; that establishes a representative body to develop and administer programs for police; and that establishes financial support for local police training.

This legislation should prohibit any individual from performing the police function unless he is certified as having met the minimum standards.

In addition to traditional basic police subjects, training should include instruction in law, psychology, and sociology, and should involve assigned activities away from the training academy to enable the employee to gain insight into the community and the criminal justice system of government. Remedial training should be provided for individuals who are deficient in performance but have the potential to perform satisfactorily.

In calling for 400 hours of minimum training, the Commission is supporting a basic recommendation of the 1967 President's Crime Commission. A survey conducted in 1970 by the International Association of Chiefs of Police disclosed that only 19 States required more than 200 hours of instruction, and that the number of required hours ranged from 72 to 400. Basic police training programs reflect to a large degree both the police agency's commitment to quality police service and the complexity of police responsibilities. Thus, in major cities a few police agencies require more than 1,000 hours of training as a minimum for all employees.

The representative body for setting training standards could also set selection standards. Presently 33 States have commissions charged with the responsibility for setting police standards in the areas of selection and training.[5]

---

[5] Advisory Commission on Intergovernmental Relations, *State-Local Relations in the Criminal Justice System* (1971), p. 30.

Development, Promotion, and Advancement

Development, promotion, and advancement of personnel are necessary activities in achieving successful and efficient policing. Promotion and advancement of employees should be based on demonstrated ability and proven performance. Police agencies should adopt the policy of promoting to higher ranks and advancing to higher paid grades only those personnel who successfully demonstrate their abilities to assume increased responsibilities and to perform the duties of the position to which they are promoted or advanced. Police agencies should screen all personnel to identify their individual potential and guide them toward achieving full potential.

Police agencies should offer comprehensive and individualized programs of education, training, and experience designed to develop the potential of every employee.

The Commission recommends that every police agency implement programs designed to aid employees' professional growth and increase their capacity for their present and future roles within the agency.

Such programs should include, where feasible:
• Provision for internships with other police, criminal justice, and governmental agencies.
• Provision for the temporary assumption of the position, responsibility, and authority of an immediate superior.
• Provision for selective and individualized rotation of personnel to develop patrol and specialist expertise.
• Provision for rotation to areas of varying crime incidence, and to major administrative assignments.

Lateral Entry

The development of incumbent personnel is the most effective manner in which to fill senior advanced positions, but it is not the most practical or expeditious technique for every agency. Because of inattention to personnel development, it is not unusual for individual police agencies to have vacancies for which qualified replacements are unavailable within that agency. Conversely, it is not unusual for the more professional police agencies to develop what amounts to a surplus of managerial and administrative talent.

If the opportunity for lateral movement within the law enforcement profession were enhanced, manpower would be used more efficiently with commensurate benefit accruing to individual agencies

and professions as a whole. Lateral entry is particularly promising in selecting the police chief executive and in adding minority officers to the ranks.

Before the full benefits of lateral mobility can be realized, certain dynamic changes must be made within the police service. Among the necessary changes is the elimination of overly restrictive residency requirements and of civil service restrictions on eligibility for entry-level and advanced positions. Additionally, State and national provisions must be made for transferring retirement pensions and other fringe benefits so that those who desire to move laterally do not suffer financially.

Personnel should be recruited for lateral entry at any level from outside police agencies when it is necessary to do so in order to obtain the services of individuals who are qualified for a position or assignment.

Every State should provide a statewide police retirement system for all sworn personnel within the State. Reciprocal agreements should be formulated among independent, local, State, and interstate agencies to allow any police officer in the country to accept any law enforcement position available within any State and still retain his accrued retirement benefits.

Classification and Pay

Increased professionalization of the police service depends on the caliber of the people it can recruit and retain.

Many police agencies are unable to attract the officers they need because of unreasonably low salaries. The police must offer salaries to recruit and retain the caliber of personnel necessary to perform the police function.

The Commission recommends that every State and local government establish and maintain salaries that attract and retain qualified personnel capable of performing the police function.
Every State should set minimum entry-level salaries for all State and local police officers and should reimburse the employing agency for a portion of the guaranteed salary.

A salary review procedure should be established to insure the automatic annual adjustment of police salaries to reflect the prevailing wages in the local economy.

As noted earlier in this chapter, the Commission feels that the patrolman is the most vital element of the police function and that police departments should make every effort to attract and retain highly qualified patrolmen. The policies of many police agencies, however, encourage the best patrol officers to seek other assignments.

These agencies make no provisions for officers who desire to advance and earn more pay while remaining in the patrol function. As a result, qualified patrol officers often seek promotion to supervisory positions or transfer to specialist positions in order to obtain greater status and pay. In most police agencies, no distinction is made between the duties and responsibilities of the patrol officer with 1 year of service and the officer with 15 years. As a result, a highly qualified, well-motivated officer feels that he is not progressing unless he transfers from the patrol force.

A system (the Jacobs Plan) recently adopted in the Los Angeles City Police Department provides multiple pay grades within the basic patrol rank, granting well-qualified patrol officers greater responsibilities and pay while they remain on the patrol force. The Commission would carry this plan even further and allow a patrol officer to advance to a salary level equal to that of an investigator or any other police officer at the nonsupervisory level.

The Commission also feels that proficiency pay should be given to patrol officers who train recruits in patrol duties, who coordinate activities of a patrol team, or who acquire specialist skills or experience that contribute to patrol efficiency. Competent patrol officers with greater responsibility should receive appropriate and distinctive uniform insignia.

Every local government should expand its classification and pay system to provide greater advancement within the basic patrol rank.

The system should provide:
• Multiple pay grades within the basic patrolman rank.
• Opportunity for advancement within the basic patrolman rank.
• Parity in top pay grades between patrol officers and nonsupervisory officers assigned to other operational functions.
• Proficiency pay for patrol personnel who have demonstrated expertise in specific field activities that contribute to more efficient police service.

Women in Policing

The role of women in the police service has been based largely on traditional and often outmoded ideas. Some misconceptions concerning women's ability to perform certain "masculine" tasks have been dispelled as a result of changing social attitudes. The police service should keep current with social

changes and legal requirements by reexamining the function of female police officers.

Just prior to the turn of the century, a movement to employ women as regular police officers gained support among several social action groups and culminated in the hiring of the first regularly appointed policewomen in the country. By the end of World War II, more than 200 cities employed policewomen. These women, however, have been assigned mainly to duties that do not involve patrol. Most policewomen work in clerical jobs or in jobs related to juvenile delinquency, family crises, missing persons, runaways, and sex offenses.

Within the past 2 to 3 years, police departments in some major cities have been moving toward using policewomen in all functions performed by the police and particularly in patrol. More and more departments are assigning women to patrol duties and some departments have developed promotional policies requiring that when a vacancy occurs the next eligible person be elevated, regardless of sex.

The Commission recommends that every police agency immediately insure that there exists no agency policy that discourages qualified women from seeking employment as sworn or civilian personnel or that prevents them from realizing their full employment potential.

Agencies should institute selection procedures to facilitate employment of women and should insure that recruitment, selection, training, and salary policies do not discriminate against women.

Agencies should require career paths for women, allowing each individual to obtain a position commensurate with her particular degree of experience, skill, and ability.

Use of Civilian Employees

Police agencies traditionally have staffed the majority of positions with sworn police officers. Policemen have been assigned clerical tasks, general maintenance, and even construction duties.

The term "sworn police officers" refers to those individuals in a police department who are authorized to make arrests and who have peace officer status under applicable provisions of State and local laws. Civilian or nonsworn personnel include all other individuals employed by a police department.

Civilian personnel can be an important addition to the operations of a police agency. They can free police from routine tasks for more effective assignment in line operations.

Additionally, civilians capable of performing routine tasks often do not command the salaries of trained policemen and often have specialized skills needed in police work.

The Dallas, Tex., Police Department, for example, has made extensive use of civilian personnel. It has established the positions of "police service officer" and "community service officer" to perform nonenforcement functions. Civilians are used by Dallas as helicopter pilots, radio dispatchers, communications aides, property control and supply officers, and jail aides, and are used for issuing traffic citations and for performing traffic patrol and control duties.

Police agencies should explore all possible uses of civilians and should be innovative in determining the functions they could perform.

In addition to the functions set out above, in some departments civilians are employed as evidence-gathering technicians, lab technicians, personnel specialists, and photographers.

Employee Relations and Police Employee Organizations

The police chief executive is usually held more accountable by the public for the activities of his personnel than are most other public agency officials. The conduct of police employees depends, in turn, upon the attitudes and programs of the police chief executive. His reaction toward employees encourages their cooperation.

The police chief executive must promote an atmosphere of effective cooperation and employee relations. He must create an atmosphere that encourages an employee to do a good job, and the employee must feel that he is contributing to the agency's success.

Every police chief executive should develop methods to obtain information from police employees who have daily contact with operational problems in order to assist him in reaching decisions on personnel and operational matters.

In addition, every police chief executive should develop fair and effective grievance procedures to consider the complaints of all police employees. Every police chief executive should have employee relations specialists available to him. He must be prepared for collective negotiation and must establish effective working relationships with employee organizations.

The Commission notes that one of the most innovative methods of employee participation is occurring in Kansas City, Mo. The police department has established numerous task forces directed by patrolmen and other line personnel to explore and develop new methods for crime reduction. Funds are provided for the work of the task forces, and police employees are involved in planning and designing projects.

The Commission recommends that every police chief executive acknowledge the right of his agency's officers to join employee organizations.

Legislation should be enacted to authorize every police agency and all employees to engage in collective negotiations in arriving at terms and conditions of employment, police service effectiveness, and equitable representation for police employees and management. Such legislation should specifically prohibit strikes, work stoppages, and concerted job actions, and should provide for the retention of management rights including the setting of management policies, the direction of employees' work, and the setting of hiring, firing, and promotion policies.

MAXIMUM USE OF TECHNOLOGY AND SUPPORT SERVICES

In addition to allocating human resources in the most efficient manner possible, police agencies need to concentrate on obtaining and applying sophisticated technological and support resources. Communications systems, information systems, and criminal laboratories are tools that multiply the effectiveness of police officers.

Only token progress has been made in the application of available modern technology in police work. Another surge of technological innovation is needed if law enforcement is to respond adequately to the increasing sophistication of the criminal element.

Communications Systems

The time it takes a patrol car to respond to a call for service is critical to successful apprehension of criminals. Police communications systems are vital to improving this response time.

The elapsed time in the communications center is a significant part of the total time it takes for police to respond to a call for service. A study done by the 1967 President's Crime Commission showed that patrol cars took an average of 3.8 minutes to reach the scene of a crime after the initial call was placed. The communications center delay thus accounted for as much as 50 percent of the total delay.

Many police communications systems are actually chaotic assemblies of independent radio networks that somehow manage to move a monumental volume of radio traffic despite considerable inefficiency. They operate on the threshold of collapse, with radio traffic overloads the rule rather than the exception. In a major civil disorder, disaster, or other massive emergency, most police communications systems will break down.

The first element of a police communications system is the telephone. Substantial improvements are needed in telephone systems linking police to the community. To most people in the United States, the policeman is usually no farther away than the telephone. Yet police agencies often fail to give enough thought to the importance of a successful telephone call and a prompt response. Inefficient telephone and radio communications can result in serious injury or loss of life to the victim of a crime or accident and can hamper apprehension of criminal offenders. In an emergency, the public should be able to contact the police immediately by making a single telephone call.

States and units of local government should undertake to provide a single universal telephone number for all calls for emergency, police, and other municipal services in a given geographic area.

The second element of a communications system is the radio system. The degree to which agencies achieve communications with their field units is critical. It affects the success of the agencies' efforts to preserve life and property and increases the potential for apprehension of criminal suspects.

The Commission recommends that every police agency immediately establish command and control centers for the operation of their communications systems and provide a 24-hour, two-way radio capability for continuous communications between the command and control communications center and the field units.

Where necessary smaller agencies should contract for services or consolidate operations with those of larger agencies. The elapsed time between receipt of a complaint emergency call at the communications center and the time of radio message transmission should not exceed 2 minutes. As soon as possible, this elapsed time should not exceed 1 minute. Upon receiving an emergency call patrol cars should reach the scene of the call within a minimum of three minutes.

All patrol cars should be equipped with two-way radios, and every police agency should equip all on-duty uniformed officers with a portable two-way radio capable of being carried with reasonable comfort on the person of the officer.

Research has shown that digital communications may have the potential for vastly increasing the efficiency of police operations. Digital communications systems can provide instantaneous dispatch of routine operational messages and can provide field units with direct access to computer data banks. They can reduce frequency congestion and can allow field units to query computer-based information systems directly, without going through a dispatcher. They also can be used to inform dispatchers whether field units are available for assignment.

In a system tried in Oakland, Calif., police officers utilized a "touch map" mounted on a police vehicle dashboard. This device allowed the policeman to touch a specific point on the map, which automatically, by a digital communication, activated a light showing his unit number and location on a similar map in front of a dispatcher.

The components of a fully automated digital communications system have been used independently or in various combinations but never have been brought together in an integrated system. The individual development of these sophisticated and complex devices should not continue on a random and uncoordinated basis. Coordinated research and development will result in considerable savings of time and money.

The Commission recommends that the Law Enforcement Assistance Administration (LEAA) initiate a competitive research and development effort for the study, design, manufacture, and operation of pilot digital communications systems.

The systems should include the use of vehicular

visual display devices with printed computer readouts, automated vehicle locater devices, and real-time unit status reporting devices.

Evidence Gathering and Crime Laboratories

An efficient and productive crime laboratory can be an invaluable aid to the police investigation process. Forensic science applies the principles of physical and biological disciplines to solving crimes. Few police agencies have taken full advantage of developments in this field. Police services need to become more familiar with the extent to which an efficient forensic science program can contribute to police effectiveness.

In order to solve many crimes the police agency must be able to identify, collect, and preserve physical evidence at the crime scene. In recent years, court decisions and more effective criminal defense have placed a stronger burden on police agencies to prove their cases. Greater efficiency in gathering evidence is necessary.

The Commission recommends that every police agency provide all incoming police personnel with a formalized basic training course in forensic science and evidence-gathering techniques, and that every police agency also develop and deploy specially trained personnel to gather physical evidence 24 hours a day.

Every State should establish a consolidated criminal laboratory system composed of local, regional, or State facilities capable of providing the widest possible range of forensic science services to police agencies.

COORDINATION WITH OTHER CRIMINAL JUSTICE AGENCIES

Success in protecting society is not measured by the length of time it takes the police to respond to a crime scene, by the number of arrests they make, or by the number of arrestees successfully prosecuted or sentenced. Rather, success or failure is determined by the degree to which society is free of crime and disorder.

This is but another way of saying that no element of the criminal justice system completely discharges its responsibility simply by achieving its own immediate objectives. The police, the prosecutor, the courts, and probation, parole, and corrections agencies must cooperate with each other if the system is to operate effectively. This requires an effort on the part of each element to communicate with the other elements, even though this is sometimes difficult because of legal and administrative separation of powers and responsibilities.

Case Preparation Unit

An essential element in cooperation between the police and prosecutor is the development of evidence necessary to obtain the conviction or acquittal of arrested individuals. The police department in Detroit, Mich., has found that by establishing a special unit for case preparation it could relieve precinct investigators from spending excessive time in court and on court-related activities. This unit has also considerably improved the quality of court case preparation and improved the working relationship among the police, the prosecutor's office, and the courts. The case preparation unit has saved the department almost 875 man-hours per month in patrol and investigative measures.

The Commission recommends that police departments in major metropolitan areas utilize case preparation specialists to insure that all evidence that may lead to conviction or acquittal of defendants is systematically prepared and presented for review by the prosecutor.

Procedures for case preparation should be developed in cooperation with the representatives of the local prosecutorial and judicial systems to establish a format and procedure beneficial to all agencies. Procedures should include the establishment of case files which clearly document all legal action on the case from the first police action to final disposition. The files should constitute a firm foundation upon which police agency recommendations on diversion, bail, release on recognizance, sentencing, probation, and even parole can be based.

Major Violations and Criminal Case Followup

Police agree that the sequential processing of defendants through the criminal justice system has contributed to the common but erroneous belief that, except for police appearances as witnesses, their function ends when a criminal complaint is issued. Police agencies, however, have undertaken a more active role in the disposition of criminal cases.

Police departments in New York and Washington, D.C., have initiated Major Violator Programs to focus attention on suspected offenders who they believe are responsible for a large amount of crime. An example of a major violator might be an individual who has been found to be responsible for a large number of burglaries or robberies in a given area. By concentrating on those individuals the police departments, in cooperation with prosecutors and the courts, have been able to pinpoint and concert prosecution efforts on individuals who might pass unnoticed through congested courts. Prosecution agencies in New York and Washington, D.C., have generally agreed to cooperate in avoiding plea negotiations in cases involving major offenders and to give them priority handling.

In determining major violators many factors are considered, including police expenditure of resources to solve the crime, defendant's alleged responsibility for a number of crimes, and seriousness of the offense or the situation in the area where the crime occurred. Additionally, police departments in New York and Washington have established followup procedures to correct improper handling of cases in cooperation with the local courts and prosecuting agencies.

Every police agency in cooperation with local courts, prosecutors, and corrections agencies should provide for the adequate followup of criminal cases.

Police agencies should identify major violators and should follow the progress of these individuals through the criminal justice system. Police agencies should review all major criminal cases that prosecutors refuse to prosecute or later cause to be dismissed, in order that administrative action may be taken to correct any police actions that may have weakened the case. The review procedure should also serve to inform the prosecuting office of deficiencies that the police may feel the prosecution has made in the case in order that the prosecutor may correct those inconsistencies.

The programs described above may be more effective in the court systems of large urban areas. Every police agency may, however, use the case followup procedure to encourage outside evaluation of the quality of case preparation and courtroom demeanor and testimony. Police agencies should be receptive to external evaluation by prosecutors and courts and should take steps to correct reported deficiencies.

Formal Consultation with Other Criminal Justice Agencies

Among the agencies in the criminal justice system, the police are in the best position to observe the tangible effects of crime on the victim and possible disruption of order. It is rare, however, for the police to be consulted formally by other criminal justice elements attempting to arrive at decisions concerning screening, diversion, plea negotiation, probation, or parole.

This problem was highlighted in a survey of more than 3,400 criminal justice practitioners.[6] The survey showed that 2,274, or 66 percent, said that it was undesirable for the prosecutor to engage in plea negotiations without consulting the arresting officer. Yet 2,393, or 70 percent, said that this was either very probable or somewhat probable.

Information from the police regarding such matters as the effect of crimes upon the victims and the likelihood of future crimes by an arrested individual or convicted offender should be made available to and utilized by other criminal justice agencies for reference in making screening, diversion, plea negotiation, sentencing, and parole recommendations. Uniform standards and procedures should be established for making such recommendations.

Summons in Lieu of Arrest

The 1970 National Jail Census, conducted by the U.S. Bureau of the Census for the Law Enforcement Assistance Administration, found that on a given day more than 50 percent of those in the Nation's jails were awaiting trial.

These numbers can be significantly reduced and the criminal justice system better served if, in lieu of arrest and detention, police issue a citation requiring the person to attend a court hearing. In Oakland, Calif., for example, more than 10,000 misdemeanants have been issued citations in lieu of arrest by police since 1970 and recent figures show a failure-to-appear-at-trial rate of less than 5 percent.

The Commission recommends that every police agency issue, where legal and practical, written summons and citations in lieu of physical arrest. Police should establish procedures to seek out expeditiously and take into custody individuals participating in these programs who fail to appear in court.

Telephonic Search Warrants

The question of searches and seizures presents a critical problem to effective operation of the criminal justice system. The fourth amendment prohibits unreasonable searches and seizures by the police. Evidence obtained pursuant to an unreasonable seizure cannot be used against an individual and many otherwise valid criminal prosecutions fail.

---

[6] Project STAR, *Survey of Role Perceptions for Operational Criminal Justice Personnel Data Summary* (California Department of Justice, 1972), p. 179.

Judicial decisions have tended to equate a reasonable search with one conducted pursuant to a properly issued warrant. For example, *Katz* v. *United States*, 389 U.S. 347, 357 (1967), held: "Searches conducted outside the judicial process, without prior approval by judge or magistrate, are per se unreasonable under the fourth amendment subject only to a few specifically established and well delineated exceptions."

In justifying exceptions to the rule requiring warrants, police officers often mention the long delay required to obtain them from the courts. However, while this delay frequently extends up to 10 hours the courts have been reluctant to accept delay as an exception under *Katz*.

To resolve this problem, California in 1970 and Arizona in 1971 enacted legislation that allows a search warrant to be issued during a recorded telephone conversation with a judge in which the requesting officer orally makes a sworn affidavit to the judge. This affidavit is later transcribed. The requesting officer then may be permitted to sign the judge's name on a duplicate original warrant, which then serves as the officer's search warrant. Following the conversation the judge signs and files the original warrant with the court clerk. Under this procedure the issuing authority remains with the judge and the officer's role is ministerial in executing the search ordered by the judge. Following execution of the warrant and completion of the search, the officer files the duplicate original warrant, an inventory of seized property, and a transcription of the recording with the court.

The efforts of these two States are an attempt to employ existing technology in carrying out the intent of the law. The procedure has been held to be constitutional by the California Supreme Court. (See the Commission's *Report on Police* for a more detailed discussion of this subject.)

The Commission recommends that every State enact legislation that provides for the issuance of search warrants pursuant to telephone petitions and affidavits from police officers.

Court-Authorized Electronic Surveillance

The use of electronic surveillance by law enforcement agencies has been a controversial subject because of its potential for abuse of individual rights of privacy.

Efforts to enact Federal legislation in this area culminated in 1968 with the passage of Title III of the Omnibus Crime Control and Safe Streets Act. This legislation permitted limited and narrowly circumscribed court-authorized electronic surveillance. The act prohibited private electronic surveillance.

Reports filed by the Attorney General with the Administrative Office of the United States Courts indicate that Title III-authorized electronic surveillance has been used on a limited basis and that it has proved to be productive in terms of arrests and indictments of organized crime figures. The offenses investigated through the use of electronic surveillance frequently involved dangerous drugs and narcotics, gambling, and larceny. In 1971, 816 intercepts were authorized; these resulted in 2,818 arrests.

The figures quoted above include intercepts authorized by State court judges as well as those authorized by Federal judges. Title III authorized electronic surveillance by State enforcement officials if the State enacts statutes meeting the standards for intercept orders set forth in the Federal law. According to a 1972 report of the Administrative Office of the United States Courts, 19 States had enacted such legislation.

This legislation substantially strengthens the police resources utilized in the fight against bribery, corruption, organized crime, and narcotics distribution and can be a vital tool to reduce crime.

The Commission recommends that each State enact legislation prohibiting private electronic surveillance and authorizing court-supervised electronic surveillance by law enforcement officers, consistent with the provisions of Title III of the Omnibus Crime Control and Safe Streets Act of 1968.

CONCLUSION

Police decisions—whether to arrest, to make a referral, to seek prosecution, or to use force—have profound and visible effects. Many of these decisions must be made within the span of a few moments and within the context of the most aggravated social problems. Yet the police officer is just as accountable for these decisions as any other public official.

The Commission's standards are designed not only to make police decisions more rational, but also to make them more understandable to the average citizen. The standards are based on the broad currents of reform generated by other professional and governmental efforts.

The police profession has made important advances in recent years. The pace of progress should continue and accelerate.

Chapter 6

Courts

The criminal court system in the United States, which should bring swift and sure justice, has broken down under the burden of increased business while trying to operate under outmoded procedures.

The Commission, in its research and deliberations, sought to identify the underlying causes of the breakdown and to propose standards that provide realistic, meaningful solutions to the problems that plague the courts and that will be instrumental in reducing crime in the United States. Before discussing specific solutions, the complexities of the problems and the role and function of the criminal courts need to be defined.

Within the criminal justice system, the criminal court system ideally should perform the following functions:
- Swiftly determine the guilt or innocence of those persons who come before it.
- Sentence guilty offenders in such a way that their rehabilitation is possible, and that others are deterred from committing crimes.
- Protect the rights of society and the offender.

What problems cause the courts to fall short of the ideal? The Commission sees them as inconsistency in the processing of criminal defendants, uncertainty as to the results attained, unacceptable delays, and alienation of the community.

Judge presiding in court.

Uncertainty and Inconsistency

To many observers, it appears that the court processes produce inconsistent treatment in similar cases. They observe that a few defendants go to trial while the vast majority "cop pleas" to lesser charges, are placed in treatment programs without prosecution, or are handled by other nontrial procedures. The system thus appears to be unequal and suspect.

Over the years, nontrial procedures undoubtedly have been used inconsistently and without explanation to the public. Often only experts in criminal justice have understood some of the distinctions. There have been no accepted standards and few written policies against which the equality of the system could be measured.

In addition to nontrial procedures, inconsistency in sentencing has caused controversy. Sentencing disparities in many jurisdictions are pronounced.

Delay

Delay in the judicial process is harmful to both the accused offender and society at large. Delay also results in unavailable witnesses, forgotten circumstances, and dismissal of prosecutions because the defendant did not receive the speedy trial guaranteed by the Constitution.

Insofar as the apprehension and punishment of offenders have a deterrent effect upon the offenders themselves and others, the Commission believes that the more closely punishment follows a crime, the greater its deterrent value will be; the longer the delay, the smaller the deterrent effect will be. Finally, delay thwarts society's interest in incapacitating those who have committed crimes.

Examples of the effect of delay are plentiful. On January 18, 1973, as the result of a 36-month pretrial delay in one major metropolitan court, charges were dismissed against six men accused of a $128,000 robbery. And on February 2, 1973, a man who had been held in jail in a large city for more than 2 years awaiting trial was acquitted by a jury.

Public Alienation

A special poll conducted for *Newsweek* magazine by the Gallup organization found that many Americans have little faith in their courts:

"It's not the courts of justice any more."
"Lawyers use every loophole to free the guilty and the innocent suffer more than the lawbreakers."
"Convicted criminals are let off easily. I don't think all people are treated fairly by the law. The judges, the juries and the lawyers are biased."

The statistics from the *Newsweek* poll indicate that only 35 percent of blacks and 53 percent of whites believe that juries produce correct verdicts most of the time. Seventy percent of blacks and 39 percent of whites believe that a Negro suspected of a crime is more likely than a white man to be convicted and sentenced. Eighty-four percent of blacks and 77 percent of whites believe that poor people are more likely to be convicted and sentenced than those who are wealthy.[1]

These statistics and statements clearly suggest that the American public is alienated from or at best suspicious of the criminal court system. Cynicism is replacing respect.

Some criticism of the court system is well taken, as the studies of the Commission made clear and this report strives to reflect. Other criticism, however, stems from a lack of information. Many of the processes followed by judges, prosecutors, and defenders are not visible to the public. Policies, if they exist, are not published. Public perceptions of the court system are gained through the news media or through infrequent service as jurors or witnesses. Valid judicial decisions, when announced without explanation of the legal basis or rationale, are a constant source of public concern and generate further criticism.

[1] *Newsweek* (March 8, 1971).

MAJOR RECOMMENDATIONS

The need to avoid unnecessary delay in criminal processing from arrest to final appeal is emphasized throughout this chapter and in the Commission's *Report on Courts*. But efficiency and speed are not advocated to the detriment of just and equitable treatment for every person coming within the jurisdiction of the Nation's judicial system. Accordingly, the Commission's major proposals call for:
• Establishment of objective criteria for screening.
• Diversion of certain offenders into noncriminal programs before formal trial or conviction.
• An end to the practice of plea negotiation.
• Elimination of inefficient and unnecessary pretrial proceedings.
• Pretrial processing period not to exceed 60 days from arrest to trial in felony cases and 30 days in misdemeanor cases.
• Affording every convicted offender the opportunity to obtain full and fair judicial review of his conviction.
• Abolition of the trial de novo system.
• Unification of all trial courts within a State into a single court of general jurisdiction, under administrative authority of the State's highest appellate court.
• Establishment of a State court administrator responsible for setting policies for the administration of the entire State court system.
• Employment of qualified full-time prosecutors provided with the necessary personnel, fiscal resources, and support services.
• Provision of public representation to all eligible defendants from arrest to exhaustion of all avenues of relief from conviction.
• Improvement of court-community relations.
• Establishment of family courts to handle juvenile cases.
• Reform of juvenile handling procedures.

PRIORITIES

The Commission has assigned priorities to the standards, according to the importance of each in reducing crime.

First priority is given to the standards dealing with the litigated case and the review of trial court proceedings. Attaining speed and efficiency in the pretrial and trial processes and achieving prompt finality in appellate proceedings should result in increased deterrence of crime and earlier and more effective rehabilitative treatment of offenders.

As a second priority, the Commission believes that

the prosecution and defense functions must be upgraded. The public prosecutor must be able to perform fairly and adequately the screening, diversion, plea negotiation, and case preparation duties of that office. Similarly, a public defender must have the ability and the resources to handle his clients fairly and competently. High-caliber personnel in both these functions would help reinforce public faith in the American system of justice.

Third priority should go to insuring the high quality of the judiciary. Again, competent and dedicated judges would insure the proper functioning of the court system and upgrade that system in the minds of the public.

These priorities should be viewed in terms of the recommended allocation of effort. However, the Commission believes that immediate and concentrated effort should be expended on complex, high-priority actions that may require constitutional amendment or legislation. However, those standards easy to implement should be implemented quickly, regardless of priority.

The Commission's priorities pervade all the standards relating to court processes and procedures, court organization and administration, court-community relations, and juveniles. These major topics are covered in succeeding sections.

COURT PROCEDURES AND PROCESSES

Uncertainty, inconsistency, and delay in the court system frequently have their origin in outmoded or inappropriate procedures and processes. The Commission, therefore, believes that major changes must be made in pretrial, trial, and appellate processes. Two objectives, reducing criminal caseloads and insuring a fair disposition of cases, are the motivating forces behind the Commission's proposed reforms.

Reducing Caseload

Achieving efficiency in the criminal court system involves more than setting time limits. Decriminalization, screening, and diversion are important methods of reducing caseloads. The Commission endorses all three methods. Decriminalization of drunkenness and vagrancy and the administrative disposition of traffic offenses are discussed in the chapter on criminal code reform. Screening and diversion are discussed in this chapter.

Screening is a critical step in increasing the efficiency of the system. It consists of a decision by the prosecutor or the police to release the

accused unconditionally prior to trial or plea. The decision often occurs before the filing of charges.

In Philadelphia, Pa., the district attorney initiated a system of placing prosecutors in police precinct stations around the clock to review every criminal complaint prior to arrest and every search warrant prior to execution. As a result, one-third of the cases filed by the police were screened out.

Screening occurs because the evidence of guilt is insufficient to bring the accused to trial, because the evidence was improperly obtained and could not be used at trial, or because prosecution would not serve the interests of justice.

The standards encourage careful screening at the earliest possible stage of the proceedings. To assure fair and equitable screening, the Commission proposes establishment of policy guidelines. There should be a uniform basis for the screening decision —a basis that will assure decisions in the interests of society and the accused.

The Commission recommends that prosecutors establish objective criteria for screening and that police consult with the prosecutor to develop guidelines, based on these criteria, for arresting and taking persons into custody. After a person is taken into custody, the decision to proceed with formal prosecution should rest with the prosecutor.

Screening criteria should include:
• Whether the evidence is sufficient to convict.
• Whether prosecution would further the interests of the criminal justice system.
• Whether the value to society of prosecution and conviction would be commensurate with financial, social, and individual costs.

Diversion is a second means of relieving the court system of inappropriate cases. In diversion, by the prosecutor or by the court, prosecution is stopped short of conviction in exchange for the defendant's agreement to do such things as enroll in a rehabilitation program, make restitution to the victim of his crime, or enter a mental institution. Although the court may enter into the decision to divert, the agreement is usually a product of negotiation between the prosecutor and the defendant.

Project Crossroads illustrates the advantages of a diversion program.

Project Crossroads is a pretrial intervention program which began in the District of Columbia in 1968. It was designed to divert youthful first offenders from the justice process. The offender had to meet certain criteria for enrollment including offense, age, residence, employment status, and prior record. To offer an alternative to a criminal career the staff tutored, counseled, and found jobs for those enrolled in an effort to give them an alternative to a

Prosecutor in courtroom.

criminal career. After 90 days with the program, a defendant's case was dismissed if he had completed program requirements, extended if the staff and court determined that he needed further assistance, or resumed if he had failed in the program.

From April 1968 to September 1970, 824 individuals were referred to Project Crossroads. Of those, 74 were still enrolled in the program, charges against 467 had been dropped, and 283 had been returned to court for prosecution. A year after release from Project Crossroads, participants experienced a doubling in their employment rates. Former participants were earning more money in better jobs and staying in jobs longer than before, and had a lower rate of recidivism than a control group of nonparticipants.[2]

Programs utilizing the same principle were established for drug addicts in a number of cities in

---

[2] John Holahan, *A Benefit-Cost Analysis of Project Crossroads* (National Committee for Children and Youth, 1970).

1972 with the assistance of the President's Special Action Office for Drug Abuse Prevention and the Law Enforcement Assistance Administration (LEAA). The program, called "Treatment Alternatives to Street Crime" (TASC), provided community-based treatment for addicts. After police processing, TASC representatives and the prosecutor test all arrestees for addiction. A judge determines whether to release the individual outright on his own recognizance or on bail, to send the individual to detention, or to order treatment as a condition of release with diversion of the individual to TASC.

Multimodality treatment clinics throughout the community serve clients, mostly outpatients, near their homes. Failure to cooperate with these programs' regulations causes expulsion from the program and criminal prosecution. Full program participation is viewed favorably by the court and can result in dismissal of pending criminal charges against the participant.

A properly administered diversion program with full cooperation of the court offers many benefits. A court can save time and money better devoted to more serious criminals. An offender can find gainful employment and avoid a criminal record, and the community can gain contributing residents.

The Commission recommends that in appropriate circumstances offenders be diverted into noncriminal programs before formal trial or conviction.

Diversion decisions should be made as soon as adequate information is available. Diversion should be made when there is a substantial likelihood of conviction and when the benefits to society of diversion are expected to outweigh the potential dangers of nonprosecution. However, precise decision guidelines should be established and made public by the deciding agency—police or prosecutor. When the diversion program would involve substantial deprivation of liberty, a formal, court-approved diversion agreement should be executed.

PLEA NEGOTIATION

In many courts in this country, more than 90 percent of criminal convictions are obtained by pleas of guilty, not by the verdict of the jury or the decision of a judge.

Many of these guilty pleas are the result of an express agreement between the defendant and the prosecution, in which the charge and the sentence are negotiated in a process of mutual advantage-taking.

Associate Justice William Rehnquist of the U.S. Supreme Court in a commentary of plea negotiation noted:

It should be recognized at the outset that the process of plea bargaining is not one which any student of the subject regards as an ornament to our system of criminal justice. Up until now its most resolute defenders have only contended that it contains more advantages than disadvantages, while others have been willing to endure or sanction it only because they regard it as a necessary evil.[3]

In the past 10 years more and more prosecutors have come to rely upon plea negotiation to dispose of the vast majority of their cases. This is in part attributable to the dramatic increase in the amount of crime reported to the police and prosecuted in the courts. The large metropolitan courts are inundated and have unmanageable backlogs of criminal cases. The resources for prosecution, defense, and the courts simply are not adequate for handling these cases. The prosecutor with a serious case backlog and limited resources to try cases is faced with the prospect of negotiating a plea or dismissing the case.

[3] Speech before the National Conference on Criminal Justice, Washington, D.C. (January 25, 1973).

Further, in many large cities, persons accused of crime are anxious to plead guilty rather than languish in jails for months awaiting trial. Often the time spent awaiting trial is longer than the sentence. Consequently, there is a tendency, especially among the poor and ignorant, whether innocent or guilty, to plead guilty, start serving time, and get out of jail quickly. Persons receiving this treatment understandably may lose their faith in the criminal justice system. This distrust is carried over into society through their families and associates.

The public is also getting shortchanged. According to Arlen Specter, District Attorney of Philadelphia:

The bitter experience of our criminal courtrooms has demonstrated that the bargained plea is really no bargain. We should not settle for a system which simultaneously deprives the innocent defendant of the forum where the prosecutor is compelled to prove his case, and the public is victimized by excessive leniency for hard-core criminal repeaters.

Experience with plea bargaining in many jurisdictions has taught us the painful lesson, again and again, that the violent criminal who secures his freedom through plea bargaining is often encouraged to rob or rape again. The practical effect of plea bargaining unquestionably results in the violent recidivist receiving less than an adequate prison sentence.[4]

The experience in New York is illustrative. The *New York Times* reported in the fall of 1972 that the number of persons serving time in State prisons dropped from 18,000 in 1966 to 12,500 in 1972 and that suspects brought before New York City's overflowing courts received lighter sentences than those convicted of the same crime in upstate New York. The reasons for this, the *Times* states, were the judges' loss of faith in the prison system and "massive plea bargaining," in which a defendant is offered a light sentence in return for a guilty plea.

There is also a threat to defendants' rights in the plea negotiation process. A recent survey of more than 3,400 criminal justice practitioners in four States—California, Michigan, New Jersey, and Texas —reveals the potential threat to defendant rights inherent in the plea negotiation process. Sixty-one percent of the survey respondents agreed that it was very probable or somewhat probable that most defense attorneys "engage in plea bargaining primarily to expedite the movement of cases." Thirty-eight percent agreed that it was very probable or somewhat probable that most defense attorneys in plea bargaining negotiations "pressure clients into entering a plea that [the] client feels is unsatisfactory."[5]

[4] Speech before the National Conference on Criminal Justice, Washington, D.C. (January 24, 1973).
[5] Project STAR, *Survey of Role Perceptions for Operational Criminal Justice Personnel Data Summary* (California Department of Justice, 1972), pp. 238, 243.

Despite the dangers posed by plea negotiations, many experts have concluded that plea negotiation is inevitable, desirable, or both, and that efforts should be directed at improving rather than eliminating the practice. The Commission does not agree.

In the view of the Commission, the high volume of court business and the lack of resources should not and need not cause the perpetuation of undesirable practices. Neither is the plea bargain necessary to avoid the harshness of some laws or to obtain the informant's cooperation.

The experience in Philadelphia, Pa., illustrates methods of handling large caseloads without undue plea negotiation. In Philadelphia the criminal backlog has been steadily reduced in recent years from its 1965 peak. The reduction in backlog has been made possible by careful screening and diversion of cases and by a streamlined trial process. It has been achieved in the face of a firm policy against wholesale disposition through plea negotiation. Contrasted with some other major American cities where more than 90 percent of the cases are concluded by guilty pleas, Philadelphia has disposed of only 32 percent of its cases through the guilty plea. The Philadelphia experience is substantial evidence that American court systems can function effectively without heavy reliance on the negotiated plea.

It should be made clear that the Commission does not condemn the entry of guilty pleas. There is a distinction between negotiation of a plea in which the prosecution makes some concessions and the entry of a plea where there are no reasonably contestable issues.

Further, if prosecutors and defense attorneys were convinced that plea bargaining would not occur, the charges filed by prosecutors would correspond more closely to what the prosecutor reasonably thinks he can and should get as a result. (This is often not the case today.) If the defendant and his attorney agree that this is the likely result—as the Commission believes will more often be the case than under existing practice—they can and should enter a plea of guilty. If they do not agree that this is the likely result, they can and should litigate the disagreement.

In addition, if other recommendations of the Commission are followed, there should be more resources available. If the unnecessary and duplicative proceedings are eliminated and procedures are streamlined, the existing judicial personnel and facilities could properly process more criminal cases. Similarly, if pretrial discovery is expanded, many more cases should be resolved early in the proceedings, thus freeing additional judicial resources.

The Commission flatly rejects the idea that plea negotiations are needed to give flexibility to the criminal justice system and to avoid unjustifiably harsh provisions of substantive law. This Commission has recommended a reasoned, rational penalty structure. Further, if there appears to be harsh effect, a prosecutor can alleviate the problem in his selection of initial charge. To the extent that greater flexibility is desired, it should be made available as a matter of formal law, either by changes in the definitions of substantive crimes or in a modification of dispositional alternatives available to sentencing courts.

Finally, as to the value of negotiation to law enforcement, the elimination of plea negotiation need have little effect upon the exchange of leniency for information and assistance. Since the prosecutor can alter initial charge and sentence recommendations in return for law enforcement assistance, the elimination of plea negotiations will have little impact upon this situation.

The Commission condemns plea negotiation and recommends that as soon as possible, but not later than 1978, negotiations between defendants and prosecutors concerning concessions to be made in return for guilty pleas be abolished.

Until plea bargaining is eliminated, standards should be adopted that will reduce its potential for abuse, and the Commission therefore recommends that:
• The agreement on which a negotiated guilty plea is based should be presented in open court, and the record should show the judge's reasons for its acceptance or rejection.
• Each prosecutor's office should develop and publish uniform policies on plea negotiations.
• Prosecutors should be barred from making unfair inducements or threats to gain a plea of guilty.
• A time limit should be set for plea negotiation in order to avoid hasty, last-minute pleas and to permit sound management of a trial docket.
• In determining sentence, the court should not consider the fact that the defendant has entered a plea of guilty.

PRETRIAL PROCEEDINGS

Pretrial delay has been the subject of considerable writing and litigation. Commission review of the problem identified several factors which contribute to pretrial delay. These are:
• Failure to present arrested persons promptly before a judicial officer. This in turn delays appointment of

counsel, bail setting, and scheduling of other processes by the court.

• Use of preliminary hearings as evidence discovery devices and the concomitant failure to initiate informal evidence discovery without resort to formal pretrial motions.

• Use of grand jury indictment processes which do not justify the delay and inconvenience inherent in the use of a grand jury.

• Formal arraignment procedures which only duplicate the presentment process after grand jury indictment.

• Excessive filing of formal pretrial motions practice which could be avoided by rules for mutual discovery and omnibus pretrial hearings.

The Commission recommends that steps be taken immediately to eliminate inefficient and unnecessary pretrial proceedings or procedures and speed up pretrial processing so that the period from arrest to the beginning of trial of a felony generally should not be longer than 60 days. In a misdemeanor prosecution, the period from arrest to trial generally should be 30 days or less.

The Commission recommends that:

• In misdemeanor prosecutions, preliminary hearings should be eliminated.

• Grand jury indictment should not be required for any criminal prosecution, but the grand jury should be retained for its investigative functions.

• An arrested person should be brought before a judicial officer within 6 hours after arrest.

• The preliminary hearing in felony cases should be held within 2 weeks after arrest, with evidence limited to that relevant to a determination of probable cause.

• Formal arraignment (as distinguished from presentment) before a judicial officer should be eliminated.

• Disclosure of prosecution evidence to the defense in felony proceedings should take place within 5 days after the preliminary hearing and disclosure of most defense evidence to the prosecution should immediately follow resolution of pretrial motions. Strict rules should limit the admissibility at trial of undisclosed evidence. (See chart on following page.)

TRIAL

Although most public attention has been directed to pretrial delay, valuable time also is wasted during the actual trial of many cases. This not only prolongs the final disposition of the case on trial, but also ties up court facilities and personnel, preventing the trial of other cases. In a recent trial, 4 months were consumed selecting a jury; 1,035 prospective jurors were examined in the process. Less spectacular—but more frequent—delays result from early adjournments of court during routine trials, preparation of instructions, and similar matters. Similarly, there is substantial delay in the sentencing process.

The standards recommended by the Commission are directed toward insuring a fair and impartial trial while obtaining maximum utilization of all resources.

In every court where trials of criminal cases are being conducted, daily sessions should commence promptly at 9 a.m. and continue until 5 p.m. unless all business before the court is concluded at an earlier time and it is too late in the day to begin another trial.

The Commission also recommends that:

• Only the judge should conduct examinations of prospective jurors, and that the number of challenges to jurors' qualifications to serve should be strictly limited.

• Juries of fewer than 12 but at least 6 persons should be employed in cases not punishable by life imprisonment.

• Opening statements to the jury should be limited to a clear, concise, nonargumentative statement of the evidence to be presented.

• Evidence admitted should be limited to that which is directly relevant and material to the issues being tried.

• Instructions to juries should be standardized to the extent possible and clearly conveyed to the jury.

• With a view toward the development of future standards, studies should be made of the use of the exclusionary rule and of the use of video-taped evidence.

REVIEW OF THE TRIAL COURT PROCEEDINGS

Because of the social stigma and loss of liberty associated with a criminal conviction, many people believe that determining guilt and fixing punishment should not be left to a single trial court. The interests of both society and the defendant are served by providing another tribunal to review the trial court proceedings to insure that no prejudicial error was committed and that justice was done. Review also provides a means for the ongoing development of legal doctrine in the common law fashion, as well as a means of insuring evenhanded administration of justice throughout the jurisdiction. Functionally, review is the last stage in the judicial process of

The Litigated Case

SUMMARY OF COMMISSION RECOMMENDATIONS FOR STEPS TO ACHIEVE TRIAL IN A FELONY CASE WITHIN 60 DAYS OF ARREST

Pretrial delay in a criminal prosecution is a major concern of this Commission. In its *Report on Courts*, the Commission proposes standards that would structure the procedural framework for the formal processing of accused persons to achieve trial in felony cases within 60 days of arrest. This chart outlines those proposals. The time frames shown are derived from figures contained in Standards 4.5, 4.8, 4.9, and 4.10 of the *Report on Courts*; and the interested reader is referred to that report for details.

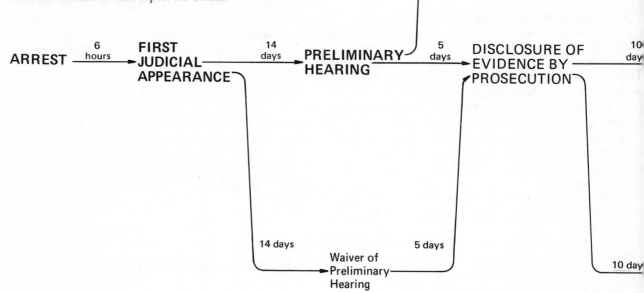

ARREST —6 hours→ FIRST JUDICIAL APPEARANCE —14 days→ PRELIMINARY HEARING —5 days→ DISCLOSURE OF EVIDENCE BY PROSECUTION —10 days→

14 days — Waiver of Preliminary Hearing — 5 days

10 days

In some felony cases, the Commission recommends that a summons or citation be issued in lieu of arrest. In such instances, there would be no first judicial appearance and the Commission calls for a preliminary hearing within 14 days of the issuance of citation or summons.

In felony cases in which there is a grand jury indictment, the Commission recommends that no preliminary hearing be held. The time limits and steps shown above as following the preliminary hearing become applicable upon apprehension of the indicted individual or service of a summons following the indictment.

PREPARATION FOR TRIAL

46 days maximum

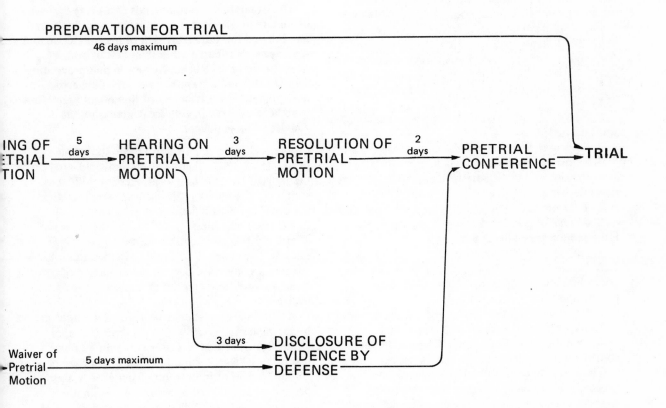

ING OF
ETRIAL
TION

5
days

HEARING ON
PRETRIAL
MOTION

3
days

RESOLUTION OF
PRETRIAL
MOTION

2
days

PRETRIAL
CONFERENCE

TRIAL

Waiver of
Pretrial
Motion

5 days maximum

3 days

DISCLOSURE OF
EVIDENCE BY
DEFENSE

determining guilt and fixing sentence. Like the trial proceeding, it should be fair and expeditious.

The review stage, like other aspects of the criminal process, is in trouble. Several decades ago appeals were taken only in a minority of cases, and collateral attacks on convictions were relatively rare. Today, in some jurisdictions more than 90 percent of all convictions are appealed, and collateral attack is almost routine in State and Federal courts. Courts are handling appeals under procedures used for the past hundred years. The process is cumbersome, fragmented, and beset with delay. Both State and Federal courts are threatened with inundation. Even now, the vast increase in workload is making it increasingly difficult for appellate courts to give to substantial questions the careful, reflective consideration necessary to the development of a reasoned and harmonious body of decisional law.

For a State criminal case, review may have as many as 11 steps, some of which can be repeated. Although not every case goes through each of these steps, they are all potentially available, and it is not uncommon for a defendant to pursue four or five. They are:

1. New trial motion filed in court where conviction was imposed;

2. Appeal to State intermediate appellate court;

3. Appeal to State supreme court;

4. Petition to U. S. Supreme Court to review State court decision on appeal;

5. Postconviction proceeding in State trial court;

6. Appeal of postconviction proceeding to State intermediate appellate court;

7. Appeal to State supreme court;

8. Petition to U. S. Supreme Court to review State court decision on appeal from postconviction proceeding;

9. Habeas corpus petition in Federal district court;

10. Appeal to U. S. court of appeals; and

11. Petition to U. S. Supreme Court to review court of appeals decision on habeas corpus petition.

The actual operations and interplay of review proceedings are more complex than this listing suggests. Some convictions are not appealed at all; others are subject to a number of these steps several times over; and with respect to some convictions, review may proceed simultaneously in both State and Federal courts.

Curiously, despite all the variations of review available, the sentence itself—often the most important feature of the case—cannot be reviewed at all in most American jurisdictions.

The result of these limitations and fragmentations is a drawn-out, almost never-ending review cycle. This in turn brings the criminal process into public disrepute and leaves convicted defendants with feelings of injustice mixed with illusory hopes that another round of review will overturn the conviction.

What is needed, in the view of the Commission, is not merely an effort to accelerate the existing review machinery. Rather, it is necessary to experiment with a restructuring of the entire process of review.

The Commission believes that there should be a single, unified review proceeding in which all arguable defects in the trial proceeding can be examined and settled finally, subject only to narrowly defined exceptional circumstances where there are compelling reasons to provide for a further review.

This is a far-reaching and controversial proposal but the Commission recommends it as a reasonable response to an escalating problem.

The Commission recommends that every convicted defendant be afforded the opportunity to obtain one full and fair judicial review of his conviction and sentence by a tribunal other than that by which he was tried or sentenced. Review in that proceeding should extend to the entire case, including errors not apparent in the trial record that might heretofore have been asserted in collateral attacks on the conviction or sentence.

The reviewing court should have a full-time professional staff of lawyers, responsible directly to the judges. The function of this staff would be to supplement the work of the attorneys representing the prosecution and defense in each case.

Review procedures should be flexible so as to afford the greatest possible fairness, expedition, and finality. The court also should have the authority to confirm a conviction despite the existence of error if to do so would not amount to a miscarriage of justice.

A criminal case should be ready for initial action by the reviewing court within 30 days after the imposition of sentence. Cases containing only insubstantial issues should be finally disposed of within 60 days of imposition of sentence. Cases presenting substantial issues should be finally disposed of within 90 days after the imposition of sentence.

After reviewing court disposition, or after a fair opportunity to gain review, a conviction and sentence should not be subject to further State or Federal review except in such limited circumstances as the following: (1) further review would serve the public interest in the development of legal doctrine or in the maintenance of uniformity in the application of decisional or statutory law; (2) newly discovered evidence raises substantial doubt as to the defendant's guilt; or (3) issue arises as to a constitutional violation which, if well founded, would undermine the basis for or the integrity of the trial or review proceeding.

A review court should always state its reasons for its decision in a criminal case, but formal publication of reasons should be allowed only if the opinion would be significant to the development of legal doctrine or if it would serve other important institutional purposes. Reducing the number of published opinions would speed adjudication by freeing for other purposes the time judges use to write opinions and by reducing the time lawyers and judges need to prepare and decide cases.

The Commission further recommends that funds be devoted to technological innovation in the field of transcript production, such as computer-aided stenotyping, sound recording, and videotaping, in order to expedite preparation of the trial record for review purposes.

The Commission also recommends that the trial de novo system, which permits an offender convicted in a lower court to demand a full retrial in a court of general jurisdiction, be abolished. All courts should be courts of record and all should follow the same appellate practices.

COURT ORGANIZATION AND ADMINISTRATION

In opening the first National Conference on the Judiciary in March 1971, President Nixon called for "genuine reform" of the Nation's courts—"the kind of reform that requires imagination and daring." At the same conference, Chief Justice Warren E. Burger emphasized that "the challenges to our system of justice are colossal and immediate and we must assign priorities." "I would begin," he said, "by giving priority to methods and machinery, to procedures and technique, to management and administration of judicial resources even over the much-needed reexamination of substantive legal institutions." [6]

Essential to "efficient management and administration of judicial resources" is the unified court system. Centralized administrative authority is the unified court system's most important feature.

Under a unified court system, issues which are systemwide in nature may be resolved in a uniform fashion; for example, through the establishment of general rules of procedure, judicial training programs, and information systems. Temporary transfer of personnel to meet changes in workloads is also made possible by a unified court system.

[6] *Proceedings, National Conference on the Judiciary,* Williamsburg, Va., March 1971 (West Publishing Co.).

Progress toward complete unification varies from State to State. Lower courts, which process minor criminal offenses and city and county ordinance violations, are often the last to come under State organization and administration. In most cases, there is no coordination of lower courts within the same State. It is not unusual, for example, for a rural justice of the peace to have little or no work while a nearby municipal judge must hold evening sessions to keep his calendar current.

The Commission believes that all courts in a State should be organized into a unified judicial system financed by the State and administered by a statewide court administrative judge under the supervision of the chief justice of the State supreme court. This fully unified court system should consolidate all trial courts into a single court of general jurisdiction. All courts within a State would be unified under the administrative authority of the State's highest appellate court.

A matter of high priority in any reexamination of court processing of criminal defendants is court administration—the management of the nonjudicial business of the court.

Court management and administration has as its goal relieving judges of some nonjudicial functions and enhancing their performance of judicial functions.

Although court administration is one of the newer fields of public administration, it has already proved itself to be a valuable tool in maximizing the efficiency of the courts. A survey undertaken by the Commission and reproduced in its *Report on Courts* shows that the Nation already has 43 State court administrators and an undetermined number of regional and trial court administrators.

The Commission believes that professional court administration is an essential function in the reform of American courts. Nevertheless, improvements are needed. More courts need professional court administrators and the manner in which administrators serve their courts needs to be upgraded. The standards in this chapter are designed to stimulate and guide these improvements.

The Commission recommends that each State have a State court administrator responsible for establishing policies for administration of the entire State court system, including budgets, personnel, information compilation and dissemination, fiscal operations, court system evaluation and remediation, assignment of judges, and external liaison. The court administrator should establish operational guidelines for local and regional trial court administrators.

Local administrative policies should be established

by the judges of each trial court within guidelines set forth by the State's highest appellate court. A presiding judge should have ultimate administrative authority over such matters.

Each trial court with five or more judges should have a full-time administrator. Trial courts with caseloads too small to justify a full-time administrator should combine into administrative regions for that purpose.

IMPROVING THE QUALITY OF THE PROSECUTION, DEFENSE, AND JUDICIARY

A system is only as good as the people who work within it. The quality of personnel working in the court system is particularly important since it has a direct impact on the quality of justice.

Significant efforts must be made to upgrade and make more professional the performance of prosecution, defense, and judicial personnel.

Prosecution

The prosecutor occupies a critical position in the criminal justice system. His office combines legal, administrative, and judicial functions which require experienced, professional personnel and a rational and efficient organizational structure. Efforts to deal with the problem of crime in America are unlikely to be successful if prosecutors' offices are poorly funded, understaffed, and ineffective.

The personnel policies, size, and organization of many prosecutors' offices are not conducive to meeting the complex demands of the criminal justice system. Most of the Nation's 2,700 prosecutors serve in small offices and have only one or two assistants. Frequently, both prosecutor and assistants are part-time officials who have outside law practices. The salaries of prosecutors and their assistants are still considerably lower than those of private-practice lawyers with similar background and experience.

The President's Crime Commission observed that "a talented attorney, even one dedicated to public service, cannot be expected to remain long in such a position if it is his only source of income." A survey conducted by the National District Attorneys Association indicated that most assistant prosecutors obtain higher paying positions in private law firms after serving an average of 2 to 4 years.[7] Because of

[7] Report on Proceedings, Recommendations, and Statistics of the National District Attorneys Association Metropolitan Prosecutors' Conference, pp. 43-44 (1971).

low salaries prosecutors therefore are faced with the continuing problem of replacing experienced assistant prosecutors with inexperienced ones.

It is thus imperative that substantial additional resources be devoted to the training and continued education of prosecutors and their assistants. Similarly, every prosecutor's office should systematically develop and review the policies and practices to be followed by all staff attorneys. Only through training and policy guidelines can the requisite standard of performance be achieved.

The Commission believes that prosecutors' offices must be alert to good management and should undertake some new duties. For example, every office should have effective filing procedures and sound statistical systems. In many jurisdictions, the prosecutor's role in criminal investigation should be enlarged to cover consumer fraud complaints, municipal corruption, and organized crime activities, and the prosecutor should specifically develop his relationships with the police and the community.

The Commission recommends that the prosecutor be a full-time professional selected on the basis of demonstrated competence and personal integrity. The prosecutor's office should be provided with the necessary personnel, fiscal resources, and support services to deal effectively and fairly with all cases coming before it and to allow proper preparation of all cases at all levels of the criminal proceeding including screening and diversion.

The Commission also recommends that:

• The prosecutor should serve for a minimum term of 4 years and be compensated on a scale equal to the presiding judge of the trial court of general jurisdiction.

• Assistant prosecutors should be actively recruited from all segments of the population and should possess demonstrated legal ability.

• Professional staff size and scheduling should permit proper preparation of cases.

• The State should establish and support an independent agency or specialized unit in the attorney general's office to provide technical assistance and supplemental support services to local prosecutors.

• Formal national and statewide educational and training programs and local in-house orientation and training programs should be established and utilized for assistant prosecutors.

• The prosecutor should have at his disposal investigatory resources sufficient to assist in case preparation, supplement police investigations, and conduct initial investigations of official corruption, organized crime, and consumer fraud.

Defense

The task of providing legal defense representation for those accused of a crime has grown tremendously, in part because of the increased functions that defense counsel must perform as a matter of constitutional mandate. The right to representation at trial no longer is confined to those defendants charged with more serious criminal offenses. In *Argersinger* v. *Hamlin,* 407 U.S. 25 (1972), the U.S. Supreme Court held that no indigent person may be incarcerated as the result of a criminal trial at which he was not given the right to be represented by publicly provided defense counsel.

In considering the provision of defense services to those accused of a crime, the Commission addressed itself almost entirely to the provision of defense services at public expense. This was done because most defense services are provided by public representation and because there is substantial controversy over the adequacy of public representation.

The best available estimates are that about 60 percent of felony defendants, and 25 to 50 percent of misdemeanor defendants, cannot pay anything toward their defense, and therefore must be represented at public expense.[8] However, the proportion of defendants who are actually represented at public expense varies from jurisdiction to jurisdiction. One recent study of several Arkansas counties, for example, found that the percentage of felony defendants represented by appointed counsel ranged from 18.2 percent to 59.5 percent.[9]

With respect to the adequacy of public representation, there has been public criticism. For example, the Administrative Office of the United States Courts issued a report in 1969 that showed that defendants who could not afford private counsel received much harsher sentences than those who had privately retained counsel.[10]

However, the Commission found no evidence that public representation is always, or even generally, worse than private representation. Nevertheless it recognizes widespread suspicion and concludes that this suspicion is itself a major problem.

After study, the Commission drew these conclusions:

---

[8] Lee Silverstein, *Defense of the Poor in Criminal Cases in American State Courts* (American Bar Foundation, 1965), pp. 8-9.

[9] Morton Gitelman, *The Relative Importance of Appointed and Retained Counsel in Arkansas Felony Cases —An Empirical Study, 24 Ark. L. Rev. 442* (Winter 1971).

[10] Administrative Office of the United States Courts, *Federal Offenders in United States District Court* (1969), p. 49.

- Lawyers provided at public expense should be experienced and well educated.
- More professional staff resources, supporting resources and staff, and education are needed.
- The entire bar should be involved in the provision of public defense services.
- Provision of defense services should be prevented from becoming the realm of a limited clique of practitioners, whether in a public defender's office or a private capacity.

There is also need to deal with the special problems raised by the provision of public defense services. The lawyer rendering services at public expense is liable to be caught between public resentment at having to pay for the defense of guilty criminals and defendants' resentment at not having available as effective a defense as those with private counsel.

The Commission recommends that each eligible defendant be provided public representation from arrest until all avenues of relief from conviction have been exhausted.

Each jurisdiction should maintain a full-time public defender organization and a coordinated assigned counsel system involving the private bar, and should divide case assignments in a manner that will encourage participation by the private bar. The standard for eligibility for public representation should be based upon ability to pay for counsel without substantial hardship. Defendants should be required to pay part of the cost of representation if they are able to do so.

The Commission further recommends that:
- The right of a defendant to represent himself should be severely limited.
- If the defendant has no attorney and no request for counsel has been made, the judicial officer at the initial appearance should provide counsel for any eligible defendant who has not made an informed waiver of the right.
- Counsel should be available to convicted offenders for appeals or collateral attacks on convictions and at proceedings concerning detention or early release, parole revocation, and probationary status.
- Organization and administration of defender services should be consistent with local needs.
- The public defender should be selected on the basis of demonstrated and high personal integrity and should serve on a full-time basis at a salary not lower than that of the presiding judge of the trial court of general jurisdiction. A regional office should be established, if necessary to warrant a full-time defender.
- Public defenders should be appointed for a term of not less than 4 years and should be eligible for

reappointment. Selection and discipline should be vested in the judicial nominating commission and the judicial conduct commission.

• Staff attorneys should be recruited from all segments of the population and should be hired, retained, and promoted on the basis of merit qualifications.

• Staff size and scheduling should be regulated to insure manageable caseloads.

• All attorneys who represent the indigent accused should participate in comprehensive national, local, and office training programs designed to impart basic and extended skills in criminal defense.

• The public defender should be sensitive to the problems of his client community, and should strive to educate the community about his role.

• The public defender should have available adequate support services including investigative and social work assistance.

Judiciary

The role of the judiciary in the Nation's efforts to reduce crime is to provide a system of unquestioned integrity and competence for settling legal disputes. If the courts are to fulfill this role, the judicial processes must use effective and up-to-date management methods. In addition, the courts must strive to preserve the American heritage of freedom and to deal thoroughly with all cases that come before them—no matter how minor or routine they may be. Procedures and court systems can be no better than the judges who administer the procedures and render the decisions.

Unless the courts reflect all of these qualities, they will be viewed with disdain, fear, or contempt. Such attitudes are incompatible with the respect for law essential to a free society.

The Commission believes that courts exercising criminal jurisdiction meet these criteria inadequately, and that the American public shares this view. The inadequate quality of some judicial personnel, especially those who exercise trial jurisdiction, is partly responsible for this situation. Rules and methods also are important, but they cannot insure a highly regarded system. Judges exercise enormous discretionary power and trial judges function with almost no direct supervision. The quality of judicial personnel thus is more important than the quality of the participants in many other systems.

The Commission views the selection process as a matter needing attention, but it also believes that other aspects of the court system contribute to the poor quality of judicial personnel. Inadequate compensation is one factor. Judicial tenure also may account for some difficulty in obtaining and retaining capable judicial officers.

These factors—selection, compensation, and tenure—relate primarily to the need to maintain high quality judges. A somewhat different aspect of the problem concerns the behavior of judges. The public loses confidence in the court system when it sees examples of gross misconduct or obvious incompetence, especially when no remedial action is taken. But even if a trial judge commits no overt act of misconduct, his demeanor can have a significant impact upon the public's opinion of the courts.

There is a need for a more effective system of discipline and removal to deal with misbehavior and incompetence among the judiciary. In less extreme situations, the Commission sees the problem as one of inadequate judicial education. The need is not for a means of imposing sanctions on offending judges but rather for a means of developing programs of educating judges and of sensitizing them to the fact that their behavior affects the entire criminal justice system.

The Commission recommends that judges be nominated by a judicial commission appointed by the Governor, and that judges stand for periodic uncontested elections in which they run against their record. The judicial commission should consist of private nonlawyer citizens and members of the legal profession.

The Commission further recommends that:

• Retirement at age 65 should be mandatory, but retired judges should be assigned to sit for limited periods at the discretion of the presiding judge of the jurisdiction.

• State and local judges should be compensated at rates commensurate with salaries and retirement benefits of the Federal trial judiciary. When appropriate, salaries and benefits should be increased during a judge's term of office.

• A judicial conduct commission staffed by judicial, legal, and lay members should be established and empowered to discipline or remove judges for sufficient cause.

• Every State should establish and maintain a comprehensive program for continuing judicial education. Participation in the program should be mandatory.

COURT-COMMUNITY RELATIONS

Because court operations are subject to public scrutiny, court-community relations inevitably exist. The quality of these relations relates directly to the courts' ability to perform their functions effectively.

Defense lawyer preparing case.

A law-abiding atmosphere is fostered by public respect for the court process. Public scrutiny should not result in public dissatisfaction.

The community's perception of the court system also may have a direct impact on court processes, as when it affects the willingness of members of the community to appear as witnesses, serve as jurors, or support efforts to provide courts with adequate resources.

Court-community relations cannot and should not be avoided. The Commission believes that favorable court-community relations cannot be accomplished without a vigorous and well-planned program to insure that courts deserve to be and are, in fact, perceived favorably by the public.

Information and Education

There are several areas of serious deficiency in present court-community relations. The first involves information and education. Courts operate in a manner which frequently leaves the public uninformed. Inadequacies here can be traced to several causes. The use of specialized terminology and procedures makes legal proceedings particularly difficult for the public to understand. Added to this is the reluctance of courts to undertake informing the public about their procedures. Courts rarely issue news releases or make public reports.

Apart from the general lack of information, there are also problems of informing participants in the process and the Commission notes the need for courthouse information services. Participation in the criminal justice process often is a confusing and traumatic experience that leaves the witness, juror, or defendant with an unfavorable impression of the system.

Use of Witnesses

Another area of deficiency involves the methods and procedures by which witnesses are used. Witnesses often are required to make appearances that serve no useful purpose. Police officers, for example, often must be present at a defendant's initial appearance, although they serve no function at this proceeding.

Witnesses often are not compensated for time spent testifying and traveling, or they are compensated inadequately. In Connecticut and South Carolina, for example, witnesses are paid 50 cents for each court appearance. In Alabama, the fee is 75 cents. In Texas courts, witnesses (other than those called as experts) receive no fee for their court appearances.

Facilities

A most serious deficiency in court-community relations involves court facilities. A study of New York civil courts, conducted by the National College of the State Judiciary, found a correlation between the adequacy of a court's physical facilities and its public image in the community.

Facilities for witnesses sometimes are inadequate or nonexistent. Testifying can be an exhausting experience, as witnesses are frequently subjected to grueling examination. The Courts Task Force of the President's Commission on Law Enforcement and Administration of Justice observed that "sensitivity to the needs of witnesses who are required to return to court again and again, often at considerable personal sacrifice, is usually lacking."

The Commission recommends that immediate steps be taken to enhance court-community relations through systematic programs of public information and education, through improved treatment of witnesses, and through provision of adequate court facilities.

The Commission specifically recommends that:
• Courthouses should be designed and placed with careful attention to function. The ability to see and hear the proceedings should be a primary design consideration.
• Comfortable waiting rooms should be provided for jurors. The jury's waiting room should be separate from the one used by prosecution and defense witnesses.
• Courthouse information desks should be provided, and manned by informed staff who are fluent in the languages of the area.
• Court personnel should be representative of the community served, especially with respect to minority-group employment.
• The court should pursue a systematic program of public information and education that includes issuance of news releases and reports, speaking appearances, and public tours.
• Judges and court personnel should participate in criminal justice planning activities.
• Provision should be made for witnesses to be on telephone alert rather than present in court.
• Witnesses should be compensated at more realistic rates than now prevail.

JUVENILES

The general rise in crime throughout the United States in the last decade has brought increasing burdens to all courts, particularly the juvenile courts. In 1960, there were 510,000 delinquency cases disposed of by juvenile courts; in 1970 there were 1,125,000 delinquency cases disposed of by juvenile courts.[11]

The question is whether or not the present juvenile court system is an effective method of controlling juvenile crime. Throughout the country, the juvenile courts vary widely in structure, procedure, and quality. In the main, however, they reflect an understanding that special treatment for the young offender is desirable.

After considerable study, the Commission concurs that the juvenile offender should have special treatment. However, the present juvenile court systems are not providing that special treatment in an adequate, fair, and equitable manner.

The Commission believes that major reform of the juvenile justice system is needed. The juvenile justice system has not obtained optimum results with young people on their first contact with the system. Further, it is the conclusion of the Commission that juvenile courts must become part of an integrated, unified court system; that the jurisdiction of the juvenile courts must be narrowed and that the relationships between the courts and juvenile service agencies must be broadened in a manner which maximizes diversion from the court system. In addition there must be reform of the procedures for handling those juveniles who are referred to court.

Reorganization of Juvenile Courts

The existence of the juvenile court as a distinct entity ignores the causal relationship between delinquency and other family problems. A delinquent child most often reflects a family in trouble—a broken family, a family without sufficient financial resources, a family of limited education, and a family with more than one child or parent exhibiting antisocial behavior. The family court concept as now utilized in New York, Hawaii, and the District of Columbia permits the court to address the problems of the family unit, be they civil or criminal.

Further, in the past juvenile courts have, by their jurisdictional authorization, intervened in areas where alternative handling of the juvenile is more successful. It is the view of the Commission that the delinquent child—the child who commits an offense which would be criminal if committed by an adult—should be the primary focus of the court system. The Commission takes no position with

respect to extension of jurisdiction to the "person in need of supervision" (PINS). The PINS category includes the runaway and truant. Jurisdiction, however, should not extend to dependent children—those needing economic, medical, or other social assistance through no fault of their parents. Dependent children should be handled outside the court system through other social agencies. Of course, provision in the court system must be made for the neglected child who must be taken from his parents and cared for due to abusive conduct of the parent, failure of the parent to provide for the child although able to do so, and those circumstances where parents are incarcerated, hospitalized, or otherwise unable to care for their children for protracted periods of time.

The Commission recommends that jurisdiction over juveniles be placed in a family court which should be a division of a trial court of general jurisdiction. The family court should have jurisdiction over all legal matters related to family life, including delinquency, neglect, support, adoption, custody, paternity actions, divorce, annulment, and assaults involving family members. Dependent children— those needing help through no fault of their parents —should be handled outside the court system.

Reform of Court Procedures

In re Gault [12] clarified the constitutional rights of juveniles to due process. The juvenile can no longer be deprived of his basic rights by adherence to a *parens patriae,* "best interests of the child" doctrine.

Reform of court procedures, however, must not be limited to the areas identified in *Gault*. There is much, much more to be done in the juvenile justice system to minimize recidivism and control juvenile crime. Reforms are needed in the areas of intake proceedings, detention of juveniles, disposition of juveniles, and transfer of juveniles to the adult system when juvenile resources are exhausted.

Intake, Detention, and Shelter Care

There are a number of studies which suggest that many children mature out of delinquent behavior. If this is true, the question is whether it is better to leave these persons alone or put them into the formal juvenile justice system. Because there are no satisfactory measures of the effectiveness of the juvenile justice system, there is a substantial body of opinion which favors "leaving alone" all except those who have had three or four contacts with the police.

Each jurisdiction should consider this phenomenon, conduct studies among its juveniles

---

[11] U.S. Department of Health, Education, and Welfare, *Juvenile Court Statistics* 1971 (1972), p. 11.

[12] *In re Gault,* 387 U.S. 1 (1967).

charged with delinquent behavior, and establish intake criteria. Each court system should have an intake unit which should determine whether the juvenile should be referred to court. This intake unit should have available a wide variety of informal dispositions including referral to other agencies, informal probation, consent decrees, etc. In addition, this intake unit should have criteria for determining the use of detention or shelter care where formal petitions are filed with the court.

The Commission recommends that each family court, in accord with written criteria, create an intake unit which should determine whether the juvenile should be referred to court or dealt with informally, and should determine whether the juvenile should be placed in detention or shelter care. In no event should a child be detained for more than 24 hours pending determination of the intake unit.

Transfer of Juveniles to Adult Court

There are some instances in which the juvenile process is not appropriate. These include instances where the juvenile has previously participated in the rehabilitative programs for juveniles; instances where the juvenile justice system has no suitable resources; and instances where the criminal sophistication of the juvenile precludes any benefit from the special juvenile programs.

It is the view of the Commission, however, that transfer of juveniles should be limited. The Supreme Court in *Kent* v. *United States*[13] has given direction on the procedures to be used and on the substantive issues to be resolved in any transfer to adult court. The procedures must meet due process standards.

The Commission recommends that family courts have authority to order the transfer of certain juveniles for prosecution in the adult courts, but only if the juvenile is above a designated age, if a full and fair hearing has been held on the transfer, and if the action is in the best interest of the public.

Adjudication and Disposition

A juvenile charged with an act which, if committed by an adult, would be a criminal offense is by law entitled to most of the procedures afforded adult criminal defendants. The juvenile is entitled to:
- Representation by counsel.
- The privilege against self-incrimination.
- Right to confront and cross-examine witnesses.
- Admission of only evidence which is competent and relevant.

---

[13] *Kent* v. *U.S.*, 383 U.S. 541 (1966).

Juvenile Court.

- Proof of the acts alleged beyond a reasonable doubt.

There remains some question as to whether juveniles should be afforded jury trials. After consideration of *McKeiver* v. *Pennsylvania*[14] and the rationale therein, this Commission concludes that the State as a matter of policy should provide nonjury trials for juveniles. The theoretical protections of a jury trial are outweighed by the advantages of informality, fairness, and sympathy which the traditional juvenile court concept contemplates.

The Commission noted, however, that where the adjudication of delinquency is in a nonjudicial forum, provision must be made for separation of the adjudication and the disposition. The disposition hearing should be separate and distinct so that the determination of guilt will not be tainted by information that should be considered in making a decision on the appropriate rehabilitative program, including the past involvement of the juvenile with the criminal justice system.

During adjudicatory hearings to determine guilt or innocence, the juvenile should have all of the rights of an adult criminal defendant except that of trial by jury.

The disposition hearing to determine a rehabilitative program for the juvenile should be separate and distinct from the adjudicatory hearing and should follow, where feasible, the procedure recommended for the sentencing of convicted adult offenders.

CONCLUSION

The criminal court system of a free nation should conform to the ideal of equal justice under law and should be typified by quality, efficiency, and fairness. These three words exemplify the standards proposed in the Commission's *Report on Courts*. Great emphasis is placed upon upgrading the quality of criminal court personnel and thereby improving the quality of justice dispensed. Efficiency in processing cases from arrest to trial to final appellate judgment is a prominent theme. But throughout the report appear standards safeguarding the rights of all persons, including witnesses, jurors, and defendants.

The Commission believes that persons committing infractions of the law should be speedily arrested, tried, afforded appellate review, and given meaningful sentences. If recidivism is to be reduced, these same persons must feel that they have been treated fairly, honestly, and impartially. The standards in the *Report on Courts* provide a mechanism for achieving both of these sets of goals.

---

[14] *McKeiver* v. *Pennsylvania*, 403 U.S. 528 (1971).

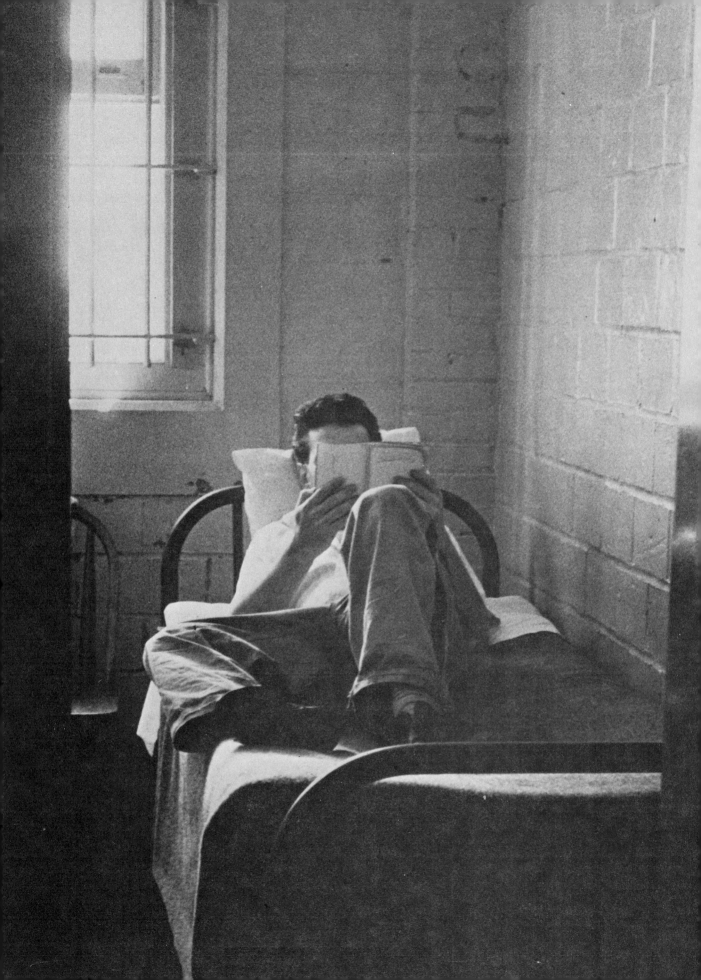

Chapter 7

Corrections

The American correctional system today appears to offer minimum protection for the public and maximum harm to the offender. The system is plainly in need of substantial and rapid change.

Figures on recidivism make it clear that society today is not protected—at least not for very long—by incarcerating offenders, for many offenders return to crime shortly after release from prison. Indeed, there is evidence that the longer a man is incarcerated, the smaller is the chance that he will lead a law-abiding life on release.

There is also evidence that many persons in prison do not need to be there to protect society. For example, when the Supreme Court's *Gideon* decision [1] overturned the convictions of persons in the Florida prison system who had not had an attorney, more than 1,000 inmates were freed. Such a large and sudden release might be expected to result in an increase in crime. To check this hypothesis, two groups of inmates released at the time were matched on the basis of individual characteristics. The one significant difference was

---

[1] *Gideon* v. *Wainwright,* 372 U.S. 335 (1963). The research is described in Charles J. Eichman, *The Impact of the Gideon Decision upon Crime and Sentencing in Florida* (Florida Division of Corrections, 1966). Mr. Wainwright's statement is quoted on pp. 4-5.

that one group of prisoners was released as a result of the *Gideon* decision and the other group at the expiration of their sentences. Over a period of 2½ years, the *Gideon* group had a recidivism rate of 13.6 percent, and the other group had almost twice that rate, 25.4 percent. Commented Louie Wainwright, director of Florida's corrections system:

> The mass exodus from prison may prove that there are many inmates presently in prison who do not need to be there in order to protect society. It may prove that many more people can be safely released on parole without fear that they will commit new crimes. This may well be the most important lesson we can learn from the *Gideon* experience.

It also seems clear that many persons can serve their sentences in the community without undue danger to the public.

There is substantial evidence that probation, fines, public service requirements, and restitution are less costly than incarceration and consistently produce lower rates of recidivism after completion of sentence.

There is also in this country a growing concern for the widespread abuses in the correctional system. Within the past decade, courts have intervened in prison management. Whole State prison systems have been declared unconstitutional as violating the eighth amendment's prohibition against cruel and unusual punishment. In other cases, courts have ruled that prisoners' civil rights have been violated.

As one court stated:

In the Court's estimation confinement itself within a given institution may amount to cruel and unusual punishment prohibited by the Constitution where the confinement is characterized by conditions and practices so bad as to be shocking to the conscience of reasonably civilized people even though a particular inmate may never be personally subject to any disciplinary action.[2]

Other courts have reached similar conclusions. In September 1972 the U.S. District Court for the Northern District of Mississippi found that the living units in the Mississippi prison system were "unfit for human habitation under any modern concept of decency" and that confinement of prisoners there under the present circumstances was "impermissible." In this case the U.S. Justice Department intervened on the side of the plaintiffs (prison inmates) after the suit was filed and asserted that the prison system was unconstitutionally segregated and violated the prisoners' rights.

The scrutiny of the courts has extended also to local jails and to those forgotten people of the criminal justice system—persons detained awaiting trial. Federal Judge Alfonso J. Zirpoli of the Northern District of California felt compelled to visit the unit of the Alameda County jail where plaintiffs were detained prior to trial. "The shocking and debasing conditions which prevailed there constituted cruel and unusual punishment for man or beast . . . the court's inescapable conclusion was that Greystone should be razed to the ground." [3]

In 1971–1972, the U.S. Supreme Court decided eight cases directly affecting convicted offenders.[4] The offender's contention prevailed in all eight cases, five of them by unanimous vote. Formal procedures are needed to revoke a person's parole, the Court said. Prisoners are entitled to access to legal materials, and prison officials must provide reasonable opportunities to all prisoners for religious worship. A judge may not use unconstitutionally obtained convictions as the basis for sentencing an offender. Prisoners need not exhaust all possible State remedies before pursuing the Federal route in order to challenge conditions of their confinement. Offenders committed under State laws pertaining to defective delinquents or sexually related offenses are entitled to formal procedures if their sentences are to be extended.

MAJOR RECOMMENDATIONS

The pressures for change in the American correctional system today are intense; it is clear that a dramatic realignment of correctional methods is needed. The Commission has made many recommendations toward that end, including:
• Enactment of laws clearly defining prisoners' rights, rules of conduct, and disciplinary and grievance procedures to be followed by correctional authorities in dealing with offenders.
• Repeal of legislation that deprives ex-offenders of civil rights and opportunities for employment.
• Elimination of disparate sentencing practices.
• Increased diversion out of the criminal justice system for certain types of offenders.
• Unification within the executive branch of all non-Federal correctional functions and programs for adults and juveniles.
• Active recruitment of corrections personnel from minority groups and among women and ex-offenders.
• Payment of competitive salaries to corrections personnel.
• Recruitment of volunteers, including ex-offenders, for correctional programs.

PRIORITIES FOR ACTION

Recognizing the inadequacies of the Nation's correctional systems, the Commission identified six goals toward which corrections must move with speed and determination. Top priority must be given to action that will achieve these ends:
• Equity and justice in corrections.
• Narrowing of the base of corrections by excluding many juveniles, minor offenders, and sociomedical cases.
• Shift of correctional emphasis from institutions to community programs.
• Unification of corrections and total system planning.
• Manpower development.
• Greater involvement of the public in corrections.

In furtherance of these six goals, the Commission recommends in its *Report on Corrections* 159 specific standards. These are discussed in summary

[2] *Holt* v. *Sarver*, 309 F. Supp. 362, 372-73 (E.D. Ark. 1970), aff'd 442 F. 2d 304 (8th Cir. 1971).

[3] *Brenneman* v. *Madigan*, 11 Crim. L. Rptr. 2248 (N.D. Cal. 1972).

[4] *Morrissey* v. *Brewer*, 408 U.S. 471 (1972); *Arciniega* v. *Freeman*, 404 U.S. 4 (1971); *Younger* v. *Gilmore*, 404 U.S. 15 (1971) affirming *Gilmore* v. *Lynch*, 319 F. Supp. 105 (N.D. Cal. 1970); *McNeil* v. *Director, Patuxent Institution*, 407 U.S. 245 (1971); *Wilwording* v. *Swenson*, 404 U.S. 249 (1971); *Cruz* v. *Beto*, 405 U.S. 319 (1972); *Humphrey* v. *Cady*, 405 U.S. 504 (1972); *U.S.* v. *Tucker*, 404 U.S. 443 (1972).

form in this chapter. Many of the standards are implicit in the recent court decisions. Others have grown out of accepted principles of public administration, such as the need for public agencies and agents to be accountable to the public they serve. Still others have come from the experience of correctional administrators across the country. A committee named by the American Correctional Association and members of the Association of State Correctional Administrators assisted the Commission by studying proposed standards and suggesting improvements.

These standards and goals for corrections cover many areas that have not traditionally been considered within the scope of correctional concern. The Commission, however, concluded that such matters as diversion from the criminal justice process, bail, and sentencing have a direct and important impact on correctional systems. These matters, together with the more traditional areas, are addressed in the following pages.

EQUITY AND JUSTICE IN CORRECTIONS

Corrections in the United States often has been—and in some areas still is—characterized by inhumane treatment of prisoners. Personnel in various correctional programs have made arbitrary and discriminatory decisions and exhibited a disregard for law. American society cannot tolerate such conditions. Moreover, it is illogical to try to train lawbreakers to obey the law in a system that does not itself respect law.

Further, correctional institutions too often are impeded by the sentencing practices of the courts. The disparity of sentences, as well as their length, determine the extent to which an offender may be rehabilitated. Rehabilitation is rarely achieved unless the offender perceives some justification for his sentence and sees his sentence as equitable—at least in terms of sentences imposed on fellow prisoners.

The Commission, in an effort to achieve equality and justice, thus offers two groups of recommendations relating to offenders' rights and sentencing practices.

Rights of Offenders

Convicted offenders should retain all rights that citizens in general have except those rights that must be limited in order to carry out the criminal sanction or to administer a correctional facility or agency.

The strategy for correctional reform must be built on a foundation of nondiscriminatory, just, and humane action that honors the legal and social rights of the offender. Moreover, it is imperative that such action be seen by the offender himself as just and fair.

The Commission's standards in the area of offenders' rights are applicable to all persons under correctional control, but many apply with special force to sentenced offenders in prisons and other correctional institutions and to persons detained awaiting trial.

Several standards deal with the right of offenders to seek protection of the law within the judicial system. Each correctional agency should develop policies and procedures to guarantee the offender's right to:

- Access to the courts.
- Access to legal services.
- Access to legal materials.

These three standards are fundamental. Guarantees of the right of access to the courts were among the first to be recognized by Federal and State courts. The result has been a dramatic increase in the number of petitions filed each year by prisoners.[5] The Commission realizes that implementing guarantees of access to legal services and legal materials presents some problems. These are dealt with in detail in the Commission's *Report on Corrections.*

Another group of standards deals with the conditions under which prisoners live and identifies the prisoner's right to:

- Protection against personal abuse at the hands of staff and other inmates.
- Healthful surroundings.
- Medical care.
- Nondiscriminatory treatment.

Among the types of personal abuse by staff which the Commission rejects are corporal punishment and solitary confinement as punishment, except as a last resort and then for not more than 10 days.

To protect prisoners from abuse by other inmates, the standards call for classification to identify violence-prone prisoners and for better supervision throughout the institution.

Courts in Arkansas, California, Mississippi, Pennsylvania, Virginia, and elsewhere have recognized the strip cell, beatings, and similar disciplinary methods as cruel and unusual punishment. Lack of medical care for prisoners was found by a court in Alabama to be "barbarous" as well as unconstitutional.[6]

---

[5] In the Federal courts alone, such petitions have risen from just over 2,000 in 1960 to more than 16,000 in 1970. In the latter year they constituted one out of every six civil filings.

[6] 12 Crim. L. Rptr. 2113 (M.D. Ala., 1972).

Group counseling session at a halfway house.

Other Commission standards deal with the discretionary power which correctional authorities exercise over offenders and how that power is to be regulated and controlled. The Commission recognizes that correctional agencies must have discretionary power, but this power must not be used arbitrarily or capriciously.

Toward this end the proper foundation for disciplinary action is a code which specifies prisoner behavior and which is easily understood. Many codes in use today are stated in terms that call for subjective and often unprovable judgments, such as prohibitions against being "untidy" or "insolent." Often the code is not explained to offenders in terms they understand.

Rules of conduct should be limited to dealing with observable behavior that clearly can be shown to have an adverse effect on the individual or corrections agency, with a full explanation to all offenders concerned.

Disciplinary procedures should allow the individual to be informed of the violation with which he is charged and, on serious charges, to have a hearing at which he may present evidence contradicting or mitigating the charge.

Grievance procedures should allow an offender to report a grievance and have it investigated by a person who is not directly involved in the incident and who is in a position to see that action is taken to mitigate grievances that appear to be warranted.

Each correctional system should have a trained person whose major function is to act as ombudsman. He should hear complaints of both inmates and employees and initiate changes to remedy justified grievances.

Recent court decisions have made clear that prisoners, pretrial detainees, probationers, and parolees have continuing rights under the first amendment. Rights to expression and association are involved in:

• Exercise of free speech.
• Belonging to and participating in organizations and engaging in peaceful assemblies.
• Exercise of religious beliefs and practices.
• Preserving identity through distinguishing clothing, hairstyles, and other items of physical appearance.

The only justification for interfering with freedom

116

of expression or association should be the showing of a compelling state interest in so doing. The degree of interference should be as little as is consistent with protecting the state's interest.

Maintenance of control in the face of an incipient riot is one obvious example of a compelling state interest as contemplated by the Commission. A parolee or probationer can be allowed more latitude than a prisoner in a tense maximum security institution. But agencies traditionally have applied a flat rule, regardless of circumstances, and the standard seeks to correct this situation.

Closely associated with freedom of expression and association is the access prisoners have to the public. Standards are provided in connection with:
• Sending and receiving mail.
• Having access to the communications media.
• Receiving visitors.

Offenders should have the right to correspond with anyone and to send and receive any material that can be lawfully mailed, without limitation on volume or frequency. Correctional authorities should have the right to inspect incoming and outgoing mail for contraband but not to read or censor mail.

Except in emergencies such as institutional disorders, offenders should be allowed to present their views to the communications media through confidential and uncensored interviews with media representatives, uncensored letters and other communications with the media, and publication of articles and books on any subject.

Several recent court decisions have recognized both the public's right to know and the offender's right to tell. Moreover, if correctional authorities are willing to allow inmates more access to the public, the Commission believes they will help to lower the walls of isolation that corrections has built around itself. To build public support, correctional authorities should support public awareness of the needs of the institutions and their inmates.

Correctional authorities should not limit the number of visitors an offender may have or the length of the visit, so long as it is in line with reasonable institutional schedules. Indeed, authorities should promote visitation by providing a suitable place for visiting by individuals and families in privacy.

Potential denial of an offender's rights does not end with the completion of his sentence. All States apply indirect sanctions to the ex-offender and most deny him the right to vote, to hold public office, and to serve on a jury. Even more important to him from an economic standpoint is the widespread practice of denying an ex-offender a license to practice occupations regulated by government. The list of such occupations is long, ranging from barber to psychiatrist.

States should adopt legislation to repeal all mandatory provisions in law or civil service regulations that deprive ex-offenders of civil rights and opportunities for employment. Each State legislature should enact a code of offenders' rights. The sentencing court should have continuing jurisdiction over the sentenced offender during the term of his sentence.

If codes are not enacted, the courts will be kept busy for years defining rights which could well be made specific by State legislation. If the one sentencing court had continuing jurisdiction, the offender could apply to the court for relief if he believed his rights were being denied.

Sentencing

Sentencing practices of the courts are of crucial importance to corrections. The sentence determines whether a convicted offender is to be confined or be supervised in the community and how long corrections is to have control over him.

If the offender is to benefit from time spent under sentence, it is essential that he feel his sentence is justifiable rather than arbitrary. The man sentenced to 10 years who shares a cell with a man convicted of the same offense under similar circumstances and sentenced to 5 years works against a handicap of bitterness and frustration. Such feelings must be accentuated if the men are of different races, or if one had money to hire a lawyer and the other did not.

The *New York Times,* in the fall of 1972, made a study of sentencing practices that highlighted sentence disparity as a major impediment to effective corrections. Among offenders sentenced to Federal prisons in 1970, whites convicted of income tax evasion were committed for an average of 12.8 months; nonwhites for 28.6 months. In drug cases, the average for whites was 61.1 months; for nonwhites, 81.1 months. The forthcoming 1973 report of the Federal Bureau of Prisons shows that in 1972 the average sentence of all persons committed to Federal prisons was 43.3 months for whites and 58.7 months for blacks. While the reader should not infer that these are all direct cause-and-effect relationships, these national statistics obviously raise questions about the equity of current sentencing practices in all jurisdictions.

Sentencing councils should be established, in which judges in multijudge courts would meet to discuss cases awaiting sentences in order to assist

the trial judge in arriving at an appropriate sentence. **Appellate review of sentencing decisions should be authorized.**

Sentencing institutes should also be set up under State auspices, at which sentencing judges, other criminal justice personnel, and possibly members of the academic community would meet regularly to discuss sentencing alternatives and criteria and reexamine sentencing procedures.

Sentencing councils were originally developed in the U.S. District Court for the Eastern District of Michigan, where sentences now tend to be less disparate. Sentencing institutes, also first developed for the Federal judiciary, are now used by several States. Appellate review of sentencing, according to the American Bar Association's study of sentencing alternatives, is now "realistically available in every serious case" in only about 15 States.[7] Even in these States, courts have moved cautiously. However, it is widely believed that, where sentence review is not available, a number of appellate courts have reversed trial courts largely because the sentence was inappropriate.

In addition, the Commission recommends the following to achieve greater equity and less disparity:
• Sentencing courts should hold a hearing prior to imposition of sentence, at which the defendant should have the right to be represented by counsel and to present arguments as to sentencing alternatives.
• Whenever the court feels it necessary—and always where long-term incarceration is a possible disposition—a full presentence report on the offender should be in the hands of the judge before the sentencing hearing.
• Sentencing courts should be required to make specific findings and state specific reasons for the imposition of sentence.

A root cause of the disparity in sentencing in the United States is inconsistency in penal codes. The American Bar Association in a study of sentencing alternatives noted that in one State a person convicted of first-degree murder must serve 10 years before he becomes eligible for parole, while one convicted of second-degree murder may be forced to serve 15 years.[8]

Many States now are undertaking massive revisions of their criminal codes that should eliminate some sentencing discrepancies.

In revising their criminal codes, the Commission recommends that States adopt a sentencing structure based on a 5-year maximum sentence unless the offender is in a special category of "persistent," "professional," or "dangerous" offenders. At present sentences are harsher in the United States than in any other Western country. This stems partly from the high maximum sentences authorized by law. To insure that the dangerous offender is removed from society, legislatures have in effect increased the possible maximum sentence for all offenders. This dragnet approach has resulted in imposition of high maximum sentences on persons who may not need them. Like disparities in sentences, this approach seriously handicaps correctional programs.

The impact of unduly long sentences on corrections is shown by studies of recidivism among offenders who have served differing lengths of sentences. A California study found that shorter incarceration was associated with no significant increase in recidivism; in some cases, it was accompanied by a decrease.[9] Among Federal parolees, a researcher found that parole violation rates increased with the length of time served. For persons serving 6 months or less before parole, the violation rate was 9 percent; among those serving 5 years or longer, the rate was 64.5 percent.[10]

The Commission recommends a maximum sentence of 5 years for most offenders, with no minimum sentence imposed by statute. The Commission recommends a maximum sentence not to exceed 25 years for a convicted offender who is:
1. **A persistent offender;**
2. **A professional criminal; or**
3. **A dangerous offender.**

A persistent offender is one who has been convicted of a third felony, two of them within the past 5 years. A professional criminal is one convicted of a felony committed as part of a continuing illegal business in which he was in a management position or an executor of violence. A dangerous offender is one whose criminal conduct shows: a pattern of repetitive behavior that poses a serious threat to the safety of others; persistent aggressive behavior without regard to consequences; or a particularly heinous offense involving infliction or threat of serious bodily injury or death.

The Commission decided not to speak on the question of using the death penalty to deter or punish murderers, because of the unresolved

[7] American Bar Association Project on Minimum Standards for Criminal Justice, *Appellate Review of Sentences* (1968), p. 13.

[8] American Bar Association Project on Minimum Standards for Criminal Justice, *Sentencing Alternatives and Procedures* (1968), p. 49.

[9] California Assembly, Committee on Criminal Procedure, *Deterrent Effects of Criminal Sanctions* (1968).

[10] Administrative Office of the U.S. Courts, *Persons under Supervision of the Federal Probation System* (1968).

constitutional and legal questions raised by recent court decisions. Resolution of this question, it believes, should be left to referendums, State legislatures, or the courts.

The American Bar Association, noting the *Gideon* study described at the beginning of this chapter and the significantly shorter average sentences imposed by Western European judges, comments that the prison sentences now authorized, and sometimes required, in this country "are significantly higher than are needed in the vast majority of cases in order to adequately protect the interests of the public." Except for a very few particularly serious offenses and under special circumstances similar to those recommended by the Commission for extended terms, the ABA standard states, "the maximum authorized prison term ought to be 5 years and only rarely 10." [11]

NARROWING THE BASE OF CORRECTIONS

The Commission believes that the public would be better served and correctional and other resources put to more effective use if many persons who now come under correctional responsibility were diverted out of the criminal justice process. More persons accused of illegal acts should be directed away from processing through the formal criminal justice system prior to adjudication by means of organized diversion programs.

Some conduct that may now result in correctional supervision or incarceration—drunkenness, vagrancy, or acts illegal only for children, for example—should be excluded from juvenile justice and criminal law, and not be brought before the courts and thus not channeled to corrections. (A more detailed discussion of the issue will be found in this report in the chapters on Criminal Code Reform and Revision and on Courts.) Other conduct, such as drug abuse or prostitution, may remain illegal, but, because corrections is not equipped to deal with it effectively, it should be handled through other resources. In short, to improve correctional services, it is imperative that corrections be given responsibility only for persons who need correctional services.

Corrections can do a better job, the Commission believes, if it does not have to handle persons with whom it is unequipped to deal. Among these are the drunks who in many jurisdictions go in and out of jail, forming the most conspicuous example of the revolving door syndrome, with perhaps two million arrests a year. Like the inebriates, drug addicts need treatment rather than the correctional mill. Similarly,

corrections is unequipped to handle the mentally disturbed who are often incarcerated.

Some States have decriminalized public drunkenness and vagrancy, and the Commission recommends that all States do so. If States follow other Commission suggestions that there be no incarceration for certain acts that do not endanger public safety, corrections can put its resources to more productive use.

Indeed, for many persons accused of criminal acts, official system processing is counterproductive. To meet the needs of these persons, planned programs must be developed as alternatives to processing into the justice system. The argument for diversion programs that occur prior to court adjudication is that they give society the opportunity to reallocate existing resources to programs that promise greater success than formal criminal sanctions.

It should be noted that the criminal justice system has never processed all persons accused of criminal acts. Criminal justice personnel have used this discretion to halt prosecution for many reasons. For example, some statutes may not be enforced because the community is not really concerned about the behavior in question. In other cases, the nature of the offense, the circumstances of its commission, the attitude of the victim, and the character and social status of the accused may cause the accused to be diverted from the criminal justice system. In still other instances, some cases are not processed because the volume of cases is so large that less serious offenders must be diverted to allow law enforcement, courts, and corrections to concentrate on the more serious cases.

These processes by which some cases are not prosecuted have sometimes operated in ways that were discriminatory. They have also been used without regard to the most effective allocation of resources. The Commission therefore endorses adoption of criteria by which equitable and logical choices can be made to exclude individuals who do not need the official attention of the system or one of its parts.

Many persons, especially the young, who are arrested for minor first offenses are not likely to repeat them, particularly if they have resources available through community agencies such as counseling, medical or mental health services, employment, and job training. Legislative or administrative action that excluded many children and youth from the justice system would force development of whatever private or community alternatives were needed. It would reduce workloads of correctional staff and offer greater opportunity for constructive work with offenders remaining within the system.

---

[11] *Sentencing Alternatives and Procedures*, p. 21.

In sum, the Commission recommends that each jurisdiction plan for diversion from the justice system of persons who are not dangerous to others, if prosecution may cause undue harm or merely exacerbate the social problem that led to the illegal act; services to meet their needs are available in the community; arrest has already served as a desired deterrent; and the needs and interests of the victims and of society are better served by diversion than by official processing. The question of diversion and the courts is discussed in Chapter 6 of this report.

EMPHASIS ON COMMUNITY-BASED PROGRAMS

The Commission believes that the most hopeful move toward effective corrections is to continue and strengthen the trend away from confining people in institutions and toward supervising them in the community. At least two-thirds of those under correctional control are already in some community-based program—probation, parole, work release, study release, or some other form of conditional release. The thrust of the Commission's *Report on Corrections* is that probation, which is now the largest community-based program, will become the standard sentence in criminal cases, with confinement retained chiefly for those offenders who cannot safely be supervised in the community.

Failure of State Institutions

There are compelling reasons to continue the move away from institutions. First, State institutions consume more than three-fourths of all expenditures for corrections while dealing with less than one-third of all offenders.[12] Second, as a whole they do not deal with those offenders effectively. There is no evidence that prisons reduce the amount of crime. On the contrary, there is evidence that they

contribute to criminal activity after the inmate is released.

Prisons tend to dehumanize people—turning them from individuals into mere numbers. Their weaknesses are made worse, and their capacity for responsibility and self-government is eroded by regimentation. Add to these facts the physical and mental conditions resulting from overcrowding and from the various ways in which institutions ignore the rights of offenders, and the riots of the past decade are hardly to be wondered at. Safety for society may be achieved for a limited time if offenders are kept out of circulation, but no real public protection is provided if confinement serves mainly to prepare men for more, and more skilled, criminality.

Confinement can be even less effective for children and youth. Some 19th century "reform schools" still exist with a full heritage of brutality.[13] Some newer institutions, also in rural settings, provide excellent education, recreation, and counseling but require expensive and extensive plants capable of providing for the total needs of children over prolonged periods.

The Commission believes that, if a residential facility for confinement of juveniles is necessary, it should be in or close to a city. It should not duplicate services that are available in the community, such as schools and clinical services, but should obtain these services for its residents by purchase or contract. In this way a child in a residential program will learn by testing himself in the community where he must live.

The Commission believes that some institutions will be necessary for the incarceration of adults who cannot be supervised in the community without endangering public safety, but there are more than enough facilities at hand for this purpose. The Commission recognizes, too, that some States will require time to develop alternatives to incarceration for juveniles.

States should refrain from building any more State institutions for juveniles; States should phase out present institutions over a 5-year period.

They should also refrain from building more State institutions for adults for the next 10 years except when total system planning shows that the need for them is imperative.

Institutions that must remain in use should be modified in order to minimize the harmful effects of the physical environment on inmates. The facilities

---

[12] These proportions were shown by the most recent nationwide survey of offenders and correctional expenditures, made in 1965 by the National Council on Crime and Delinquency and shown in the President's Commission on Law Enforcement and Administration of Justice, *Task Force Report: Corrections* (1967), p. 1. The *1970 National Jail Census* published by the Law Enforcement Assistance Administration in 1971 and the *National Prisoner Statistics,* issued by the Bureau of Prisons (Bulletin 47, 1972) show that there has been a decline in the number of inmates of Federal and State prisons and local jails since the 1965 survey. Hence it seems likely that the proportion of offenders who are under supervision in the community may be near three-fourths.

Halfway house in a large city.

[13] See Howard James, *Children in Trouble* (McKay, 1970) and the chapter on juvenile intake and detention in the Commission's *Report on Corrections.*

and functions of each institution should be reexamined at least every 5 years in connection with long-range planning for the State's entire correctional system.

The Commission believes that States should follow the example of Massachusetts, which has closed down all statewide institutions for juveniles. Several youth institutions in California have already been closed, and it is now proposed that the rest should be phased out.

All institutions or sections of institutions that do not meet health and safety standards should be closed down until such standards are met, as many courts have required. New facilities should be located close to cities from which most inmates come, so that family ties can be maintained. Such locations also make it easier to hire qualified staff and to purchase local services by contract.

Adult institutions should revamp their programs so that, among other things, the job training they offer trains for real jobs, using skilled supervision and modern machinery. Within about 5 years, prison industries should pay wages at rates prevailing in the area around the institution. In this event, it would be possible to obligate the inmate to repay the State for a reasonable share of its costs in maintaining him.

Salvaging the Jail

The conditions in local jails often are far worse than those in State prisons. Local jails are old—the national jail census made for the Law Enforcement Assistance Administration (LEAA) in 1970 showed that one out of every four cells was more than 50 years old and some were more than 100 years old. Many do not meet rudimentary requirements of sanitation—50 jails had no flush toilets and investigations in many institutions have revealed filthy cells, bedding, and food. Some jails surveyed, notably in the District of Columbia, had nearly half again as many inmates as they were designed to hold. Only half of the jails had any medical facilities.[14]

Nine out of 10 jails surveyed had no recreational or educational programs. According to inmates, one of the grimmest aspects of serving time in such places is having little or nothing to do, day after day.

Although conditions in some jails are better than those just described, the Commission believes that little improvement is likely over the country as a whole until jails are run by correctional authorities rather than local law enforcement agencies, whose personnel are largely untrained for custodial or correctional functions.

[14] Law Enforcement Assistance Administration, *1970 National Jail Census* (1971), pp. 1-5.

Jails should be part of the unified State correctional system called for later in this chapter. The Commission also urges States to develop probation for misdemeanants as an alternative to jail sentences.

As part of the correctional system, jails could provide services and programs many inmates need—education (in cooperation with local schools), vocational training, job placement, recreation, and various forms of conditional release.

Many inmates, including juveniles, are being held in local jails for long periods before coming to trial. The 1970 jail census showed that 83,000 persons (half of all the adult prisoners and two-thirds of all the juveniles) were being held prior to trial. In some institutions, the proportion was much higher—in the District of Columbia in 1971, 80 percent were being held prior to trial, some of them for as long as 36 months. These persons, all legally innocent, are held with convicted offenders.

Most of the detainees are in jail because they are too poor to make bail, and family and friends cannot help. The Commission believes that a person's financial resources should not determine whether he is detained prior to trial. The Commission commends such alternatives as issuance of citations instead of arrest; release on recognizance; and cash deposit of 10 percent of the bond with the court, a system that eliminates the bail bondsman. All of these programs have been tried in various jurisdictions in the United States, with low rates of failure to appear in court. Expediting criminal trials by requiring that a person be brought to trial not more than 30 days after a misdemeanor arrest (as recommended in Chapter 6) would also cut down on the amount of pretrial detention.

Improving Community-Based Programs

Not all the arguments for basing corrections in the community are negative ones such as the ineffectiveness and high cost of institutions. Community-based programs have important positive value in themselves.

The wide variety of correctional programs that are available—or could be made available—in communities allows a court to select one that is suited to the needs of an individual offender. A youth, for example, may be sentenced to probation under varying conditions, such as the requirement that he make restitution to the victim or work at a public service job. Or he may be sentenced to partial confinement in a residential facility (sometimes called a halfway house) under supervision during hours when he is not working or at school. An adult may be required to live in a similar facility, working during the day and returning to the halfway house at night.

Another advantage of community-based programs is that they can make use of resources that are provided to citizens in general—health, education, counseling, and employment services. This is an economical use of resources and one that keeps the offender in the community itself or helps him to return to it after incarceration.

Perhaps the major contribution of community-based programs is that they keep the offender in the community where he must ultimately live, rather than in an isolated institution where all decisions are made for him and he becomes less and less able to cope with life on the outside. Participation of volunteers will assist in keeping the offender part of the community.

The Commission makes several suggestions designed to improve and extend community-based programs:
• Both probation and parole officers should act as resource brokers to secure services for offenders in their charge, rather than acting solely as control agents.
• The casework approach, which has dominated probation, should shift to teamwork and differential assignments.
• Probation should be extended to misdemeanants.
• Both probation and parole must follow practices that offer due process to offenders threatened with revocation of their status.
• Both probation and parole need more trained workers, particularly those who come from the ethnic and racial groups which contribute heavily to the offender population.
• Correctional authorities should develop detailed procedures to assure that probationers and parolees are adequately supervised.

The Commission emphasizes that programs and services must take precedence over buildings. Communities that rush into construction to house new programs may be repeating the mistakes this country made over the past 200 years, when well-meant experiments like the penitentiary eventually produced monstrosities like Attica, San Quentin, and Parchman.

UNIFIED CORRECTIONAL PROGRAMS AND TOTAL SYSTEM PLANNING

American correction systems range in size and shape from huge State departments to autonomous one-man probation offices. Some States combine corrections with other governmental functions—law enforcement, health, or social welfare, for example. Some programs are managed in a highly professional manner, others by methods that are outmoded and ineffective.

LEAA recently reported that there are about 5,300 correctional agencies in the United States. Only one out of every six of these agencies is operated at the State level. The rest are run by counties, cities, villages, or townships, independently or in an often confusing variety of combinations.

Seeking at various times and for varying purposes to provide something more effective than prisons, State legislatures and their counterparts in counties and cities created reformatories, probation, parole, "industrial schools," and community programs for delinquent children. Agencies within the same jurisdiction often operate under contradictory assumptions, practices, and goals. With such a nonsystem, it is difficult to allocate tax dollars rationally, almost impossible to hold any one agency or agency head accountable for the results.

The Commission believes that all States should follow the example of the five States—Alaska, Connecticut, Delaware, Rhode Island, and Vermont —that now exercise control over all non-Federal correctional activities within their boundaries.

By 1978, each State should enact legislation to unify within the executive branch all non-Federal correctional functions and programs for adults and juveniles, including service for persons awaiting trial; probation supervision; institutional confinement; community-based programs, whether prior to or during institutional confinement; and parole and other aftercare programs.

The board of parole may be administratively part of the overall correctional agency, but it should be autonomous in its decisionmaking. It also should be separate from parole field services.

An integrated, State-controlled correctional system would make it possible to streamline activities and reduce waste and overlap, thus making the most effective use of tax dollars and professional talent. Uniform staff development programs, interdepartmental career opportunities, and civil service would help provide high standards of performance. Integration of correctional planning would also minimize disparities among programs that now impede the flow and quality of services to offenders. Systemwide research and evaluation would increase feedback on how programs are working and make the system accountable to the public.

The Commission emphasizes its conviction that an integrated State correctional system is not in conflict with the concept of community-based corrections.

123

The fact that a State agency makes statewide plans does not imply remote control of programs in the community. Rather it makes possible logical and systematic planning that can be responsive to changing problems and priorities. It implies maximum use of local personnel and fiscal resources to guarantee that programs will be developed to meet diverse local needs and local conditions.

Statewide planning indeed should be a stimulus to planning on the local level. At both levels, corrections needs to be seen as part of the total criminal justice system. Changes in one part of the system will require changes elsewhere. If public drunkenness is decriminalized, a detoxification center will be needed to replace the drunk tank in the local jail. Adoption of release on recognizance programs and probation for misdemeanants will reduce jail populations and allow resources to be allocated to programs for sentenced offenders. Within the corrections subsystem, sound planning will make it possible to supply services and programs on a regional basis in sparsely populated areas and, conversely, to provide a network of services in highly urbanized areas.

MANPOWER DEVELOPMENT

People are the most important resource in the fight against crime. In corrections they are the resource that is scarcest and most poorly used.

Corrections needs to use modern management techniques to analyze its manpower needs, recruit and train personnel to fill those needs, and retain staff who perform well and show interest in the job. Achieving these ends is hampered by lack of interest or information on the part of managers and by outmoded restraints and prejudices in hiring and promotions.

The Commission believes that active efforts must be made to recruit from minority groups, which are usually overrepresented among offenders and underrepresented among the staff.

At Attica in upstate New York before the 1971 riot, 54 percent of the inmates were black and 9 percent Puerto Rican, but only one black and one Puerto Rican were on the staff. More blacks and Puerto Ricans have since been hired, but the differences in the racial makeup between inmates and staff still are great.[15]

---

[15] *Attica*, Official Report of the New York State Special Commission on Attica (Bantam Books, 1972), pp. 24, 28.

Female offender (second from left) attending college seminar through a prison release project.

Some correctional administrators, like those in New York, have recognized the urgency of having an institution staff that can achieve rapport with offenders, who tend to be young, to be black, Puerto Rican, Chicano, or Indian (depending on the area), and to come from ghettos or rural slums. Much more effort must be made to interest people from these groups in careers in corrections.

Community-based correctional programs also have needs and potentials for the use of minority people. In probation, for example, the minority staff member may know the problems of the offender more intimately than do his white colleagues and often can more easily locate potential sources of help. These probabilities are increased among the staff hired to serve in paraprofessional capacities in the neighborhoods from which probationers come.

Special training programs, more intensive and comprehensive than standard programs, can be devised to replace educational and experience requirements. But it must be emphasized that training in intergroup relations is essential for all recruits to corrections, with refresher courses given as standard elements of staff development programs.

The Commission also recommends that corrections make use of other underutilized human resources, particularly women and ex-offenders.

Because women have been discriminated against in hiring and promotion throughout the corrections field, particularly in male institutions, they have been effectively eliminated from management positions except in the few institutions for females. There appears to be no good reason why women should not be hired for any type of position in corrections.

Ex-offenders have experience in corrections and often have rapport with offenders that gives them special value as correctional employees. They have been through the system and understand its effects on the individual. California, Illinois, New York, and Washington have pioneered in the use of ex-offenders in correctional work. There is obvious need for careful selection and training of ex-offenders. Their use in correctional programs may be high-risk, but it is also potentially high-gain.

Finally, there is a need to change current policies to secure and retain qualified personnel.

Correctional personnel should be paid salaries competitive with those of other criminal justice personnel who work in positions calling for comparable training and performance. Outmoded requirements of residence and physique should be eliminated. Lateral entry should also be made possible, to facilitate hiring men and women of special ability from outside a given system.

Employees with years of experience are reluctant to enter a new system if they must leave behind the pension benefits of the old. The Commission suggests a pension system that would permit benefits to accompany the employee from one agency to another, within or between States.

INCREASED INVOLVEMENT OF THE PUBLIC

The degree to which the public understands, accepts, and participates in correctional programs will determine to a large extent not only how soon, but how successfully, corrections can operate in the community and how well institutions can prepare the inmate for return to it.

Public participation is widespread in both institutional programs and community-based programs. The National Information Center on Volunteers in Courts, operating in Boulder, Colo., estimates that citizen volunteers outnumber professionals by four or five to one. According to the Center, about 70 percent of correctional agencies which deal with felons have some sort of volunteer program to aid them. Volunteer work with the misdemeanant is even more widespread.

Some volunteers supplement professional activities, as in teaching, while others play roles unique to volunteers in friendship situations, such as big brothers to delinquent youngsters. Other citizens serve as fundraisers or organizers of needed services, goods, and facilities.

In recent years institution doors have been opened to volunteer groups, including Alcoholics Anonymous and other self-help groups, ethnic organizations, and churches. Such programs have the double effect of involving citizens in the correctional system and providing services that inmates need.

Intensive efforts should be made to recruit volunteers from minority groups, the poor, inner city residents, ex-offenders who can serve as success models, and professionals who can bring special expertise to correctional programs.

Training should be provided to volunteers to instill understanding of lifestyles common among offenders and to acquaint them with the objectives and problems of corrections. A paid coordinator of volunteers should be hired in each program using volunteer help.

Although corrections has succeeded in bringing citizen participants into many institutions, it has often met resistance when it has tried to set up residential facilities in communities. Opinion surveys have shown that people who register general approval of halfway houses, drug treatment centers, and similar facilities, are often alarmed at the thought of such a facility in their own neighborhood, fearing it would jeopardize public safety or depreciate property values.

The Commission recommends that institutions plan for programs that bridge the gap between institutions and community residents. Institutions should actively develop maximum interaction between the community and the institution, involving citizens in planning and activities.

Work-release programs should involve advice from employer and labor groups. Offenders should be able to participate in community educational programs, and, conversely, community members with special interest in educational or other programs at the institution should be able to participate in them. The institution should cultivate active participation of civic groups and encourage the groups to invite offenders to become members.

For such activity to become widespread, there will have to be a general change in the attitude of corrections itself. The correctional system is one of the few public services today that is isolated from the public it serves. Public apathy toward improving the system is due in part to the tendency of corrections to keep the public out—literally by walls, figuratively by failure to explain its objectives. If corrections is to receive the public support it needs, it will have to take the initiative in securing it. This cannot be achieved by keeping the public ignorant about the state of corrections and thus preventing it from developing a sense of responsibility for the correctional process.

SETTING THE PROGRAM IN MOTION

The program of action outlined in this chapter will require a major national commitment on many fronts. Measures to be taken are interrelated; the effectiveness of each depends on accomplishments of the others.

Adequate Financing

Corrections is in difficulty today partly because not enough money has been provided to support even existing programs adequately. Nothing is left for investment in change.

Anyone familiar with State and local corrections knows that it is at the end of the line when legislators and county commissioners are parceling out available

tax funds. States and localities combined now are spending about $1.5 billion a year on corrections, an amount that just maintains the system at its present grossly deficient level of operation. The Federal Government contributes, through LEAA, about $200 million a year.

The Commission believes that a large increase in funding—possibly double the amounts now appropriated—is essential if corrections is to become a more effective part of the criminal justice system. All levels of government—particularly the Federal level—should increase their contributions substantially.

Needed Legislation

State and Federal penal and correctional codes are striking examples of the problems created by passing laws to meet specific situations without considering other laws already in force. For the most part, these codes have been enacted piecemeal over generations and follow no consistent pattern or philosophy. Indeed, the lack of a basic philosophy of the purpose of corrections is as crippling to operation of the system as are contradictions between statutes. The Commission calls attention to the 1972 action of

the Illinois legislature in passing a unified code of corrections and urges all States to do so.

Reform of penal and correctional codes will require time. If it is to be done in the 5-year period suggested by the Commission, the entire code of a State should be redrafted and considered legislatively as a package.

As each jurisdiction has its own history and traditions regarding the legislative process, success in reforming a penal and correctional code will depend on careful planning from the start and the involvement of progressively larger groups of legislators, administrators, judges, and other citizens as the drafting progresses.

Manpower

This Commission has emphasized the importance of qualified manpower throughout the criminal justice system. Nowhere is the lack of educated and trained personnel more conspicuous than in corrections.

A major problem is to attract capable people to corrections in the first place. They can be persuaded to enter the field only if the image of regimentation and failure is changed to one of potential success in changing offenders and reducing crime. Changing the

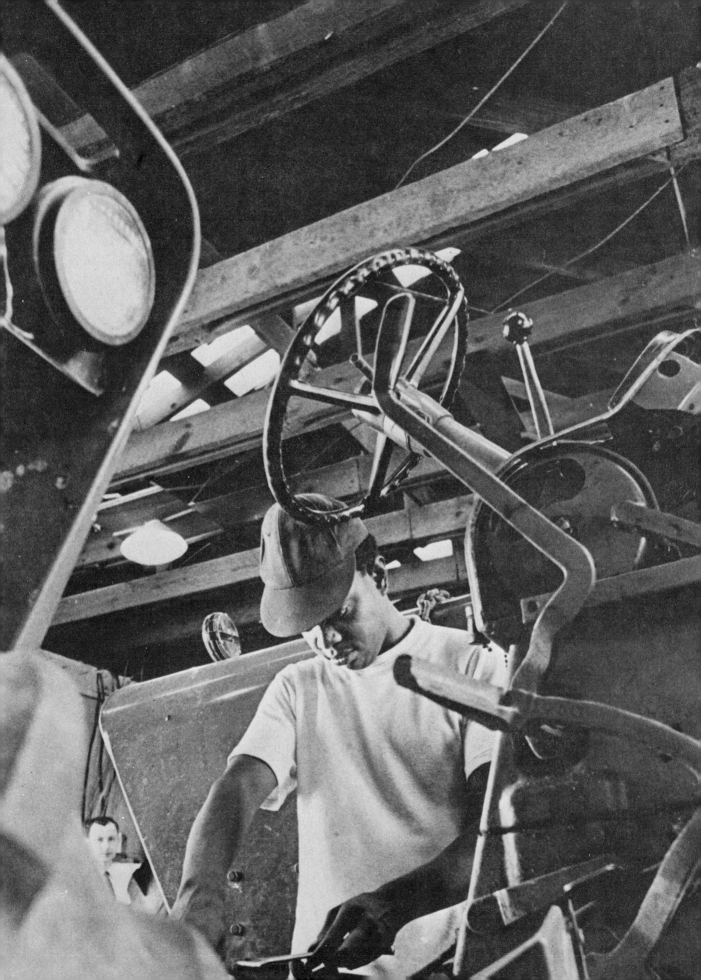

image will depend in large measure upon the present personnel in corrections.

Availability of education to prepare students for careers in corrections is also essential. Federal funds are available for scholarships. States must take responsibility for insuring that criminal justice curriculums with correction-oriented components are available throughout the State and that efforts are made to recruit graduates into State and local programs.

National Institute of Corrections

A national academy of corrections has been proposed for many years. At the National Conference on Corrections held in Williamsburg, Va., in December 1971, the Attorney General directed LEAA and the Bureau of Prisons to work with the States in developing such an academy, to be called the National Institute of Corrections.

Among other proposed functions, the Institute would serve as a clearinghouse for information on crime and corrections; provide consultant services; fund training programs; and coordinate and fund correctional research. At present none of these functions is being satisfactorily fulfilled on a national basis.

A national institute with the authority and funds for this wide range of activities could serve as a powerful force for coordinating and implementing a national effort to reform corrections. The Commission urges immediate action to make it a reality.

Accreditation of Corrections Agencies

An accreditation system for corrections would be used to recognize and maintain standards of service, programs, and institutions, and eventually to bring about higher levels of quality.

One function of the accreditation system would be to hold the correctional administrator accountable for results. In the past, custodial institutions have been required only to keep offenders until ordered to release them. Probation and parole agencies have been required to list offenders in their charge and

report violations. In short, unless riots, escapes, and scandals occurred, the correctional administrator had satisfied requirements.

But if accountability is to be a basic principle of correctional management, as the Commission recommends, the manager must have tools by which to measure. It is a waste of public funds to impose penal terms without either knowing the goals to be achieved or having some method to measure accomplishments.

The Commission urges the implementation of an accreditation plan for corrections which would help measure accomplishment of individual institutions and generally elevate standards of performance in correctional programs.

CONCLUSION

A national commitment to change is essential if there is to be any significant reform of corrections, for this is a formidable task. High recidivism rates, riot and unrest in prisons, revelations of brutality and degradation in jails, increasing litigation against correctional officials, and indignant public reactions attest to the need for change in corrections.

The chairman of the U.S. Board of Parole said in an address to the American Correctional Association in the summer of 1972:

> To put it bluntly, the field of corrections is experiencing a crisis in public confidence, and the crisis shows no sign of abating. Unlike times past, we can't expect to handle the problem by letting it wear itself out.

Corrections must commence reform now. But corrections cannot accomplish the needed reform in its traditional isolation. It must act vigorously to enlist the support of legislators, local officials, law enforcement personnel, community agencies, and various other public and private groups.

Reform in corrections will also require changes in public values and attitudes. The public must recognize that crime and delinquency are related to the kind of society in which offenders live. Reduction of crime may therefore depend on basic social change.

Youth learning valuable skills in a training program.

Chapter 8

Criminal Code Reform And Revision

Gambling, marijuana use, trafficking in pornography, prostitution, sexual acts between consenting adults in private—the mere mention of these activities may generate an emotional response in almost every American.

Some citizens may be angry, embarrassed, or frightened because these activities take place in society. Other citizens may express resentment that these activities, which they may consider to be relatively harmless, are condemned and punished at all. Still other citizens may condemn one of these activities while at the same time practicing one of the others.

Another group of crimes—drunkenness, vagrancy, and minor traffic violations—are a constant source of irritation and dismay to society in general and to the criminal justice system in particular. For example, the FBI reports that in 1971 there were an estimated 1.8 million arrests for public drunkenness.[1]

The criminal justice system is ill-equipped to deal with these offenses. These crimes place a heavy and unwelcome burden on law enforcement resources throughout the Nation. And the laws regulating these offenses are open to abuse and, increasingly, to constitutional challenge.

[1] Federal Bureau of Investigation, *Uniform Crime Reports—1971* (1972), p. 118.

The crime of public drunkenness.

MAJOR RECOMMENDATIONS

The Commission looked at these two categories of crimes and concluded that States should consider substantive changes in their statutes dealing with these crimes. Detailed recommendations in these areas are set out in this chapter, but in general the Commission recommends that:

• States review criminal statutes dealing with gambling, marijuana use and possession for use, pornography, prostitution, and sexual acts between consenting adults in private, to determine if current laws best serve the purposes of the State and the needs of the people; and, as a minimum, States remove incarceration as a penalty for these offenses, except when these offenses involve a willful attempt to affect others in these areas, such as pandering, public lewdness, and sale or possession for sale of marijuana.

• States decriminalize drunkenness and vagrancy and dispose of minor traffic offenses administratively rather than through criminal process in court.

• States whose codes have not been revised within the past decade initiate complete revision, including, when necessary, a revamped penalty structure.

• States create criminal law commissions to review new legislative proposals bearing criminal penalties.

There has been considerable activity in the area of criminal code reform in recent years. At least nine

States and the District of Columbia have enacted the Uniform Alcoholism and Intoxication Act which abolishes drunkenness as a crime. The possession of marijuana is now a misdemeanor in most States, and two States, Illinois and Connecticut, have made consensual homosexual acts legal.[2]

REEVALUATION OF LAWS

The Commission believes that the criminal code should reflect a more rational attitude toward current social practices and a more realistic appraisal of the capabilities of the criminal justice system.[3]

Gambling, marijuana use and possession for use, pornography, prostitution, and sexual acts in private often are punished by incarceration. The Commission questions whether incarceration serves as a deterrent to these types of behavior.

The existing criminal justice system was designed to deter potential offenders by the threat of punishment, to punish and rehabilitate offenders, and to protect society by incarcerating persons who pose a threat to others. The system has failed to some extent in almost every respect.

The Commission recommends that States reevaluate their laws on gambling, marijuana use and possession for use, pornography, prostitution, and sexual acts between consenting adults in private. Such reevaluation should determine if current laws best serve the purpose of the State and the needs of the public.

The Commission further recommends that, as a minimum, each State remove incarceration as a penalty for these offenses, except in the case of persistent and repeated offenses by an individual, when incarceration for a limited period may be warranted.

The recommendation insofar as it deals with removal of incarceration as a penalty does not apply

---

[2] Norval Morris, "Crimes Without Victims: The law is a busybody," *The New York Times Magazine* (April 1, 1973).

[3] A thorough investigation and discussion of code reform is beyond the reach of this survey. A variety of studies have been undertaken by other organizations, such as the National Commission on Marihuana and Drug Abuse; the Department of Health, Education, and Welfare; the Joint Conference on Alcohol Abuse and Alcoholism; and the National Council on Crime and Delinquency.

Other studies are mentioned elsewhere in this report. It was not within the purview of this Commission to initiate detailed studies of the activities in question, but in light of its mandate to develop a national strategy to reduce crime, the Commission has weighed the arguments on each side of each issue, noting the impact of current laws on the operations of the criminal justice system.

to behavior in which a willful attempt is made to affect others in areas such as pandering, soliciting, public lewdness, and the sale or possession for sale of marijuana.

The Commission emphasizes that it is not necessarily recommending decriminalization of these five activities. It is up to each State to determine whether or not such behavior should be classified as criminal in nature. Some States may decide, upon reevaluation of existing laws, to retain the laws or to modify or repeal them altogether.

The Commission is aware that both prostitution and gambling may be associated with organized crime, and it urges States to take appropriate safeguards when enacting legislation. There also may be some need to control pornography where children could be exposed to explicit sexual material.

The Commission, however, recommends that States that do not decriminalize these activities reexamine the effectiveness of incarceration in enforcing the laws. The Commission has made such an examination and concludes that incarceration is an ineffective method of enforcement. The Commission believes that incarceration should be abandoned and that probation, fines, commitment to community treatment programs, and other alternative forms of punishment and treatment be substituted for incarceration.

Incarceration is clearly not an infallible deterrent. For example, the threat of punishment did not end the use of liquor, and today it does not keep an estimated 15 to 20 million Americans a year from experimenting with or using marijuana, or prevent countless cases of illegal gambling. Evidence shows that incarceration itself does not deter; study after study documents that the majority of crimes are committed by persons who previously had been incarcerated.

The characterization of prisons as "schools of crime" needs little substantiation. Prisons often do not rehabilitate or change inmates, but instead may send back to society hardened, frustrated, alienated individuals who return quickly to patterns of crime and other antisocial conduct. Thus, incarceration may backfire: rather than protect society, it may perpetuate a threat to society.

Stricter sentences are not necessarily the solution. When sentences seem too severe for a particular crime, a jury may balk at a finding of guilty and may return a finding of not guilty or of guilty of a lesser offense.

The use of alternative forms of treatment is even more essential in the case of these crimes. Because these are the least serious crimes, long sentences rarely are applied and convicted offenders often are shuttled in and out of jail—with no benefit to the offender and at a high cost to the taxpayer.

Furthermore, these acts usually consist of behavior that does not pose a direct threat to others, but that often generates strong social disapproval. Therefore, as social problems these crimes are best dealt with by social institutions capable of treating the problem and of integrating the offender into society, rather than by a criminal justice system that could further alienate the offender by treating him the same as it would a violent criminal.

The approach recommended here already is practiced by many judges and courts; adoption of the recommendation merely would regularize that practice. The uniform application of penalties will eliminate discrimination against or harassment of certain classes of individuals; it also will prevent situations in which an individual is given an unusually severe penalty as an example to others, or as a demonstration to the public of seemingly efficient law enforcement.

DECRIMINALIZATION

The Commission believes that the criminal justice system would benefit from the removal of drunkenness as a crime, the repeal of vagrancy laws, and the administrative disposition of minor traffic offenses. The benefits from these changes that would accrue to the criminal justice system would be immediate and far ranging.

The following sections contain the Commission's recommendations in these three areas, plus a discussion of the rationale for the proposed changes.

Public Drunkenness

The Commission recommends that public drunkenness in and of itself no longer be treated as a crime. All States should give serious consideration to enacting the Uniform Alcoholism and Intoxication Act.

In *Crimes With No Victims,* Edwin Kiester, Jr., portrays the existence of the Skid Row drunk:

He has been drinking steadily since his teens; and he lives on Skid Row, that run-down jumble of shabby taverns, insect-infested flophouses, religious missions dispensing free meals and lodging, cafeterias selling cheap soup, and employment agencies that specialize in dishwashers and busboys. John has no ties to anyone; and he has forgotten what trades he ever knew. He panhandles for pennies and wipes the windshields of cars stopped by a red light in hopes of a handout; occasionally he works in a restaurant kitchen hauling out garbage or washing dishes. Whatever he earns goes for cheap wine or rotgut liquor at the cut-rate Skid Row bars.[4]

---

[4] Edwin Kiester, Jr., *Crimes With No Victims* (Alliance for a Safer New York, 1972).

The plight of such persons has not been improved by laws designating the alcoholic as a criminal. For the public drunk, the deterrence factor of a criminal sanction is virtually inoperative. Alcoholism is a problem for which social services, not the penal-correctional process, are indicated. Aggression that manifests itself in other criminal conduct, accompanied by drunkenness, should remain punishable.

In 1967, *The Challenge of Crime in a Free Society,* a report by the President's Commission on Law Enforcement and Administration of Justice, began its discussion of drunkenness offenses with this paragraph:

Two million arrests in 1965—one of every three in America—were for the offense of public drunkenness. The great volume of these arrests places an extremely heavy load on the operations of the criminal justice system. It burdens police, clogs lower criminal courts, and crowds penal institutions throughout the United States.[5]

The President's Crime Commission doubted that drunkenness should continue to be treated as a crime.

In the 6 years since that report, there has been a slight decrease in the number of arrests for drunkenness; according to the Federal Bureau of Investigation's *Uniform Crime Reports,* there were approximately 1.8 million such arrests in 1971.[6]

That decrease is insignificant considering the amount of money and police and court time spent on each arrest. In 1971, the San Francisco Committee on Crime noted the inordinate amount of time spent on chronic recidivist drunks. In discussing the costs of handling drunkenness by criminal process, the Committee said:

The futility and savagery of handling drunkenness through the criminal process is evident. The cost to the city of handling drunks in that way cannot be determined with exactness. Only approximation is possible. The Committee's staff has computed that in 1969 it cost the city a *minimum* of $893,500. The computation was that $267,196 was spent in making the arrests and processing the arrested person through sentence, and that roundly $626,300 was spent in keeping the drunks in county jail at San Bruno. And these figures do not include the costs to the city when a drunk is taken to San Francisco General Hospital from either the city prison or county jail. While our staff has concluded that it costs the city between $17 and $20 to process each drunk from arrest through sentencing, an estimate by a police officer assigned as liaison to the Drunk Court put the cost at $37 per man through the sentencing process. Thus, if anything, our estimates are low.[7]

---

[5] President's Commission on Law Enforcement and Administration of Justice, *The Challenge of Crime in a Free Society* (1967).

[6] *Uniform Crime Reports—1971.*

[7] The San Francisco Committee on Crime, "Basic Principles—Public Drunkenness," *A Report on Non-Victim Crime in San Francisco* (April 26, 1971).

The Committee said that "it cost the taxpayers about $2,500 to run one morning's 'crop' of drunks through the criminal process. The split-second decision of a judge to dismiss, sentence or suspend, may cost the city anywhere from $125 to $150." The Committee concluded: "If these expenditures achieved some social or public good, they should be gladly borne. But they do not."[8]

The San Francisco figures, when multiplied by the annual 1.8 million arrests for drunkenness, present an intolerable bill paid by Americans each year for the corralling and locking up of the public drunk.

A significant step to rectify this situation has been taken by the National Conference of Commissioners on Uniform State Laws. The Conference has drafted model legislation, the Uniform Alcoholism and Intoxication Treatment Act, that calls for decriminalization of alcoholism and public drunkenness and provides States with legal guidelines for dealing more rationally with public drunkenness. At least nine States and the District of Columbia have enacted this law, which was endorsed by the American Bar Association in 1972.

The uniform act calls for the development of a department in the State government to deal with alcoholism. It authorizes police officers to take a person incapacitated by alcohol into protective custody rather than arrest him. The act provides for a comprehensive program for treatment of alcoholics and intoxicated persons—including emergency, inpatient, intermediate, outpatient, and followup treatment—and authorizes appropriate facilities for such treatment. This Commission recommends that all States consider the adoption of this act.

As noted in the preface to the uniform act, society's attitude toward alcohol abuse has changed. There is also increasing recognition that current laws discriminate against the poor and pose possible constitutional problems.

The alternative to reform in this area is more of the same of what society faces today. The Commission urges that appropriate measures be taken to relieve the police, courts, and jails of the futile job of dealing with a massive problem best handled by social services.

Vagrancy

The Commission recommends that each State review its laws and repeal any law that proscribes the status of living in idleness without employment and having no visible means of support, or roaming or wandering.

[8] *Ibid.*

One of the faults inherent in existing vagrancy statutes is that they are too vague to provide a reasonable degree of guidance to citizens, police, and courts as to what constitutes the offense. Thus, these statutes are constitutionally suspect. Their constitutional validity is even more in doubt when they touch the rights of assembly and free association. Yet in 1971, the FBI estimated there were 91,600 arrests for vagrancy.[9]

Another serious objection to vagrancy statutes is that they discriminate against the poor and may be enforced arbitrarily. The adverse results of this situation were stated well in *Task Force Report: The Courts,* a report of the President's Crime Commission. The report states:

One of its consequences is to communicate to the people who tend to be the object of these laws the idea that law enforcement is not a regularized, authoritative procedure, but largely a matter of arbitrary behavior by the authorities. The application of these laws often tends to discriminate against the poor and subcultural groups in the population. It is unjust to structure law enforcement in such a way that poverty itself becomes a crime. And it is costly for society when the law arouses the feelings associated with these laws in the ghetto, a sense of persecution and helplessness before official power and hostility to police and other authority that may tend to generate the very conditions of criminality society is seeking to extirpate.[10]

Vagrancy statutes often are used as a device for taking into custody persons suspected of other offenses. In an exhaustive article on vagrancy laws, Professor Caleb Foote discussed this misuse of the law:

One cannot escape the conclusion that the administration of vagrancy-type laws serves as an escape hatch to avoid the rigidity imposed by real or imagined defects in criminal law and procedure. To the extent that such rigidity presents a real problem and that the need for a safety valve is not merely the product of inefficiency on the part of police or prosecutors, such a problem should not be dealt with by indirection. If it is necessary to ease the prosecution's burden of proof or to legalize arrests for mere suspicion, then the grave policy and constitutional problems posed by such suggestions should be faced. If present restrictions on the laws of attempts or arrests place too onerous a burden upon the police because of the nature of modern crime, then such propositions should be discussed and resolved on their merits. . . .[11]

The Commission recognizes that police departments in many jurisdictions have relied upon the vagrancy statute as a means of controlling disruptive conduct in public. But removal of criminal penalties for vagrancy ought not to leave police

[9] *Uniform Crime Reports—1971,* p. 115.

[10] President's Commission on Law Enforcement and Administration of Justice, *Task Force Report: The Courts* (1967).

[11] Caleb Foote, 104 *University of Pennsylvania Law Review,* 603, 649 (1956).

Officers questioning suspected vagrant.

wholly without constitutionally valid means of dealing with the rowdy and brawling individual.

Therefore, the Commission recommends that each jurisdiction enact legislation that clearly defines disorderly conduct.

The Commission commends the Model Penal Code of the American Law Institute as an example of a sound approach to a disorderly conduct statute.[12] The Model Penal Code redefines the crime to include only that behavior that is in itself disorderly and removes from the law behavior that "tends to provoke a breach of the peace." To constitute disorderly conduct, the defined disturbances must be genuinely public.

Elimination of the vagrancy statute and redefinition of the disorderly conduct statute may appear to eliminate or decrease police ability to protect themselves and to investigate and deal with criminal behavior on the street. The Commission, however, notes the stop-and-frisk procedure that has been upheld by the Supreme Court. The Commission recommends that each State enact legislation in accordance with *Terry* v. *Ohio,* 88 S. Ct. 1968, 1884–85 (1968). The stop-and-frisk procedure and its constitutional limits are explained in Chapter 9, Handguns in American Society, of this report.

Minor Traffic Offenses

The Commission recommends that all minor traffic offenses, except driving while intoxicated, reckless driving, and driving with a suspended or revoked license, be made infractions subject to administrative disposition. Penalties for such infractions should be limited to fines, suspension or revocation of the

[12] American Law Institute, *Model Penal Code: Proposed Official Draft* (1962).

driver's license, or compulsory attendance at traffic school. Provision should be made for administrative disposition of such infractions by an agency other than the court of criminal jurisdiction. The right of appeal from administrative decisions should be assured.

The Commission strongly believes that adoption of this recommendation would result in an immediate beneficial impact upon the criminal justice system. This recommendation is discussed in detail in Chapter 8 of the *Report on Courts,* a report of the Commission.

The Commission does not belittle the significance of traffic offenses; because automobile accidents are responsible for thousands of deaths and injuries annually, minor traffic violations cannot be ignored. Repeated violations indicate that a driver is incompetent. Some form of sanction is necessary as a deterrent and to protect society and the individual. Records of violations are essential for determining which persons should be forbidden the use of an automobile.

The volume of minor traffic violations clogs lower courts, preventing the speedy and efficient consideration of serious offenses. The administrative procedure recommended is an example of a viable alternative to the criminal justice system for the necessary regulation of conduct that is per se harmless.

The Commission notes that the right of appeal from administrative decisions should be assured. Recommendations for the appeal procedure appear in the *Report on Courts* of the Commission.

The extent of the burden for the courts can be seen in the fact that in fiscal year 1969, 78 percent of all criminal cases in California adult misdemeanant courts were traffic cases. More

recently, more than half of the new criminal cases filed in the District of Columbia Superior Court were traffic cases.[13] A study in 1970 of the lower criminal courts of metropolitan Boston showed that approximately 75 percent of the charges were either for drunkenness or petty traffic offenses. The same study showed that 63 percent of all charges brought in the Commonwealth of Massachusetts in the lower criminal courts were for petty traffic offenses.[14]

It is obvious in view of these statistics that administrative disposition of minor traffic offenses could free valuable criminal court resources and could contribute significantly to speeding up the disposition of other criminal cases.

CRIMINAL CODE REVISION

Criminal statutes may overlap one another, use words in an inconsistent fashion, and carry inconsistent punishments. For example, after a particularly notorious or offensive case, legislatures may enact penalties that are excessive in day-to-day application.

A State's criminal justice system may be a model of contemporary efficiency; but if its basic criminal law is the outmoded product of legislative or judicial processes of an earlier generation, the protection afforded the citizen through criminal law processes can be much less than it ought to be.

States whose criminal codes have not been revised in the last decade should initiate revisions; these revisions should be complete and thorough, not partial, and the revision should include where necessary a revamped penalty structure.

Much of the benefit of revision is likely to be lost unless revision is a continuing process, through which omissions or duplications in coverage can be remedied, defects in administration cured, and the inevitable urge to pass new statutes resisted. Legislatures sometimes have a tendency to enact new statutes without determining whether existing statutes suffice, or whether administrative sanctions or other control devices are likely to afford greater protection

than new criminal statutes. Legislatures do not always have time within the pressures of a legislative session to spot duplications and contradictions in proposed legislation. The establishment of law review commissions can remedy this problem.

The Commission recommends that States create permanent criminal law review commissions to review all legislative proposals bearing criminal penalties in order to ascertain whether a need for them actually exists. These review commissions should propose draft statutes for legislative consideration whenever functional gaps in criminal law enforcement appear.

The membership of the review commission should reflect the experience of all branches of the legal profession, corrections, law enforcement, and community leadership. Placement of the review commission within the legislative or executive branch should be made in view of each State's governmental and political needs. Freedom to issue objective opinions without excessive political pressure is important.

Those who revise criminal codes should be warned of the potential danger to the revision process posed by emotional issues such as abortion or the death penalty. Because criminal code revision efforts too frequently founder on one or two such issues that may be quite incidental to the overall revision effort, States should consider these issues in legislation that is introduced separately from legislation calling for criminal code revision. A more complete discussion of this area is contained in Chapter 13 of the Commission's *Report on the Criminal Justice System*.

CONCLUSION

The reforms suggested in this chapter will benefit the criminal justice system and society in general.

The reforms will help reduce court caseloads; they will lessen the unnecessary costs of futile incarceration; and they simultaneously will address the underlying behavioral problems associated with the crimes discussed in this chapter.

The Commission therefore recommends that implementation of the recommendations presented here be carried out by State legislatures on a priority basis.

---

[13] District of Columbia Courts, *Annual Reports, 1971*, p. A-2.

[14] Stephen R. Bing and S. Stephen Rosenfeld, *The Quality of Justice in the Lower Criminal Courts of Metropolitan Boston* (Lawyers Committee for Civil Rights Under Law, 1970).

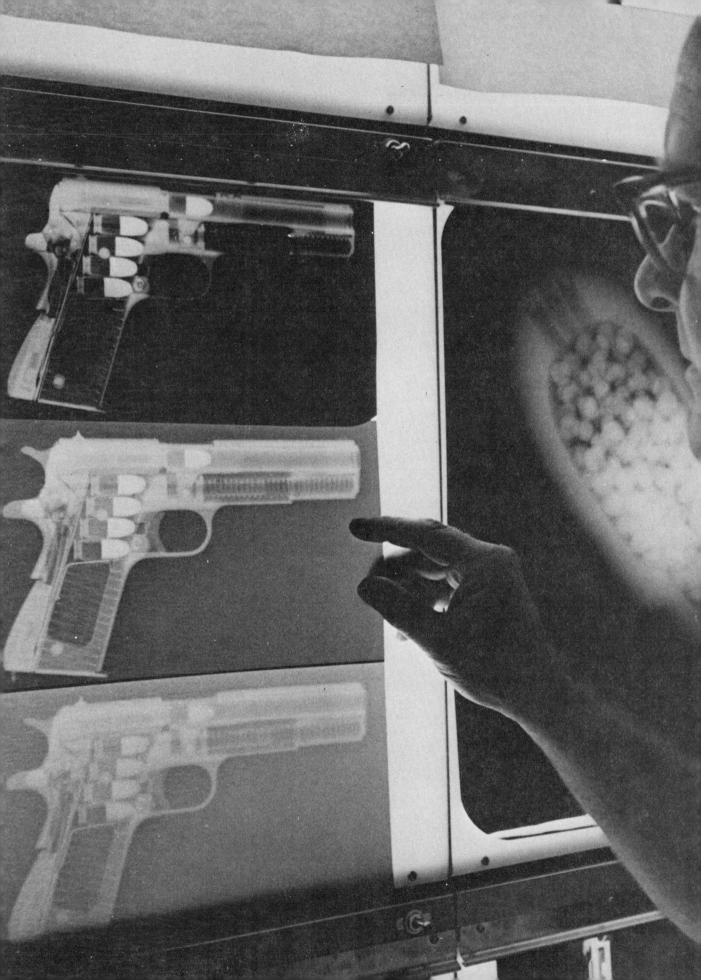

Chapter 9

Handguns In American Society

Americans are accumulating handguns at a rate estimated at more than 1.8 million weapons a year.[1] The national arsenal of privately owned handguns is estimated to be as high as 30 million.[2]

Nowhere in the world is the private ownership of handguns, on a per capita basis, as high as in the United States. Similarly, nowhere among the industrial nations of the world is the criminal homicide rate as high as in the United States.

In the United States, during 1971 alone, approximately 9,000 Americans,[3] including 94 police officers,[4] were murdered with handguns. In 1971, more than 600 accidental deaths resulted from the improper use of handguns.[5]

In the past few years, handguns have also had a searing effect on American political life. In 1968, Senator Robert F. Kennedy of New York was killed by a handgun. In 1972, Governor George C. Wallace of Alabama was wounded and crippled by a handgun. Early in 1973, Senator John C. Stennis of Mississippi was wounded seriously by a handgun.

Not surprisingly, the American public is concerned about gun control. The polls show that the vast majority of American citizens favor firearm control. As long as modern polling has existed, the polls have shown majority support for firearms control. Never have less than two-thirds of those polled favored gun control.[6] Most recently, in a 1972 Gallup Poll, 71 percent of all persons polled, and 61 percent of all gun owners polled, indicated they were in favor of gun control.[7]

This citizen concern has been recognized by Congress and by the President. In 1968, Congress enacted the Gun Control Act; and since taking office, President Nixon has expressed his support for legislation banning the possession of cheap handguns.

For these reasons, and because the members of the Commission are dedicated to the goal of reducing crime and violence in America, the Commission believes that it would be derelict in its duties if it did

---

[1] Data received from the Bureau of Alcohol, Tobacco, and Firearms, Department of the Treasury.

[2] George Newton and Franklin Zimring, *Firearms and Violence in American Life,* A Staff Report to the National Commission on the Causes and Prevention of Violence (1969), p. 6.

[3] Federal Bureau of Investigation, *Uniform Crime Reports—1971,* pp. 7, 8.

[4] *Ibid.,* p. 44.

[5] Estimates made by the National Safety Council from data contained in "Accidental Facts, 1972."

[6] Hazel Erskine, "The Polls: Gun Control." *Public Opinion Quarterly* (Fall 1972), p. 455.

[7] *Ibid.*

not address the vital issue of handguns in today's society.

Prohibition on Handguns

The Commission believes that the violence, fear, suffering, and loss caused by the use of handguns must be stopped by firm and decisive action. The Commission therefore recommends that, no later than January 1, 1983, each State should take the following action:

• The private possession of handguns should be prohibited for all persons other than law enforcement and military personnel.
• Manufacture and sale of handguns should be terminated.
• Existing handguns should be acquired by States.
• Handguns held by private citizens as collector's items should be modified and rendered inoperative.

The recommendations of the Commission apply only to handguns, a term which for the purposes of this chapter refers to a firearm designed to be fired with one hand. The term also includes the personal possession or control of a combination of parts from which a handgun can be assembled. The term includes both pistols (sometimes referred to as automatics) and revolvers, but does not include antique firearms.

The Commission believes that laws currently in force regarding rifles and long guns require no change. The Commission does not wish to curtail the use of rifles and long guns by hunters and other legitimate users.

Further, the Commission makes recommendations for State and local units of government only, not for the Federal Government. Congress is on record on the subject of firearms; it has passed some controls and has encouraged States and local units of government to enact their own laws and adopt their own ordinances. It remains for the State and local governments to address the problems surrounding the public possession of handguns.

In an effort to prohibit possession of handguns, the Commission encourages States to examine and implement all recommendations proposed in this chapter. The recommendations are intended to be an operative package.

Some States, however, may want to implement the recommendations in stages. They are urged to do so in the order in which they are presented in this chapter. Further, some States may already have taken steps proposed in the recommendations. In keeping with these local variances, the Commission urges each State to work out a combination of steps best suited to complete control of handguns.

Toward this end, it is the recommendation of the Commission that States study their present laws regulating handguns and take measures to insure that existing laws are enforced fully and are adhered to scrupulously by their citizens. Next, the Commission recommends that the penalties attached to committing a crime with the use of a handgun be increased. Further, to safeguard the lives of police officers, States should enact stop-and-frisk laws to authorize search of persons and automobiles when the officer has reasonable suspicion to believe that he is in danger due to a suspect's possession of and access to a weapon.

As an additional step, the Commission recommends that States prohibit the manufacture, importation, or sale of all handguns other than those for use by law enforcement or military personnel. States should also establish agencies authorized to purchase handguns from private individuals for a just price, and further authorized to modify rare and valuable guns that owners wish to retain as collector's items. Finally, States should prohibit the private possession of all handguns other than those which have been designated as collector's items and rendered inoperative.

WHY HANDGUNS MUST BE CONTROLLED BY THE STATES

To maintain an orderly society, a government must regulate certain of its citizens' acts. Rights and freedoms cannot exist without recognition that one person's rights exist only to the degree they do not infringe on those of another.

Such a balance must be maintained in the possession and use of handguns. The Commission believes that private use and possession of handguns infringes on the right of the American public to be free from violence and death caused by the use of handguns. Public welfare does not permit the civilian possession of machineguns, flame throwers, handgrenades, bombs, or sawed-off shotguns; neither can it any longer tolerate the private possession of handguns.

Removing the handgun from American society will not eliminate crime and violence, but documentation shows there is a strong correlation between the number of privately owned handguns and the corresponding use of guns in crimes of violence.

Nationally, the handgun is the principal weapon used in criminal homicide. Reported crime statistics for 1971 indicate that 51 percent of all murders and nonnegligent manslaughters were committed with the use of a handgun.[8]

Handguns are also an important instrument in other crimes of violence. Possibly a third of

[8] *UCR—1971*, p. 8.

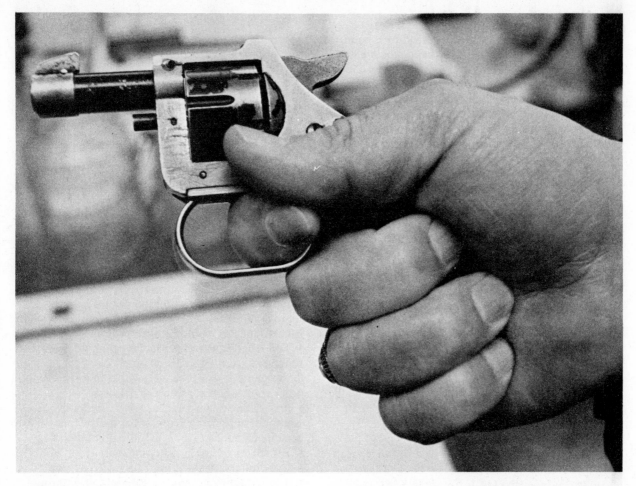

Saturday night special.

all robberies and one-fifth of all aggravated assaults are committed with handguns.[9]

Countries that have restrictive regulations on the private possession of handguns have considerably lower homicide rates than does the United States. For example, in Tokyo, Japan, a congested metropolis of more than 11 million people, and where it is illegal to own, possess, or manufacture handguns, there was only one handgun homicide reported in 1971.[10] In contrast, during the same time period, Los Angeles County, Calif., with a population of just over 7 million, reported 308 handgun homicides.[11]

Cultural differences account for some of this disparity but this explanation alone cannot account for the wide difference in homicide rates nor for the fact that Japanese statistics reflect a consistent yearly decrease in the number of crimes committed with

firearms since the 1964 national prohibition against all firearms.[12]

In the past 10 years in the United States, 722 police officers were murdered while performing in the line of duty; 73 percent of them were murdered with handguns. During the same 10 years, nine police officers were killed by handguns in Great Britain, 26 in Japan, and in France, "not enough to make a percentage." These countries all have stringent handgun control laws.[13]

The Commission is aware that many persons keep firearms in their homes because they fear for the lives and safety of themselves and their families. It should be known, however, that many "gun" crimes are family killings—not the "stranger" crimes where protection is needed. In 1971, one-fourth of all murders were "intra-family" in which a family member seized the weapon at hand. When a gun was seized, the fatality rate was five times higher than by an attack with any other weapon.[14]

[9] Newton and Zimring, *Op. cit.*, pp. 70, 73.
[10] Data received from the Metropolitan Police Department, Tokyo, Japan.
[11] Telephone Survey of Los Angeles County, Calif., Police Departments (conducted by the Los Angeles County Sheriff's Department, 1972).

[12] Data received from the Japanese National Police Agency.
[13] National Conference of Christians and Jews, *Hot Line* (November 1972), p. 6.
[14] Newton and Zimring, *Op. cit.*, p. 44.

Further, the self-protection afforded by a handgun often is illusory. Although many handguns are acquired to defend family and property from intruders, a handgun in the home is more likely to kill a member of the family than it is to provide life-saving protection from burglars and robbers. A survey conducted in Detroit, Mich., indicated that more people are killed in household handgun accidents in 1 year than die as a result of home burglaries and robberies in 4½ years.[15]

RECOMMENDATIONS

In the following section the Commission sets out its detailed recommendations for the control of handguns. Each recommendation is followed by explanatory notes.

Enforcement of Current Laws

The Commission recommends that existing Federal, State, and local laws relating to handguns be strenuously enforced. It further recommends that States undertake publicity campaigns to educate the public fully about laws regulating the private possession of handguns.

Federal laws, if utilized, present a sound legislative base for control of handguns. The Federal Gun Control Act of 1968 (18 U.S.C. 900–928) encourages States to enact their own legislation in the area of firearms, and provides two key statutory incentives to do so.

First, Congress provides assistance for State and local gun control by prohibiting interstate gun transactions by any person in violation of local laws. In section 922(b)(2) of the Gun Control Act, Congress provided:

(b) It shall be unlawful for any licensed importer, licensed manufacturer, licensed dealer, or licensed collector to sell or deliver—

(2) any firearm or ammunition to any person in any State where the purchase or possession by such person of such firearm or ammunition would be in violation of any State law or any published ordinance applicable at the place of sale, delivery or other disposition, unless the licensee knows or has reasonable cause to believe that the purchase or possession would not be in violation of such State law or such published ordinance.

Federal law becomes a seal at the border of the State, prohibiting licensed importers, manufacturers, dealers, or collectors from selling or delivering firearms to such persons in violation of State law or local ordinance.

[15] *Ibid.*, p. 64.

Second, Congress encourages States to enact their own firearms legislation. Congress said:

No provision of this chapter shall be construed as indicating an intent on the part of the Congress to occupy the field in which such provision operates to the exclusion of the law of any State on the same subject matter, unless there is a direct and positive conflict between such provision and the law of the State so that the two cannot be reconciled or consistently stand together.

Thus, States may legislate freely in the area of gun control, and only when Federal and State law are in direct conflict will the doctrine of Federal preemption come into play.

The Gun Control Act of 1968 contains other provisions critical to an effective national policy of handgun control. These are:
• A ban on interstate transactions of firearms and ammunition, and a prohibition against any person receiving firearms and ammunition from out of State; licensed dealers would be exempt from this provision.
• The requirement that a buyer submit a sworn statement attesting to his competence and setting out the essential facts of the transaction in interstate mail order shipment and receipt of firearms.
• Prohibition against sale of rifles, shotguns, or ammunition to persons under 18, and of handguns to persons under 21.
• Establishment of licensing provisions for manufacturers, dealers, importers, and collectors.
• The requirement that several types of firearms, including short-barreled shotguns and machine guns, be registered with the Federal Government.
• Prohibition of sale of firearms to convicted felons, fugitives from justice, or persons under indictment for crimes punishable by more than 1-year imprisonment.

Many States and units of local government have statutes or ordinances that make it illegal with varying limitations to carry a handgun on or about the person or in a vehicle, and in some areas a handgun can be carried only by a person possessing either a special permit and/or registration.

The Commission firmly believes that the enforcement of these existing laws—Federal, State, and local—would substantially reduce the availability of handguns to criminals and incompetents, and effect a reduction in the level of violence in America today.

The Commission, however, does not include current laws dealing with mandatory minimum sentences within the scope of this recommendation.

The Commission believes that some of these laws are inconsistent with current knowledge about incarceration and its effect on rehabilitation. Also, juries are sometimes reluctant to convict a defendant if they must in effect impose an exceedingly long prison term. For these reasons, the Commission recommends instead prison sentences up to 25 years but with no mandatory minimum.

The public should also be educated fully about the laws in force through State publicity campaigns, through enlisting the aid of print, radio, and television media, and by making information easily available to interested citizens and citizen groups.

Penalties for Crimes Committed with a Handgun

The Commission urges enactment of State legislation providing for an extended prison term with a maximum term of 25 years for committing a felony while in possession of a handgun.

Because of its ease of portability and concealment, the handgun is by far the principal weapon of criminal gun use. Although nationally handguns constitute only one-fourth of all privately owned firearms, they account for more than three-fourths of all criminal gun violence. If the public ever is to experience a feeling of relative safety and well-being, there must be positive and effective measures enacted to remove and eliminate the constant threat of the criminal use of handguns.

The Commission does not intend that legislatures mandate minimum sentences for those committing a felony while in possession of a handgun. Rather, this recommendation provides that extended prison sentences may be imposed if there are circumstances warranting their application.

This proposal allowing for increased prison sentences is consistent with the rest of the Commission's recommendations. In its *Report on Corrections,* the Commission recommends against incarceration beyond terms of 5 years except for dangerous and repeating offenders, for whom terms of up to 25 years may be appropriate. The Commission believes that individuals who perpetrate felonies while in possession of a handgun clearly fall within the defined exceptions, and should be subject to the imposition of an extended sentence.

The benefits to be derived from enactment of legislation providing extended sentences for persons possessing firearms while commiting felonies are twofold. First, the gun-wielding criminal would be removed from society for a substantial time period; and, second, many criminals, considering the risk too great, would be dissuaded from the continued use and possession of handguns.

Most Americans appear to agree with this approach. On February 16, 1969, the Gallup Poll conducted a survey using the following question:

It has been suggested that anyone who commits a crime with a gun be given double the regular sentence. Does this sound like a good idea to you, or a poor idea?

The answers indicated that 58 percent of respondents thought that it would be a good idea.[16]

Stop-and-Frisk Searches

The Commission urges the enactment of State legislation providing for police discretion in stop-and-frisk searches of persons and searches of automobiles for illegal handguns.

The fourth amendment provides that "The right of people to be secure in their persons, homes, papers, and effects, against unreasonable searches and seizures shall not be violated."

The Commission believes that police discretion to stop and frisk persons and to search automobiles for handguns is reasonable in situations where there are articulable reasons to believe that a police officer's life is in danger. In suspicious circumstances, officers, for their own safety, must have the right to search the person and portion of the vehicle accessible to the occupants for deadly weapons, especially handguns.

In *Firearms and Violence in American Life,* a staff report to the National Commission on the Causes and Prevention of Violence, the problem is stated as follows:

Firearms are not only the most deadly instrument of attack, but also the most versatile. Firearms make attacks possible that simply would not occur without firearms. They permit attacks at greater range and from positions of better concealment than other weapons. They also permit attacks by persons physically or psychologically unable to overpower their victim through violent physical contact. It is not surprising, therefore, that firearms are virtually the only weapon used in killing police officers.

The policeman, himself armed, is capable of defending against many forms of violent attack. He is trained and equipped to ward off attacks with blunt instruments, knives, or fists, and his firearm is usually sufficient to overcome his attacker, even if surprised at close range. It is, therefore, the capacity of firearms to kill instantly and from a distance that threatens the lives of police officers in the United States.[17]

Stop-and-frisk legislation should include broad police powers to search for weapons where strong articulable suspicion exists to indicate that the suspect is engaged in criminal conduct and there is suspicion that he is armed. This is consistent with the holding of the U.S. Supreme Court in *Terry* v. *Ohio,* 88 S.Ct. 1868 (1968).

---

[16] Erskine, *Op. cit.,* p. 468.

[17] Newton and Zimring, *Op. cit.*

Speaking for the court in the *Terry* decision, Chief Justice Earl Warren stated:

The crux of this case, however, is not the propriety of Officer McFadden's taking steps to investigate petitioner's suspicious behavior, but rather, whether there was justification for McFadden's invasion of Terry's personal security by searching him for weapons in the course of that investigation. We are now concerned with more than the governmental interest in investigating crime; in addition, there is the more immediate interest of the police officer in taking steps to assure himself that the person with whom he is dealing is not armed with a weapon that could unexpectedly and fatally be used against him. Certainly it would be unreasonable to require that police officers take unnecessary risks in the performance of their duties. American criminals have a long tradition of armed violence, and every year in this country many law enforcement officers are killed in the line of duty, and thousands more are wounded.

Virtually all of these deaths and a substantial portion of the injuries are inflicted with guns and knives.

In view of these facts, we cannot blind ourselves to the need for law enforcement officers to protect themselves and other prospective victims of violence in situations where they may lack probable cause for an arrest. When an officer is justified in believing that the individual whose suspicious behavior he is investigating at close range is armed and presently dangerous to the officer or to others, it would appear to be clearly unreasonable to deny the officer the power to take necessary measures to determine whether the person is in fact carrying a weapon and to neutralize the threat of physical harm.

Justice John M. Harlan, concurring, stated:

If the State of Ohio were to provide that police officers could, on articulable suspicion less than probable cause, forcibly frisk and disarm persons thought to be carrying concealed weapons, I would have little doubt that action taken pursuant to such authority would be constitutionally reasonable.[18]

Prohibiting the Manufacture of Handguns

The Commission urges the enactment of State legislation prohibiting the manufacture of handguns, their parts, and ammunition within the State, except for sale to law enforcement agencies or for military use.

Effective immediately upon the enactment of the legislation, and under penalty of fine or imprisonment or both, all manufacturers within the State should be required to cease production of handguns, their parts, and ammunition, other than those designated or destined for sale to law enforcement agencies or to the Federal or State government for use by military personnel.

---

[18] See also *Adams* v. *Williams,* 92 S. Ct. 1921 (1972).

Any attempt to eliminate the private possession of handguns should necessarily begin with obstruction at the primary source, the firearms manufacturer. The usefulness of handguns would be greatly lessened by the elimination of the availability of handgun ammunition.

Legislation should be effective immediately in order to preclude the possibility of stockpiling handguns and ammunition.

The Commission urges the enactment of State legislation prohibiting the importation into a State of all handguns, their parts, and ammunition.

Effective immediately upon enactment of the legislation, and under penalty of fine or imprisonment or both, imports of all handguns, their parts, and ammunition should be prohibited. Importation of handguns for law enforcement and military agencies would be permitted.

This legislation, when combined with the preceding section prohibiting the manufacture of firearms, their parts, and ammunition, would eliminate all legal sources of handguns and ammunition in a State except where the gun is already in existence in the State.

Effective enforcement of statutes prohibiting the manufacture or importation into a State of firearms or ammunition would restrict the handgun problem to those already in the hands of citizens. Of all handguns, law enforcement officials consider the so-called "Saturday night special" to be the most common and most dangerous in criminal use. This is a handgun cheaply and quickly cast in metal; it has a relatively short life span and, with normal attrition, should disappear eventually from use.

Prohibiting the Sale of Handguns

The Commission urges the enactment of State legislation prohibiting the sale of handguns, their parts, and ammunition to other than law enforcement agencies or Federal or State governments for military purposes.

The Commission believes that any legislation to eliminate the private possession of handguns should require an immediate cessation of all handgun sales. Although a ban on production and importation of handguns and their parts would eliminate the source of any new handguns, there is a vast number of used handguns available for sale to the public. This legislation would eliminate the potential use of these second-hand weapons. Perhaps more significantly, it would also preclude any tendency to stockpile handguns in anticipation of the prohibition of their possession.

Establishing a State Gun Control Agency

The Commission urges the enactment of State legislation establishing and funding a State agency authorized to purchase all voluntarily surrendered handguns, and further authorized to register and modify handguns to be retained by private citizens as curios, museum pieces, or collector's items.

The Commission believes that the best way to obtain compliance with any prohibitive regulation is to offer a reasonable and practical alternative.

Many handguns presently in private possession represent a substantial financial investment, and the possessor would have an understandable reluctance to forfeit possession without receiving remuneration. The convenience of having easy access to a certain and proper buyer, willing to pay a fair price, would tend to discourage efforts to negotiate private sales, and at the same time would offer a positive motivation to comply with the law.

The program can be effective only if all persons, regardless of social or economic position, are aware of the existence of the program, the location of the purchasing centers, and the time constraints involved. All communication media should be encouraged to inform the public about the program to exchange handguns for monetary compensation.

Utilization of this agency should be voluntary. Purchasing centers should operate with the single determination to achieve the goal of substantially reducing the number of handguns in private possession. If, because of the absence of the threat of prosecution, a stolen handgun or one that had been used in a crime were forfeited, and thus eliminated from potential use in another crime, then certainly it would be to the benefit of society.

Some handgun owners have collections that are both rare and valuable; the Commission does not believe these handguns should be forfeited, or the collections diminished. Personnel at the purchasing centers should be authorized, upon a sworn statement that the handgun was intended for use as a curio, museum piece, or collector's item, to modify the firing mechanism to render the weapon inoperable as a firearm. Modified weapons should be fully registered and identified, with a copy of the registration constituting authorization for possession. Any future alteration to the firing mechanism enabling the handgun to be used again as a firearm would result in a forfeiture of the authorization for possession and subject the owner to prosecution for violation of any possession laws then in effect.

Prohibiting the Private Possession of Handguns

The Commission further urges the enactment of State legislation not later than January 1, 1983, prohibiting the private possession of handguns after that date.

Effective on January 1, 1983, and under penalty of fine or imprisonment or both, possession of a handgun should be made illegal for any person other than law enforcement or military personnel, or those persons authorized to manufacture or deal in handguns for use by law enforcement or the military.

All of the arguments against prohibiting the private possession of handguns become, by comparison, subordinate to the death, tragedy, and violence that abound in the absence of such legislation.

CONCLUSION

The Commission hopes that its position on handguns will be well received and widely supported by the American people. It recognizes, however, that there may be some initial opposition from citizens who have strong convictions in favor of private possession of all kinds of firearms, including handguns. The Commission respects the opinions of these persons and urges a full airing of all views, and open and thorough debate on the handgun issue in public forums, the press, and other appropriate places at the State and local levels.

It would be easy for the Commission to sidestep this issue altogether and to limit its recommendations to the popular and uncontroversial.

After lengthy discussion and careful deliberation, however, the Commission concludes that it has no choice other than to urge the enactment of the recommendations proposed in this chapter. The Commission believes that the American people are willing to make the personal sacrifices necessary to insure that the level of crime and violence in this Nation is diminished.

Chapter 10

A National Commitment To Change

This Commission has sought to formulate a series of standards, recommendations, priorities, and goals to modernize and unify the criminal justice system, and to provide a yardstick for measuring progress. Its purpose has been the reduction of crime.

But the Commission's work is only the first step. It remains now for citizens, professionals, and policy makers to mount the major effort by implementing the standards proposed in the six volumes of the Commission's work.

A beginning of that effort was made at the National Conference on Criminal Justice, which brought together more than 1,500 State and local leaders, criminal justice practitioners, and concerned laymen, for a major meeting and discussion of the Commission's work. That conference was held in Washington, D.C., on January 23-26, 1973.

This chapter describes some of the ways in which States and local jurisdictions can continue and expand the implementation effort. It contains, among others, proposals for:
• Efforts by the Federal Government to encourage implementation of the Commission's standards and goals at the State and local levels.
• Methods by which State and local governments can examine the standards and goals concept with the aim of possible implementation.
• Contributions that professional, civic, and educational groups can make to develop support for the standards and goals.

Plenary session of the National Conference on Criminal Justice, held in January 1973.

Each jurisdiction will, of course, analyze the reports and apply goals and standards in its own way and in the context of its own needs.

This Commission does not pretend to have the authority, responsibility, or competence to mandate the method of implementation of the goals and standards. Nor is there need to enact legislation making compliance with the standards a prerequisite to receipt of Federal funds or a requirement on the States in any other form. Such Federal control is not consistent with American practices in law enforcement.

FEDERAL ENCOURAGEMENT

While Federal endorsement of these standards is not recommended, there is still much the Federal Government, particularly the Law Enforcement Assistance Administration (LEAA), can do in translating the Commission's work into action.

Permanent Advisory Committee

The Commission believes that the effort it has begun should be carried on by a permanent group of citizens which can monitor implementation of the standards over the long term. The Commission believes that the Federal Government, through LEAA, should continue to perform a catalytic role in this regard.

The Commission recommends that LEAA establish an Advisory Committee on Criminal Justice Standards and Goals to support the standards and goals implementation effort.

This committee would provide continuing guidance, information exchange, background information, and evaluation to all jurisdictions. The group should consist of private citizens, government leaders, criminal justice professionals, and community crime prevention practitioners.

The Commission recommends that the Advisory Committee perform the following functions:
• Assess progress by States in implementing the standards.
• Evaluate progress by LEAA in using the standards in its review and approval process, its discretionary grant process, and its research and development programs conducted by the National Institute of Law Enforcement and Criminal Justice.
• Assess standards in terms of their soundness, applicability, success; decide on the necessity of eliminating unsound standards; add new ones; and refine those where experience has dictated the necessity to do so.
• Provide an annual evaluation and information exchange.
• Provide further implementation recommendations.
• Provide encouragement to States to adopt the standards.

The Advisory Committee could be supported by a small permanent staff of professionals and support personnel. The cost of forming and maintaining the staff should be met by LEAA and the staff should be located in LEAA headquarters.

The staff would provide continuing guidance, information exchange, and evaluation to the Advisory Committee members and to all jurisdictions. It could provide background information to aid the States in implementing standards.

LEAA Block Grants or Revenue Sharing Payments

The Commission believes that LEAA should use the block grant award process (or the revenue sharing payment process if law enforcement revenue sharing is enacted) to monitor implementation of its standards and goals. This process involves comprehensive plans that are developed by each State with the assistance of LEAA funds. These comprehensive plans are required to be submitted to LEAA. The purpose of the planning phase is to encourage States to plan their own priorities for crime reduction.

The Commission recognizes that LEAA, under its present authority and under the proposed Law Enforcement Revenue Sharing Act of 1973, does not and will not have authority to require States to adopt the standards and goals. Under present and proposed authority, however, LEAA can review and comment on the comprehensive plans.

Accordingly, the Commission recommends that LEAA use its review of the comprehensive plans and award of grants to inquire as to how States propose to use the Commission's standards in their planning process. If a plan does not address the standards and the State asks for LEAA assistance, LEAA should guide the State in making use of the standards.

LEAA Discretionary Grants

The Commission believes that the discretionary grant process affords LEAA a special opportunity to encourage States to consider implementation of the standards and goals. These grants are awarded by LEAA at its discretion for innovative and meritorious State and local projects that otherwise would not receive LEAA grant funds. LEAA is authorized to award 15 percent of its action funds as discretionary grants.

The Commission believes that LEAA could require discretionary grantees to explain how their programs relate to the standards and goals. Grantees could be asked to formulate updated standards as a requirement of applying for the grant. When standards do not exist in the area in question, the applicant should be required to formulate new standards.

ACTION AT THE STATE AND LOCAL LEVELS

With over 500 standards on such diverse subjects as referral criteria for youth services bureaus, privacy and security requirements for information systems, and bilingual capabilities for police departments, State planning agencies (SPA's) and other criminal justice agencies wishing to use intelligently the Commission's reports will have to set priorities among the many standards.

Getting the Facts

Priority-setting must begin with an assessment of a State or locality's major crime problems and the criminal justice system's response to those problems. Program funding decisions may change drastically depending on whether the crime problem given top

Participants at the National Conference on Criminal Justice.

requirements for 7-day-a-week, 24-hour-a-day services, minimum starting salaries for sworn personnel, compliance with FBI Uniform Crime Reporting procedures, and a minimum of 10 full-time sworn officers per department. Police agencies in Maryland must meet these standards to be eligible for funding assistance in the form of Safe Streets subgrants and other State grants.

While most SPA's have not set standards for the types of operating agencies that might be eligible for Safe Streets assistance, several States have taken actions similar to Maryland's in the police area or plan to do so in the immediate future. The Commission urges SPA's not to stop with police services, but to adopt standards for courts, corrections, and prevention efforts as well.

Standard-setting efforts should be limited to those human resources, physical resources, and management and operations requirements that are clearly essential to the achievement of the goals of the criminal justice system. SPA's may have to resist the temptation to be too detailed in their standard-setting efforts. The Commission does not believe all of its standards are of such importance that they should be made rigid conditions for grants. It does believe, however, that there are elements readily identifiable in certain standards that are essential to any effective criminal justice system, and these elements serve as the basis for minimum standards for funding assistance.

priority is white collar crime, burglary, or various types of violent crime.

The Commission recommends, as a first step in implementing standards and goals, that each jurisdiction analyze its own unique crime problems. Such an analysis should result in the establishment of quantifiable and time-phased goals for the reduction of priority crimes, such as those adopted by this Commission. Once this has been accomplished, an assessment of the Commission's standards and recommendations should be made in terms of their individual impact on the selected priority crimes.

Setting Minimum Statewide Standards

SPA's bear a special responsibility for the formation of minimum statewide standards. If SPA's are to be agents of reform, they must provide incentives for desirable practices and avoid subsidizing clearly undesirable ones.

In Maryland the Police Standards Committee of the SPA in 1972 held hearings throughout the State on the desired quantity and quality of police services. The standards initially established included

Evaluating Programs

One of the most striking characteristics of present criminal justice operations is how little is known about what works and what does not work. The Commission at the outset of its effort undertook a survey of innovative criminal justice projects throughout the country. The survey utilized news clippings, articles in professional journals, and Federal grant applications which described potentially successful programs. Commission staff members queried more than 400 agencies for information.

The agency responses, although often enthusiastic, were nonetheless not particularly useful. The outcome of some projects was described in letters and not formally set forth in documents suitable for public dissemination. Many evaluation reports contained ill-defined objectives providing no specific standards by which to judge the project. Claims of success were generally couched in subjective and intuitive statements of accomplishments.

Even when quantitative measures were used, they were frequently not accompanied by analysis and by adequate explanation.

The Commission's surveys provided direct evidence that program and project evaluation is not considered important by most public officials. The Commission believes that this lack of emphasis is unfortunate. Although many of the Commission's standards are based on a solid foundation of previous knowledge, others are more experimental. As criminal justice agencies begin putting the Commission's standards into practice, serious attention must be given to evaluating how well they contribute to the goals of the criminal justice system and particular agencies.

In implementing important standards or groups of standards, the Commission urges that evaluation plans be designed as an integral part of all projects.

In its *Report on the Criminal Justice System*, the Commission underscores appropriate evaluation strategies in an appendix on "Program Measurement and Evaluation." It commends that section to the reader in regard to evaluation of programs in general.

Other State Implementation Measures

As noted in Chapter 3, honest disagreement in the criminal justice system is common and sometimes severe. Reaching consensus on basic issues presented in the Commission's report will be difficult, but necessary. The Commission believes that acceptance of its work may be reached through publicity, education, and analysis programs initiated by Governors, State supreme court chief justices, and SPA's. These programs include:
• State sponsorship of workshops in the State's regions and major urban areas attended by individuals from all criminal justice components.
• Publicizing the report and encouraging and supporting conferences or workshops sponsored by private voluntary organizations.
• Encouraging and supporting conferences or workshops under the sponsorship of the several criminal justice components: the judiciary council, the corrections department or association, and police groups and associations.
• Encouraging and supporting legislative hearings, debate, and legislation, particularly on those standards requiring legislative action.

PROFESSIONAL, CIVIC, AND EDUCATIONAL SUPPORT

The Commission believes that substantial assistance for implementing its standards and goals can be obtained from a variety of concerned groups.

The Commission recommends that national professional and civic groups and appropriate university interests support implementation of the standards and goals.

It is hoped that these groups will place discussion of the standards and goals high on their agendas and that their conclusions, recommendations, and support will be transmitted to State and local decisionmakers.

The Commission believes that national and local professional and civic associations can play a particularly valuable role in stimulating implementation of standards. Through their initiative and leadership, these groups can exert considerable influence on standards implementation.

The associations and their members have contributed much to the formulation of standards, but the magnitude of the task of implementing them demands the energy to educate and encourage community leaders and criminal justice system practitioners to adopt the standards, and legislators to provide the necessary resources and authorizations where required.

Perhaps the best existing model for professional association participation is the effort of the American Bar Association (ABA) to stimulate adoption of their recent Standards for Criminal Justice. The ABA has provided speakers for a diversity of citizen and professional groups. It has provided educational materials for implementation. It has planned, programed, and participated in State judicial conferences, sessions, and workshops. It has cooperated in joint endeavors with other criminal justice groups and has pursued an active program both to enlist young lawyers and to stimulate law school participation. With both private and LEAA funds, it has assisted implementation efforts in several pilot States, and future plans call for the establishment of programs for measuring impact and evaluating the practical benefits of implementation.

The Commission suggests that all professional associations consider developing programs of a similar nature and that LEAA, within the limits of its capabilities, provide funding to the best of these programs.

Colleges and universities should play an effective role in standards implementation. Law schools, universities, criminal justice departments, and institutes should find the standards valuable for inclusion in their curriculums, seminars, workshops, and research projects. These efforts can play a central role in training both young students and more experienced practitioners who can carry the implementation message back to their agencies. They can also contribute to improving the standards, drafting model codes, and evaluating the impact and efficacy of standards as they are implemented.

Finally, the Commission urges the National Governors' Conference, the Regional Governors' Conference, the National League of Cities, and the National Association of Counties to call on each State and unit of local government to review its criminal justice system and to compare that system with the standards developed by the National Advisory Commission with a view toward making such changes as each State or unit of local government deems appropriate and desirable.

COST OF CRIME REDUCTION

The Commission examined the issue of the dollar cost of implementing its standards and recommendations. It recognizes that for all States and units of local government, the cost of implementing these standards and recommendations could be substantial, at least in the short term.

Nonetheless, the Commission urges elected officials, administrators, and planners to accept the heavy responsibility of presenting the taxpaying public with the facts of the situation and winning the public support necessary to raise the funds. The Commission believes that voting and taxpaying citizens in all jurisdictions will vigorously support sound programs of crime reduction of the sort proposed in this report.

In addition, the Commission points out that some action elements in its plan will save money. Major efficiencies and savings can be effected by implementing new administrative approaches proposed by the Commission. Programs of diversion of individuals out of the criminal justice process may result in actual savings. Indeed, some standards and recommendations probably can be implemented without any cost at all.

The Commission points out, too, that its proposals were developed in large part by working practitioners. These are not "blue-sky" recommendations dreamed up in an atmosphere of utopian unreality. They are the solid and often field-tested proposals of professionals in the criminal justice system.

In the last analysis, however, the Commission believes that the cost of crime reduction must be weighed against the cost of crime itself. New techniques of measurement are beginning only now to tell the American people how much crime they actually endure, crime that takes its toll in human lives, in personal injury and suffering, in stolen money and property. This cost must reach substantial levels in all jurisdictions.

Less crime will mean fewer victims of crime and will result in genuine, demonstrable savings, both to potential victims and to the whole society.

POSTSCRIPT

On January 23, 1973, the Administrator of the Law Enforcement Assistance Administration convened the first National Conference on Criminal Justice at which 1,500 representatives of the criminal justice system and the public reviewed the Commission's work.

A major objective of the conference was to initiate State and local criminal justice reform using the Commission's standards as a vehicle for discussion.

At this writing, the initial steps toward action on the Commission's recommendations are being taken in many States. A post-conference survey by LEAA revealed that at least 35 States plan to have seminars or conferences on the Commission's reports. A number of these States have either established or are in the process of establishing State commissions and task forces to review the standards of the Commission.

Finally, the National Governors' Conference in June 1973 adopted the following policy statement:

"The National Governors' Conference commends the National Advisory Commission on Criminal Justice Standards and Goals for its efforts in developing a comprehensive and detailed series of goals, standards, and priorities for reducing crime in America.

"The National Governors' Conference endorses the goals of reducing in 10 years the rate of high-fear crime by 50 percent from its 1973 level. As used in this context, high-fear crime refers to homicide, rape, aggravated assault, and robbery committed by people who are strangers to their victims. High-fear crimes also include all burglaries.

"In order to reach this goal, the National Governors' Conference calls on every State and unit of local government in that State to evaluate immediately its criminal justice system, to compare its criminal justice system with the standards and goals developed by the National Advisory Commission, and make such changes in their criminal justice system as are deemed necessary and appropriate by that State or unit of local government."

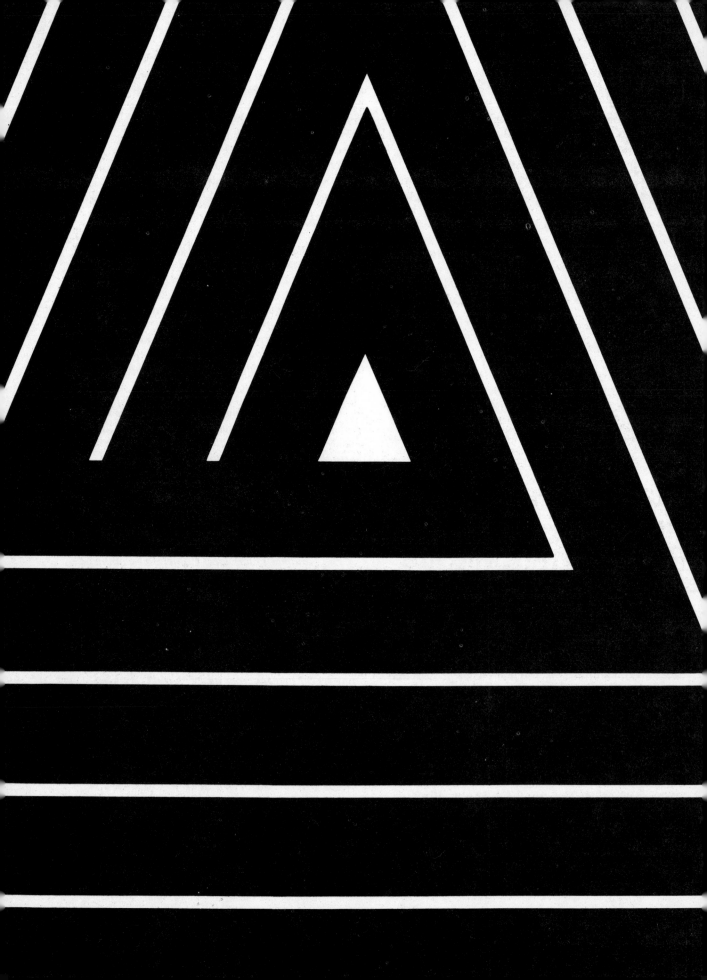

Synopses
Of
Standards
And
Recommendations

This volume, *A National Strategy to Reduce Crime,* is the summary report of the National Advisory Commission on Criminal Justice Standards and Goals. As such, it contains narrative descriptions of the major proposals of the Commission, but it does not contain any of the detailed "black letter" standards and recommendations that the Commission developed in its nearly 2 years of work.

Those detailed standards and recommendations—numbering almost 400 in all—appear in the five companion volumes to this report. The five volumes are entitled *Criminal Justice System, Police, Courts, Corrections,* and *Community Crime Prevention.* The reader is urged to consult those volumes for the precise standards and recommendations in question.

This section presents synopses of the standards and recommendations in a form that is easily understood by the layman as well as the professional. These synopses present a

capsulized version of the Commission's work. By design, they are neither comprehensive nor exhaustive. The actual standards and recommendations themselves may run to many hundreds of words and cover considerably more subjects than indicated in the synopses.

The intention in presenting the synopses is to give the reader an overview of the standards and recommendations which should be carried out in order to achieve the crime reduction goals proposed by the Commission and to show the scope of the Commission's effort and the sweeping range of its proposals.

Synopses are keyed by book, chapter, and standard or recommendation number to the appropriate volume of the Commission's report.

Some chapters contain no standards or recommendations and accordingly are so listed in the text.

CRIMINAL JUSTICE SYSTEM

Chapter 1: Planning for Crime Reduction

Standards

1.1 Assure that criminal justice planning is crime-oriented.
1.2 Improve the linkage between criminal justice planning and budgeting.
1.3 Set minimum statewide standards for recipients of criminal justice grants and subgrants.
1.4 Develop criminal justice planning capabilities.
1.5 Encourage the participation of operating agencies and the public in the criminal justice planning process.

Recommendation

1.1 Urge the Federal Government to apply these standards in its own planning.

Chapter 2: Requirements for Criminal Justice Information

Contains no standards or recommendations.

Chapter 3: Jurisdictional Responsibility

Standards

3.1 Coordinate the development of criminal justice information systems and make maximum use of collected data.
3.2 Establish a State criminal justice information system that provides certain services.
3.3 Provide localities with information systems that support the needs of local criminal justice agencies.
3.4 Provide every component of the criminal justice system with an information system that supports interagency needs.

Chapter 4: Police Information Systems

Standards

4.1 Define the proper functions of a police information system.
4.2 Utilize information to improve the department's crime analysis capability.
4.3 Develop a police manpower resource allocation and control system.
4.4 Specify maximum allowable delay for information delivery.
4.5 Insure that all police agencies participate in the Uniform Crime Reporting Program.
4.6 Expand collection of crime data.
4.7 Insure quality control of crime data.
4.8 Establish a geocoding system for crime analysis.

Chapter 5: Courts Information Systems

Standards

5.1 Provide background data and case history for criminal justice decisionmaking.
5.2 Provide information on caseflow to permit efficient calendar management.
5.3 Provide capability to determine monthly criminal justice caseflow and workloads.
5.4 Provide data to support charge determination and case handling.
5.5 Create capability for continued research and evaluation.
5.6 Record action taken in regard to one individual and one distinct offense and record the number of criminal events.

Chapter 6: Corrections Information Systems

Standards

6.1 Define the needs of a corrections information system.
6.2 Apply uniform definitions to all like correctional data.
6.3 Design a corrections data base that is flexible enough to allow for expansion.
6.4 Collect certain data about the offender.
6.5 Account for offender population and movement.
6.6 Describe the corrections experience of the offender.
6.7 Evaluate the performance of the corrections system.

Chapter 7: Operations

Standards

7.1 Provide for compatible design of offender-based transaction statistics and computerized criminal history systems.

154

7.2	Develop single data collection procedures for offender-based transaction statistics and computerized criminal history data by criminal justice agencies.
7.3	Develop data bases simultaneously for offender-based transaction statistics and computerized criminal history systems.
7.4	Restrict dissemination of criminal justice information.
7.5	Insure completeness and accuracy of offender data.
7.6	Safeguard systems containing criminal offender data.
7.7	Establish computer interfaces for criminal justice information systems.
7.8	Insure availability of criminal justice information systems.

Chapter 8: Privacy and Security

Standards

8.1	Insure the privacy and security of criminal justice information systems.
8.2	Define the scope of criminal justice information systems files.
8.3	Limit access and dissemination of criminal justice information.
8.4	Guarantee the right of the individual to review information in criminal justice information systems relating to him.
8.5	Adopt a system of classifying criminal justice system data.
8.6	Protect criminal justice information from environmental hazards.
8.7	Implement a personnel clearance system.
8.8	Establish criteria for the use of criminal justice information for research.

Chapter 9: Technical System Design

Standards

9.1	Insure standardized terminology following the National Crime Information Center example.
9.2	Establish specific program language requirements for criminal justice information systems.
9.3	Assure adequate teleprocessing capability.

Chapter 10: Strategy for Implementing Standards

Standards

10.1	Take legislative actions to support the development of criminal justice information systems.
10.2	Establish criminal justice user groups.
10.3	Establish a plan for development of criminal justice information and statistics systems at State and local levels.
10.4	Consolidate services to provide criminal justice information support where it is not otherwise economically feasible.
10.5	Consider conformity with all standards of this report as a condition for grant approval.

Chapter 11: Evaluation Strategy

Standards

11.1	Monitor the criminal justice information system analysis, design, development, and initial steps leading to implementation.
11.2	Monitor the implementation of the system to determine the cost and performance of the system and its component parts.
11.3	Conduct evaluations to determine the effectiveness of information system components.

Chapter 12: Development, Implementation, and Evaluation of Education Curriculums and Training Programs for Criminal Justice Personnel

Standards

| 12.1 | Develop, implement, and evaluate criminal justice education and training programs. |
| 12.2 | Establish criminal justice system curriculums. |

Chapter 13: Criminal Code Revision

Standards

| 13.1 | Revise criminal codes in States where codes have not been revised in the past decade. |
| 13.2 | Complete revision of criminal codes. |

13.3	Simplify the penalty structure in criminal codes.	13.7	Support drafted criminal law legislation with interpretive commentaries.
13.4	Revise corrections laws.	13.8	Assure smooth transition to the new law through education.
13.5	Create a drafting body to carry out criminal code revision.	13.9	Continue law revision efforts through a permanent commission.
13.6	Revise criminal procedure laws.		

COMMUNITY CRIME PREVENTION

Chapter 1: Citizen Action

Contains no standards or recommendations.

Chapter 2: Citizen Involvement and Government Responsiveness in the Delivery of Services

Recommendation

2.1 Distribute public service on the basis of need.
2.2 Dispense government services through neighborhood centers.
2.3 Enact public right-to-know laws.
2.4 Broadcast local government meetings and hearings.
2.5 Conduct public hearings on local issues.
2.6 Establish neighborhood governments.
2.7 Create a central office of complaint and information.
2.8 Broadcast local Action Line programs.

Chapter 3: Youth Services Bureaus

Standards

3.1 Coordinate youth services through youth services bureaus.
3.2 Operate youth services bureaus independent of the justice system.
3.3 Divert offenders into youth services bureaus.
3.4 Provide direct and referral services to youths.
3.5 Hire professional, paraprofessional, and volunteer staff.
3.6 Plan youth program evaluation and research.
3.7 Appropriate funds for youth services bureaus.
3.8 Legislate establishment and funding of youth services bureaus.

Chapter 4: Programs for Drug Abuse Treatment and Prevention

Recommendations

4.1 Adopt multimodality drug treatment systems.

4.2 Create crisis intervention and drug emergency centers.
4.3 Establish methadone maintenance programs.
4.4 Establish narcotic antagonist treatment programs.
4.5 Create drug-free therapeutic community facilities.
4.6 Organize residential drug treatment programs.
4.7 Encourage broader flexibility in varying treatment approaches.
4.8 Enable defendants to refer themselves voluntarily to drug treatment programs.
4.9 Establish training programs for drug treatment personnel.
4.10 Plan comprehensive, community-wide drug prevention.
4.11 Coordinate drug programs through a State agency.
4.12 Coordinate Federal, State, and local drug programs.

Chapter 5: Programs for Employment

Recommendations

5.1 Expand job opportunities for disadvantaged youth.
5.2 Broaden after-school and summer employment programs.
5.3 Establish pretrial intervention programs.
5.4 Expand job opportunities for offenders and ex-offenders.
5.5 Remove ex-offender employment barriers.
5.6 Create public employment programs.
5.7 Expand job opportunities for former drug abusers.
5.8 Target employment, income, and credit efforts in poverty areas.
5.9 Require employers' compliance with antidiscrimination laws.
5.10 Increase support of minority businesses.
5.11 Alleviate housing and transportation discrimination.

Chapter 6: Programs for Education

Recommendations

6.1 Adopt teacher training programs for parents.
6.2 Exemplify justice and democracy in school operations.
6.3 Guarantee literacy to elementary school students.

6.4   Provide special language services for bicultural students.

6.5   Develop career preparation programs in schools.

6.6   Provide effective supportive services in schools.

6.7   Offer alternative education programs for deviant students.

6.8   Open schools for community activities.

6.9   Adopt merit training and promotion policies for teachers.

Chapter 7: Programs for Recreation

Recommendation

7.1   Develop recreation programs for delinquency prevention.

Chapter 8: Programs for Religion

Recommendations

8.1   Enlist religious community participation in crime prevention.

8.2   Encourage religious institutions to educate their constituencies about the crime problem.

8.3   Enlist religious institution support of crime prevention.

8.4   Open church facilities for community programs.

8.5   Promote religious group participation in the justice system.

Chapter 9: Programs for Reduction of Criminal Opportunity

Recommendations

9.1   Design buildings that incorporate security measures.

9.2   Include security requirements in building codes.

9.3   Improve streetlighting in high-crime areas.

9.4   Adopt shoplifting prevention techniques in retail establishments.

9.5   Legislate car theft prevention programs.

9.6   Involve citizens in law enforcement.

Chapter 10: Conflicts of Interest

Standards

10.1   Adopt an Ethics Code for public officials and employees.

10.2   Create an Ethics Board to enforce the Ethics Code.

10.3   Disclose public officials' financial and professional interests.

10.4   Include conflicts of interest in the State criminal code.

Chapter 11: Regulation of Political Finances

Standards

11.1   Disclose candidates' receipts and expenditures.

11.2   Limit political campaign spending.

11.3   Prohibit campaign contributions from government-connected businessmen.

11.4   Prohibit campaign gifts from unions, trade groups, and corporations.

Chapter 12: Government Procurement of Goods and Services

Standard

12.1   Establish a State procurement agency.

Chapter 13: Zoning, Licensing, and Tax Assessment

Standards

13.1   Develop equitable criteria for zoning, licensing, and tax assessment.

13.2   Formulate specific criteria for government decisionmaking.

13.3   Publicize zoning, licensing, and tax assessment actions.

Chapter 14: Combating Official Corruption and Organized Crime

Standards

14.1   Set capability and integrity standards for local prosecutors.

14.2   Create a State office to attack corruption and organized crime.

POLICE

Chapter 1: The Police Role

Standards

1.1 Formulate policies governing police functions, objectives, and priorities.
1.2 Publicize and respect the limits of police authority.
1.3 Formalize police use of discretion.
1.4 Improve communication and relations with the public.
1.5 Enhance police officers' understanding of their role and of the culture of their community.
1.6 Publicize police policies and practices.
1.7 Promote police relations with the media.

Chapter 2: Role Implementation

Standards

2.1 Develop workable agency goals and objectives.
2.2 Establish written policies to help employees attain agency goals and objectives.
2.3 Establish a formal police inspection system.

Chapter 3: Developing Community Resources

Standards

3.1 Establish geographic team policing.
3.2 Involve the public in neighborhood crime prevention efforts.

Chapter 4: Criminal Justice Relations

Standards

4.1 Coordinate planning and crime control efforts with other components of the criminal justice system.
4.2 Develop cooperative procedures with courts and corrections agencies.
4.3 Formalize diversion procedures to insure equitable treatment.
4.4 Utilize alternatives to arrest and pretrial detention.

4.5 Develop court followup practices for selected cases.

Recommendations

4.1 Divert drug addicts and alcoholics to treatment centers.
4.2 Allow telephoned petitions for search warrants.
4.3 Enact State legislation prohibiting private surveillance and authorizing court-supervised electronic surveillance.

Chapter 5: Planning and Organizing

Standards

5.1 Establish a police service that meets the needs of the community.
5.2 Consolidate police agencies for greater effectiveness and efficiency.
5.3 Implement administrative and operational planning methods.
5.4 Assign responsibility for agency and jurisdictional planning.
5.5 Participate in any community planning that can affect crime.
5.6 Assign responsibility for fiscal management of the agency.
5.7 Develop fiscal management procedures.
5.8 Derive maximum benefit from government funding.

Recommendations

5.1 Formalize relationships between public and private police agencies.
5.2 Form a National Institute of Law Enforcement and Criminal Justice Advisory Committee.
5.3 Develop standardized measures of agency performance.

Chapter 6: Team Policing

Standards

6.1 Determine the applicability of team policing.
6.2 Plan, train for, and publicize implementation of team policing.

Chapter 7: Unusual Occurrences

Standards

7.1 Plan for coordinating activities of relevant agencies during mass disorders and natural disasters.

7.2 Delegate to the police chief executive responsibility for resources in unusual occurrences.

7.3 Develop an interim control system for use during unusual occurrences.

7.4 Develop a procedure for mass processing of arrestees.

7.5 Legislate an efficient, constitutionally sound crisis procedure.

7.6 Implement training programs for unusual occurrence control procedures.

Chapter 8: Patrol

Standards

8.1 Define the role of patrol officers.

8.2 Upgrade the status and salary of patrol officers.

8.3 Develop a responsive patrol deployment system.

Chapter 9: Operations Specialization

Standards

9.1 Authorize only essential assignment specialization.

9.2 Specify selection criteria for specialist personnel.

9.3 Review agency specializations annually.

9.4 Provide State specialists to local agencies.

9.5 Formulate policies governing delinquents and youth offenders.

9.6 Control traffic violations through preventive patrol and enforcement.

9.7 Train patrol officers to conduct preliminary investigations.

9.8 Create a mobile unit for special crime problems.

9.9 Establish policy and capability for vice operations.

9.10 Develop agency narcotic and drug investigative capability.

9.11 Develop a statewide intelligence network that has privacy safeguards.

Chapter 10: Manpower Alternatives

Standards

10.1 Employ civilian personnel in supportive positions.

10.2 Employ reserve officers.

Chapter 11: Professional Assistance

Standards

11.1 Establish working relationships with outside professionals.

11.2 Acquire legal assistance when necessary.

11.3 Create a State police management consultation service.

Chapter 12: Support Services

Standards

12.1 Train technicians to gather physical evidence.

12.2 Consolidate criminal laboratories to serve local, regional, and State needs.

12.3 Establish a secure and efficient filing system for evidential items.

12.4 Guarantee adequate jail services and management.

Recommendation

12.1 Establish crime laboratory certification standards.

Chapter 13: Recruitment and Selection

Standards

13.1 Actively recruit applicants.

13.2 Recruit college-educated personnel.

13.3 Insure nondiscriminatory recruitment practices.

13.4 Implement minimum police officer selection standards.

13.5 Formalize a nondiscriminatory applicant-screening process.

13.6 Encourage the employment of women.

Recommendations

13.1 Develop job-related applicant tests.

13.2 Develop an applicant scoring system.

Chapter 14: Classification and Pay

Standards

14.1 Maintain salaries competitive with private business.

14.2 Establish a merit-based position classification system.

Chapter 15: Education

Standards

15.1 Upgrade entry-level educational requirements.

15.2 Implement police officer educational incentives.

15.3 Affiliate training programs with academic institutions.

Recommendation

15.1 Outline police curriculum requirements.

Chapter 16: Training

Standards

16.1 Establish State minimum training standards.

16.2 Develop effective training programs.

16.3 Provide training prior to work assignment.

16.4 Provide interpersonal communications training.

16.5 Establish routine inservice training programs.

16.6 Develop training quality-control measures.

16.7 Develop police training academies and criminal justice training centers.

Chapter 17: Development, Promotion, and Advancement

Standards

17.1 Offer self-development programs for qualified personnel.

17.2 Implement formal personnel development programs.

17.3 Review personnel periodically for advancement.

17.4 Authorize police chief executive control of promotions.

17.5 Establish a personnel information system.

Chapter 18: Employee Relations

Standards

18.1 Maintain effective employee relations.

18.2 Formalize policies regulating police employee organizations.

18.3 Allow a collective negotiation process.

18.4 Prohibit work stoppages by policemen.

Chapter 19: Internal Discipline

Standards

19.1 Formulate internal discipline procedures.

19.2 Implement misconduct complaint procedures.

19.3 Create a specialized internal discipline investigative unit.

19.4 Insure swift and fair investigation of misconduct.

19.5 Authorize police chief executive adjudication of complaints.

19.6 Implement positive programs to prevent misconduct.

Recommendation

19.1 Study methods of reducing police corruption.

Chapter 20: Health Care, Physical Fitness, Retirement, and Employee Services

Standards

20.1 Require physical and psychological examinations of applicants.

20.2 Establish continuing physical fitness standards.

20.3 Establish an employee services unit.

20.4 Offer a complete health insurance program.

20.5 Provide a statewide police retirement system.

Recommendation

20.1 Compensate duty-connected injury, death, and disease.

Chapter 21: Personal Equipment

Standards

21.1   Specify apparel and equipment standards.
21.2   Require standard firearms, ammunition, and auxiliary equipment.
21.3   Provide all uniforms and equipment.

Chapter 22: Transportation

Standards

22.1   Evaluate transportation equipment annually.
22.2   Acquire and maintain necessary transportation equipment.
22.3   Conduct a fleet safety program.

Recommendation

22.1   Test transportation equipment nationally.

Chapter 23: Communications

Standards

23.1   Develop a rapid and accurate telephone system.
23.2   Insure rapid and accurate police communication.
23.3   Insure an efficient radio communications system.

Recommendations

23.1   Conduct research on a digital communications system.
23.2   Set national communications equipment standards.
23.3   Evaluate radio frequency requirements.

Chapter 24: Information Systems

Standards

24.1   Standardize reports of criminal activity.
24.2   Establish an accurate, rapid-access record system.
24.3   Standardize local information systems.
24.4   Coordinate Federal, State, and local information systems.

COURTS

Chapter 1: Screening

Standards

1.1 Screen certain accused persons out of the criminal justice system.
1.2 Formulate written guidelines for screening decisions.

Chapter 2: Diversion

Standards

2.1 Utilize, as appropriate, diversion into non-criminal-justice programs before trial.
2.2 Develop guidelines for diversion decisions.

Chapter 3: The Negotiated Plea

Standards

3.1 Prohibit plea negotiation in all courts by not later than 1978.
3.2 Document in the court records the basis for a negotiated guilty plea and the reason for its acceptance.
3.3 Formulate written policies governing plea negotiations.
3.4 Establish a time limit after which plea negotiations may no longer be conducted.
3.5 Provide service of counsel before plea negotiations.
3.6 Assure proper conduct by prosecutors in obtaining guilty pleas.
3.7 Review all guilty pleas and negotiations.
3.8 Assure that a plea of guilty is not considered when determining sentence.

Chapter 4: The Litigated Case

Standards

4.1 Assure that the period from arrest to trial does not exceed 60 days in felonies and 30 days in misdemeanors.
4.2 Maximize use of citations or summonses in lieu of arrest.
4.3 Eliminate preliminary hearings in misdemeanor proceedings.
4.4 Adopt policies governing use and function of grand juries.
4.5 Present arrested persons before a judicial officer within 6 hours after arrest.
4.6 Eliminate private bail bond agencies; utilize a wide range of pretrial release programs, including release on recognizance.
4.7 Adopt provisions to apprehend rapidly and deal severely with persons who violate release conditions.
4.8 Hold preliminary hearings within 2 weeks after arrest; eliminate formal arraignment.
4.9 Broaden pretrial discovery by both prosecution and defense.
4.10 File all motions within 15 days after preliminary hearing or indictment; hear motions within 5 days.
4.11 Establish criteria for assigning cases to the trial docket.
4.12 Limit granting of continuances.
4.13 Assure that only judges examine jurors; limit the number of peremptory challenges.
4.14 Adopt policies limiting number of jurors to fewer than 12 but more than six in all but the most serious cases.
4.15 Restrict evidence, testimony, and argument to that which is relevant to the issue of innocence or guilt; utilize full trial days.

Recommendations

4.1 Study the exclusionary rule and formulate alternatives.
4.2 Study the use of videotaped trials in criminal cases; establish pilot projects.

Chapter 5: Sentencing

Standard

5.1 Adopt a policy stipulating that all sentencing be performed by the trial judge.

Chapter 6: Review of the Trial Court Proceedings

Standard

6.1 Provide the opportunity to every convicted person for one full and fair review.
6.2 Provide a full-time professional staff of lawyers in the reviewing court.
6.3 Assure that review procedures are flexible and tailored to each case.

6.4   Establish time limits for review proceedings.

6.5   Specify exceptional circumstances that warrant additional review.

6.6   Assure that reviewing courts do not readjudicate claims already adjudicated on the merits by a court of competent jurisdiction.

6.7   Assure that determinations of fact by either a trial or reviewing court are conclusive absent a constitutional violation undermining the factfinding process.

6.8   Assure that claims that were not asserted at trial or that were disclaimed at trial by the defendant are not adjudicated in further reviews.

6.9   Assure that a reviewing court always states the reasons for its decision; limit publication to significant cases.

Recommendations

6.1   Develop means of producing trial transcripts speedily.

6.2   Study causes of delay in review proceedings.

6.3   Study reports and recommendations of the Advisory Council for Appellate Justice.

Chapter 7: The Judiciary

Standards

7.1   Select judges on the basis of merit qualifications.

7.2   Establish mandatory retirement for all judges at age 65.

7.3   Base salaries and benefits of State judges on the Federal model.

7.4   Subject judges to discipline or removal for cause by a judicial conduct commission.

7.5   Create and maintain a comprehensive program of continuing judicial education.

Chapter 8: The Lower Courts

Standards

8.1   Assure that State courts are unified courts of record, financed by the State, administered on a statewide basis, and presided over by full-time judges admitted to the practice of law.

8.2   Dispose administratively of all traffic cases except certain serious offenses.

Chapter 9: Court Administration

Standards

9.1   Establish policies for the administration of the State's courts.

9.2   Vest in a presiding judge ultimate local administrative judicial authority in each trial jurisdiction.

9.3   Assure that local and regional trial courts have a full-time court administrator.

9.4   Assure that ultimate responsibility for the management and flow of cases rests with the judges of the trial court.

9.5   Establish coordinating councils to survey court administration practices in the State.

9.6   Establish a forum for interchange between court personnel and the community.

Chapter 10: Court-Community Relations

Standards

10.1   Provide adequate physical facilities for court processing of criminal defendants.

10.2   Provide information concerning court processes to the public and to participants in the criminal justice system.

10.3   Coordinate responsibility among the court, news media, the public, and the bar for providing information to the public about the courts.

10.4   Assure that court personnel are representative of the community served by the court.

10.5   Assure that judges and court personnel participate in criminal justice planning activities.

10.6   Call witnesses only when necessary; make use of telephone alert.

10.7   Assure that witness compensation is realistic and equitable.

Chapter 11: Computers and the Courts

Standards

11.1   Utilize computer services consistent with the needs and caseloads of the courts.

11.2   Employ automated legal research services on an experimental basis.

Recommendation

11.1   Instruct law students in the use of automated legal research systems.

Chapter 12: The Prosecution

Standards

12.1 Assure that prosecutors are full-time skilled professionals, authorized to serve a minimum term of 4 years, and compensated adequately.

12.2 Select and retain assistant prosecutors on the basis of legal ability; assure that they serve full time and are compensated adequately.

12.3 Provide prosecutors with supporting staff and facilities comparable to that of similar-size private law firms.

12.4 Establish a State-level entity to provide support to local prosecutors.

12.5 Utilize education programs to assure the highest professional competence.

12.6 Establish file control and statistical systems in prosecutors' offices.

12.7 Assure that each prosecutor develops written office policies and practices.

12.8 Assure that prosecutors have an active role in crime investigation, with adequate investigative staff and subpena powers.

12.9 Assure that prosecutors maintain relationships with other criminal justice agencies.

Chapter 13: The Defense

Standards

13.1 Make available public representation to eligible defendants at all stages in all criminal proceedings.

13.2 Assure that any individual provided public representation pay any portion of the cost he can assume without undue hardship.

13.3 Enable all applicants for defender services to apply directly to the public defender or appointing authority for representation.

13.4 Make counsel available to corrections inmates, indigent parolees, and indigent probationers on matters relevant to their status.

13.5 Establish a full-time public defender organization and assigned counsel system involving the private bar in every jurisdiction.

13.6 Assure that defender services are consistent with local needs and financed by the State.

13.7 Assure that public defenders are full time and adequately compensated.

13.8 Assure that public defenders are nominated by a selection board and appointed by the Governor.

13.9 Keep free from political pressures the duties of public defenders.

13.10 Base upon merit, hiring, retention, and promotion policies for public defender staff attorneys.

13.11 Assure that salaries for public defender staff attorneys are comparable to those of associate attorneys in local private law firms.

13.12 Assure that the caseload of a public defender office is not excessive.

13.13 Assure that the public defender is sensitive to the problems of his client community.

13.14 Provide public defender offices with adequate supportive services and personnel.

13.15 Vest responsibility in the public defender for maintaining a panel of private attorneys for defense work.

13.16 Provide systematic and comprehensive training to public defenders and assigned counsel.

Chapter 14: Juveniles

Standards

14.1 Place jurisdiction over juveniles in a family court, which should be a division of the general trial court.

14.2 Place responsibility in an intake unit of the family court for decisions concerning filing of petitions and placement in detention or diversion programs.

14.3 Place authority in the family court to transfer certain delinquency cases to the trial court of general jurisdiction.

14.4 Separate adjudicatory hearings from dispositional hearings; assure that hearings have all the protections of adult criminal trials.

14.5 Assure that dispositional hearing proceedings are similar to those followed in sentencing adult offenders.

Chapter 15: Mass Disorders

Standards

15.1 Assure that every plan for the administration of justice in a mass disorder contains a court processing section.

15.2 Assure that the court plan is concerned with both judicial policy and court management.

15.3 Assure that a prosecutorial plan is developed by the local prosecutor(s).

15.4 Assure that the plan for providing defense services during a mass disorder is developed by the local public defender(s).

CORRECTIONS

Chapter 1: Corrections and the Criminal Justice System

Contains no standards or recommendations.

Chapter 2: Rights of Offenders

Standards

2.1 Guarantee offenders' access to courts.
2.2 Guarantee offenders' access to legal assistance.
2.3 Guarantee offenders' access to legal materials.
2.4 Protect offenders from personal abuse.
2.5 Guarantee healthful surroundings for inmates.
2.6 Guarantee adequate medical care for inmates.
2.7 Regulate institutional search and seizure.
2.8 Assure nondiscriminatory treatment of offenders.
2.9 Guarantee rehabilitation programs for offenders.
2.10 Legislate safeguards for retention and restoration of rights.
2.11 Establish rules of inmate conduct.
2.12 Establish uniform disciplinary procedures.
2.13 Adopt procedures for change of inmate status.
2.14 Establish offenders' grievance procedures.
2.15 Guarantee free expression and association to offenders.
2.16 Guarantee offenders' freedom of religious beliefs and practices.
2.17 Guarantee offenders' communication with the public.
2.18 Establish redress procedures for violations of offenders' rights.

Chapter 3: Diversion from the Criminal Justice Process

Standard

3.1 Implement formal diversion programs.

Chapter 4: Pretrial Release and Detention

Standards

4.1 Develop a comprehensive pretrial process improvement plan.
4.2 Engage in comprehensive planning before building detention facilities.
4.3 Formulate procedures for use of summons, citation, and arrest warrants.
4.4 Develop alternatives to pretrial detention.
4.5 Develop procedures for pretrial release and detention.
4.6 Legislate authority over pretrial detainees.
4.7 Develop pretrial procedures governing allegedly incompetent defendants.
4.8 Protect the rights of pretrial detainees.
4.9 Establish rehabilitation programs for pretrial detainees.
4.10 Develop procedures to expedite trials.

Chapter 5: Sentencing

Standards

5.1 Establish judicial sentencing of defendants.
5.2 Establish sentencing practices for nondangerous offenders.
5.3 Establish sentencing practices for serious offenders.
5.4 Establish sentencing procedures governing probation.
5.5 Establish criteria for fines.
5.6 Adopt policies governing multiple sentences.
5.7 Disallow mitigation of sentence based on guilty plea.
5.8 Allow credit against sentence for time served.
5.9 Authorize continuing court jurisdiction over sentenced offenders.
5.10 Require judicial visits to correctional facilities.
5.11 Conduct sentencing councils, institutes, and reviews.
5.12 Conduct statewide sentencing institutes.
5.13 Create sentencing councils for judges.
5.14 Require content-specified presentence reports.
5.15 Restrict preadjudication disclosure of presentence reports.
5.16 Disclose presentence reports to defense and prosecution.
5.17 Guarantee defendants' rights at sentencing hearings.
5.18 Develop procedural guidelines for sentencing hearings.
5.19 Impose sentence according to sentencing hearing evidence.

Chapter 6: Classification of Offenders

Standards

6.1   Develop a comprehensive classification system.
6.2   Establish classification policies for correctional institutions.
6.3   Establish community classification teams.

Chapter 7: Corrections and the Community

Standards

7.1   Develop a range of community-based alternatives to institutionalization.
7.2   Insure correctional cooperation with community agencies.
7.3   Seek public involvement in corrections.
7.4   Establish procedures for gradual release of inmates.

Chapter 8: Juvenile Intake and Detention

Standards

8.1   Authorize police to divert juveniles.
8.2   Establish a juvenile court intake unit.
8.3   Apply total system planning concepts to juvenile detention centers.
8.4   Evaluate juvenile intake and detention personnel policies.

Chapter 9: Local Adult Institutions

Standards

9.1   Undertake total system planning for community corrections.
9.2   Incorporate local correctional functions within the State system.
9.3   Formulate State standards for local facilities.
9.4   Establish pretrial intake services.
9.5   Upgrade pretrial admission services and processes.
9.6   Upgrade the qualifications of local correctional personnel.
9.7   Protect the health and welfare of adults in community facilities.
9.8   Provide programs for adults in jails.
9.9   Develop release programs for convicted adults.
9.10   Evaluate the physical environment of jails.

Chapter 10: Probation

Standards

10.1   Place probation under executive branch jurisdiction.
10.2   Establish a probation service delivery system.
10.3   Provide misdemeanant probation services.
10.4   Develop a State probation manpower unit.
10.5   Establish release on recognizance procedures and staff.

Chapter 11: Major Institutions

Standards

11.1   Seek alternatives to new State institutions.
11.2   Modify State institutions to serve inmate needs.
11.3   Modify the social environment of institutions.
11.4   Individualize institutional programs.
11.5   Devise programs for special offender types.
11.6   Provide constructive programs for women offenders.
11.7   Develop a full range of institutional religious programs.
11.8   Provide recreation programs for inmates.
11.9   Offer individual and group counseling for inmates.
11.10   Operate labor and industrial programs that aid in reentry.

Chapter 12: Parole

Standards

12.1   Establish independent State parole boards.
12.2   Specify qualifications of parole board members.
12.3   Specify procedure and requirements for granting parole.
12.4   Specify parole revocation procedures and alternatives.
12.5   Coordinate institutional and field services and functions.
12.6   Develop community services for parolees.
12.7   Individualize parole conditions.
12.8   Develop parole manpower and training programs.

Chapter 13: Organization and Administration

Standards

13.1 Professionalize correctional management.
13.2 Develop a correctional planning process.
13.3 Train management in offender and employee relations.
13.4 Prohibit, but prepare for, work stoppages and job actions.

Chapter 14: Manpower for Corrections

Standards

14.1 Discontinue unwarranted personnel restrictions.
14.2 Recruit and employ minority group individuals.
14.3 Recruit and employ women.
14.4 Recruit and employ ex-offenders.
14.5 Recruit and use volunteers.
14.6 Revise personnel practices to retain staff.
14.7 Adopt a participatory management program.
14.8 Plan for manpower redistribution to community programs.
14.9 Establish a State program for justice system education.
14.10 Implement correctional internship and work-study programs.
14.11 Create staff development programs.

Chapter 15: Research and Development, Information, and Statistics

Standards

15.1 Maintain a State correctional information system.
15.2 Provide staff for systems analysis and statistical research.
15.3 Design an information system to supply service needs.

15.4 Develop a data base with criminal justice system interface.
15.5 Measure recidivism and program performance.

Chapter 16: The Statutory Framework of Corrections

Standards

16.1 Enact a comprehensive correctional code.
16.2 Enact regulation of administrative procedures.
16.3 Legislate definition and implementation of offender rights.
16.4 Legislate the unification of corrections.
16.5 Define personnel standards by law.
16.6 Ratify interstate correctional agreements.
16.7 Define crime categories and maximum sentences.
16.8 Legislate criteria for court sentencing alternatives.
16.9 Restrict court delinquency jurisdiction and detention.
16.10 Require presentence investigations by law.
16.11 Formulate criteria and procedures for probation decisions.
16.12 Legislate commitment, classification, and transfer procedures.
16.13 Lift unreasonable restrictions on prison labor and industry.
16.14 Legislate authorization for community-based correctional programs.
16.15 Clarify parole procedures and eligibility requirements.
16.16 Establish pardon power and procedure.
16.17 Repeal laws restricting offender rights.

Chapter 17: Priorities and Implementation Strategies

Contains no standards or recommendations.

Commission Members

Russell W. Peterson

Russell W. Peterson was elected Governor of Delaware in 1968.

Prior to his election, Governor Peterson spent 26 years with the DuPont Company in Delaware, advancing through a variety of management posts in research, manufacturing, and sales. In 1963 he was named to organize and head a new division responsible for launching the DuPont Company into new fields. He also served as Chairman of the Board of the Textile Research Institute in Princeton, N.J.

Governor Peterson has taken part in numerous community and political activities. In 1961 he led the Kiwanis Club of Delaware to organize the Three-S-Citizens Campaign against crime.

For his work in environment areas, especially the passage of legislation to ban oil refineries from the Delaware coast, he was named "Conservationist of the Year" by the National Wildlife Federation in 1971 and was given the Gold Medal of the World Wildlife Fund.

Governor Peterson has made many changes in the management of State government, including the conversion of Delaware's executive branch from a commission to a cabinet form of government. He was National Chairman of the Education Commission of the States during 1971–1972. He also served as Chairman of the Crime Reduction Committee of the National Governors' Conference (1971–1972).

Governor Peterson graduated from the University of Wisconsin with B.S. and Ph.D. degrees.

Peter J. Pitchess

Peter J. Pitchess is currently serving his fourth 4-year term as Sheriff of Los Angeles County.

Sheriff Pitchess served 12 years as a special agent with the Federal Bureau of Investigation. He was appointed Undersheriff of Los Angeles County in 1953 and was elected Sheriff following the retirement of his predecessor in 1958.

Sheriff Pitchess has participated in many civic, professional, and fraternal organizations among which are: Past President and member of the Executive Committee of the California Peace Officers' Association; California State Sheriffs' Association; Past President of Los Angeles County Peace Officers' Association.

He holds B.S. and J.D. degrees from the University of Utah.

Richard R. Andersen

Richard R. Andersen was appointed Chief of Police of Omaha, Neb., on Nov. 1, 1967.

Chief Andersen joined the Police Division in

1951, becoming Deputy Chief in 1965. Chief Andersen has served in all phases of the police service, with a majority of his time in rank served within the Detective Bureau.

Chief Andersen attended Nebraska University, and graduated from the University of Omaha with a degree in Law Enforcement and Education. He is also a graduate of the first police management course held at the School of Business Administration at Harvard University in 1966.

Forrest H. Anderson

Forrest H. Anderson was elected Governor of Montana in 1968. He did not seek reelection in 1972.

Governor Anderson began his political career by serving two terms as a member of the Montana State House of Representatives in 1943 and 1945. Shortly thereafter he was elected as Lewis and Clark County Attorney. He was elected to the Montana Supreme Court in 1952 and served as an Associate Justice until 1956, when he won election to the Office of Attorney General. He served as Attorney General until his nomination for the governorship in 1968.

The Governor was educated at the University of Montana at Missoula and the Columbus University Law School in Washington, D.C.

Sylvia Bacon

Sylvia Bacon is a trial judge of the District of Columbia Superior Court, which has general jurisdiction over criminal prosecutions, civil actions, and family matters. She has served on the court since 1970.

Prior to coming to the bench, Judge Bacon was the Executive Assistant U.S. Attorney for the District of Columbia and had served in that office as a trial attorney. She also served as Associate Director of the President's Commission on Crime in the District of Columbia.

Judge Bacon has been a Bar Examiner for the District of Columbia, a member of the Board of Directors of the District of Columbia Bar Association, and a trustee of the District of Columbia Bar Association Research Foundation and of the National Home Library Foundation. She has taught Juvenile Court Practice at Georgetown University Law Center.

Judge Bacon was educated at Vassar College and at the Harvard Law School. She also obtained an LL.M. from the Georgetown University Law Center and is a graduate of the National College of the State Judiciary.

Arthur J. Bilek

Arthur J. Bilek has been Chairman of the Illinois Law Enforcement Commission since early 1969. He is on leave-of-absence from the University of Illinois at Chicago Circle where he holds the academic rank of Professor of Criminal Justice and has served as Director and Founder of the Administration of Criminal Justice Curriculum.

Mr. Bilek was Chief of Police for the Cook County Sheriff's Department from 1962 to 1966. From 1953 to 1962, he served with the Chicago Police Department, advancing from Patrolman to Lieutenant. He also has been a Special Investigator for the Cook County State's Attorney's Police and a special agent in the U.S. Army Counter Intelligence Corps.

He is a member of the board of the Law in American Society Foundation and is a member of several professional organizations including the International Association of Chiefs of Police, the American Academy of Forensic Sciences, the American Sociological Association, and the American Society of Criminology.

He is a graduate of Loyola University in Chicago, which granted him B.S. and M.S.W. degrees.

Frank Dyson

Frank Dyson was appointed Chief of Police of the Dallas, Tex., Police Department in 1969.

Chief Dyson began his police career in 1950 as a patrolman for the Dallas Police Department. He rose through the ranks becoming Assistant Chief in June 1969, and Chief of Police on December 15, 1969.

Chief Dyson has instructed at El Centro Junior College, and is a member of the faculty at Southwestern Police Academy.

He is a member of the Texas Police Association, the FBI National Academy Association, and the International Association of Chiefs of Police, and has served as a member of the Texas Criminal Justice Council.

Chief Dyson holds a B.S. degree from Sam Houston State University.

Caroline E. Hughes

Caroline E. Hughes was appointed a member of the National Advisory Council on Vocational Education by President Nixon in April 1971.

Mrs. Hughes has also been a member since 1967 of the Oklahoma State Advisory Council on Vocational Education, and served as Chairman of that council in 1969. She has been an elected member of the Board of Education of the Central Oklahoma Area Vocational and Technical School District since 1967.

Mrs. Hughes is also on the Executive Board of the Governor's Link Committee which counsels the Department of Corrections in Oklahoma. She is a member of several local civic and service clubs, including the Cushing, Okla., Chamber of Commerce and the Daughters of the American Revolution. Mrs. Hughes is also active as a consultant in the field of vocational education.

Mrs. Hughes holds a B.S. degree from Oklahoma State University.

Howard A. Jones

Howard A. Jones was appointed Chairman of the Narcotic Addiction Control Commission, State of New York, by Governor Rockefeller on July 1, 1971. He has been a member of that commission since May 1970.

Prior to joining the commission, Commissioner Jones served for 7 years as a member of the New York State Board of Parole. From 1962 to 1963 he was assistant counsel to Governor Rockefeller. From 1953 to 1960, Commissioner Jones was an Assistant District Attorney in New York County.

Commissioner Jones also has served on the New York Temporary State Commission on Revision of the Penal Law and Criminal Code, and on the Select Committee on Correctional Institutions and Programs. He is a member of several professional, charitable, and civic organizations.

He served as a World War II combat infantryman. He attended the City College of New York and New York University and holds a law degree from St. John's University Law School.

Robert J. Kutak

Robert J. Kutak is a partner in the law firm of Kutak, Rock, Cohen, Campbell, & Peters in Omaha, Neb.

Before joining the firm, Mr. Kutak was Administrative Assistant to U.S. Senator Roman L. Hruska of Nebraska. He also served as a law clerk to Judge Richard E. Robinson of the U.S. District Court for the District of Nebraska.

Mr. Kutak was a member of the President's Task Force on Prisoner Rehabilitation in 1969–1970. He was a member of the United States delegation to the Fourth World Congress on Prevention of Crime and Treatment of Offenders in 1970. He is a member of the National Advisory Panel to the Director of the

Bureau of Prisons and is Vice Chairman of the American Bar Association Commission on Correctional Facilities and Services; Mr. Kutak also serves on other committees of the American Bar Association.

Mr. Kutak holds degrees from the University of Chicago and the University of Chicago Law School.

Richard G. Lugar

Richard G. Lugar was elected Mayor of Indianapolis, Ind., in 1967, and reelected in 1971.

Mayor Lugar entered public life in 1964 when he was elected to the Board of School Commissioners in Indianapolis; he served as Vice President of that board in 1965. From 1960 to 1967, he was Vice President and Treasurer of Thomas L. Green and Company, and has served as Secretary-Treasurer of that company from 1968 to the present. Since 1960, he also has acted as Treasurer of Lugar Stock Farms, Inc.

Mayor Lugar is Vice Chairman of the Advisory Commission on Intergovernmental Relations, and former President of the National League of Cities. He is a member of the Board of Directors of the National Association of Counties.

Mayor Lugar graduated first in his class from Denison University, and, as a Rhodes Scholar, received his B.A. and M.A. from Oxford University (Pembroke College). He has served as a Lieutenant in the U.S. Navy.

Ellis C. MacDougall

Ellis C. MacDougall was appointed Director of the State Board of Corrections in Georgia in January 1971.

Mr. MacDougall also has served as the Commissioner of Corrections for the State of Connecticut, as Director of the South Carolina Department of Corrections, and as the Director of Prison Industries in the South Carolina Department of Corrections. He has served as Deputy Warden and Business Manager of the South Carolina Penitentiary, and in several other positions in the corrections field.

Mr. MacDougall is a member and Past President of the American Correctional Association, is the Past President of the Southern States Prison Association, and is a member of the National Council on Crime and Delinquency.

Mr. MacDougall holds a B.A. degree from Davis and Elkins College, an M.A. from New York University, and an Honorary LL.D. from Davis and Elkins College.

Henry F. McQuade

Henry F. McQuade was appointed to the Supreme Court of the State of Idaho in December 1956, and has been reelected to that office to the present time. He was Chief Justice of that court for the years 1964–1965 and 1971–1972.

Between 1951 and 1956, Justice McQuade served as District Judge of the Fifth (now the Sixth) Judicial District of Idaho. He also has served as Prosecuting Attorney of Bannock County, and as a Justice of the Peace in Latah County. During World War II, Justice McQuade attained the rank of Captain in the United States Army.

Justice McQuade received both his B.A. and LL.B. degrees from the University of Idaho.

Gary K. Nelson

Gary K. Nelson was appointed Attorney General of Arizona on July 1, 1968, and has been elected and reelected to that office to the present time.

Mr. Nelson has been in the Office of the Attorney General since 1964, first in the Highway Legal Division and later as Chief of the Criminal Appeals Division and Chief Trial Counsel. He has also been an associate in the firm of Kramer, Roche, Burch, Streich, and Cracchiolo, and a law clerk to Justice Fred C. Struckmeyer, Jr., of the Arizona Supreme Court.

Mr. Nelson has been the Chairman of the Arizona State Justice Planning Agency since 1969. He is also a member of the Law Enforcement Officers Advisory Council, President of the National Association of Attorneys General, and a member of the President's Consumer Advisory Council. He is Past Chairman of the Conference of Western Attorneys General.

Mr. Nelson graduated from Arizona State University with a B.S. degree, and from the University of Arizona with a J.D. degree. He served in the U.S. Army with the rank of Captain.

Charles L. Owen

Charles L. Owen has been the Director of the Kentucky Crime Commission since it was established in July 1967. He has also served for the past 2 years as Chairman of the National Conference of State Planning Agency Directors, which administers funds under the Omnibus Crime Control and Safe Streets Act.

A graduate of Princeton University and the University of Virginia Law School, Mr. Owen served as Assistant United States Attorney for the District of Columbia before assuming his present position in Kentucky.

Ray Pope

Ray Pope was appointed Commissioner of the Department of Public Safety in the State of Georgia on January 12, 1971. He has responsibility for administering the State's largest law enforcement agency, consisting of the Georgia State Patrol, the Georgia Bureau of Investigation, the State Crime Laboratory, and the Georgia Police Academy.

Colonel Pope began his law enforcement career in 1939. Since that time he has held several law enforcement positions, the most recent being a Program Specialist for the Law Enforcement Assistance Administration. He was also Chief of the Waycross, Ga., Police Department for 8 years.

Colonel Pope has served as Vice-Chairman of the Georgia Crime Commission and as a member of the Georgia Organized Crime Prevention Council. During his career he also has been President of the Peace Officers' Association of Georgia, President of the Georgia Association of Chiefs of Police, and Chairman of the Georgia Law Enforcement Planning Agency Supervisory Board. He is a member of the National Council on Crime and Delinquency's Law Enforcement Council.

Colonel Pope attended the University of Georgia and South Georgia College, from which he received a degree in Criminal Justice. He also has studied Police Administration at the Southern Police Institute. During World War II, Colonel Pope served 3 years with the U.S. Navy Shore Patrol.

Reverend Elmer J. C. Prenzlow, Jr.

Elmer J. C. Prenzlow, Jr., has been Campus Chaplain of the University Lutheran Chapel of the Metropolitan Milwaukee Campus Ministry for the South Wisconsin District of the Lutheran Church, Missouri Synod, for 11 years. He is Chairman of the Humanities Department of Spencerian Business College in Milwaukee.

Reverend Prenzlow also works as a consulting psychologist in residential treatment centers for the emotionally disturbed. He has held a number of denominational offices and responsibilities in the Wisconsin Evangelical Lutheran Synod and in the Lutheran Church, Missouri Synod.

Among his professional and civic activities, Reverend Prenzlow is a member of the American Personnel and Guidance Association and a member of the American Psychological Association, and was member of the Wisconsin Legislative Advisory Committee on the Kerner Report.

Reverend Prenzlow holds a B.A. from Northwestern College, a B.D. from the Wisconsin Evangelical Lutheran Seminary, an M.S. in psychology from the University of Wisconsin, and has done extensive postgraduate work in his field.

Milton G. Rector

Milton G. Rector is President of the National Council on Crime and Delinquency and has been its executive officer since 1959.

Prior to assuming the directorship, Mr. Rector was Western Consultant and Assistant Director of the Council from 1946 to 1959.

Mr. Rector has been a delegate to the United Nations for the Second, Third and Fourth World Congresses on Prevention of Crime and Treatment of Offenders. He was a member of the President's Advisory Council on Juvenile Delinquency from 1960 to 1966, a consultant to the President's Commission on Law Enforcement and Administration of Justice and a member of the Advisory Committee to the National Commission on Reform of Federal Criminal Laws. He is at present a member of the New York City Coordinating Council for Criminal Justice.

Mr. Rector is on the Board of Directors of the American Correctional Association, the Osborne Association, and several other professional organizations. He is author of a syndicated newspaper column, "Of Crime and Punishment."

Mr. Rector received a B.A. degree from the University of Southern California, and did graduate work at Columbia University and at the University of California at Berkeley.

Arlen Specter

Arlen Specter was elected District Attorney of Philadelphia, Pa., in November 1965 and has been reelected to that office to the present time. Mr. Specter also serves as a Lecturer in Law at the Temple University Law School.

Before his election, Mr. Specter was a Special Assistant Attorney General of Pennsylvania. He has also served as Assistant Counsel of the Warren Commission, and as an Assistant District Attorney of Philadelphia.

He is a member of the National Advisory Council of the Peace Corps, and was a delegate to the White House Conference on Youth in 1971. He is a member of the American Bar Association, the Pennsylvania Bar Association, and the Philadelphia Bar Association.

Mr. Specter received a B.A. from the University of Pennsylvania and an LL.B. from Yale University Law School.

Reverend Leon H. Sullivan

Leon H. Sullivan has been pastor of the Zion Baptist Church in Philadelphia, Pa., since 1950.

In 1964, Reverend Sullivan founded the Opportunities Industrial Center, a program that sponsors job training and retraining, and which operates in more than 100 cities in the United States and in four African countries. Reverend Sullivan also founded the Zion Investment Associates in Philadelphia, and Progress Aerospace Enterprises, Inc.

Reverend Sullivan is Founder and Chairman of the Board of the National Progress Association for Economic Development which is doing economic development planning and other urban planning in 40 cities around the country.

He is a director of several organizations and companies, including the Boy Scouts of America, the United Way of America, and the General Motors Corporation.

Reverend Sullivan holds a B.A. from West Virginia State College, an M.A. from Columbia University, and several honorary degrees.

Donald F. Taylor

Donald F. Taylor has been President of Merrill Manufacturing Corporation since 1939. He is also President of three subsidiary companies: Basic Wire Products in Ohio; Taylor Insulation Company in Wisconsin; and Bay Insulation Company in Wisconsin.

Mr. Taylor has been a Director of the Chamber of Commerce of the United States since 1966. He is also Chairman of the Crime Prevention and Control Panel of the Chamber. He is a Past Director and Past President of the Wisconsin State Chamber of Commerce. He is also Past Director of the Wisconsin Council of Safety.

Mr. Taylor received his education at the Merrill Commercial College and at the University of Wisconsin Management Institute.

Richard W. Velde (ex officio)

Richard W. Velde was appointed Associate Administrator of the Law Enforcement Assistance Administration by President Nixon in March 1969.

A meeting of the National Advisory Commission on Criminal Justice Standards and Goals.

Prior to joining LEAA, Mr. Velde served as Minority Counsel of the Senate Subcommittee on Criminal Law. He also served as Minority Counsel of the Subcommittee on Juvenile Delinquency. He engaged in the private practice of law in Washington, D.C., from 1961 to 1965. From 1958 to 1960, he served as Legislative Assistant to U.S. Representative Robert H. Michel of Illinois. He served 5 years in the U.S. Air Force, attaining the rank of Captain.

Mr. Velde received a B.S. degree in political science and an M.A. in speech from Bradley University in Peoria, Ill. He attended the University of Illinois College of Law, and received his J.D. degree from George Washington University Law School. He was also a Ph.D. candidate in government and public administration.

The Commission's Origins And Work

In early 1971, the Attorney General asked the Law Enforcement Assistance Administration (LEAA) to take the initiative in developing goals and standards for criminal justice agencies. LEAA subsequently conducted two planning conferences of criminal justice experts which recommended the creation of a national commission as the most appropriate means to carry out the Attorney General's directive.

On October 20, 1971, the Administrator of LEAA, Jerris Leonard, established the National Advisory Commission on Criminal Justice Standards and Goals.

Thomas J. Madden, General Counsel of LEAA, was detailed to work for the Commission in November 1971. In December 1971, the Commission voted unanimously to appoint him their Executive Director.

The Commission created a number of task forces, each consisting of from 10 to 20 experts and informed citizens, to carry out its research into what was workable and practicable for crime control. Within guidelines and directions set forth by the Commission, four major task forces—on Police, Courts, Corrections, and Community Crime Prevention—undertook the preparation of individual studies in their respective areas. Funding for staff and consultants for each of these four operational task forces was provided by LEAA through the State Criminal Justice Planning Agencies of California, Massachusetts, Texas, and Virginia. The mandate given each task force by the Commission and LEAA was to draft goals and standards for State and local agencies that would reduce crime and improve the quality of justice. They were charged with finding successful models for action if they existed and, if no model existed, they were charged with developing one.

In addition to the four operational task forces, the Commission and LEAA also established eight advisory task forces on: Juvenile Delinquency; Organized Crime; Drug Abuse; Community Involvement; Civil Disorders; Research and Development; Education, Training, and Manpower Development; and Information Systems. These task forces, comprised of experts and professionals, met several times to advise the Commission and the Task Forces on Police, Courts, Corrections, and Community Crime Prevention.

The advisory task forces worked without staff support, with the exception of the Information Systems Task Force. They performed recommending and reviewing functions as contrasted with drafting and research functions. The Information Systems Task Force, however, was assisted by a staff and produced a report that serves as a major section of the Commission's *Report on the Criminal Justice System*.

Commission staff was assigned by the Executive Director to administer each of the operational task force grants and to work with each task force to assure that the Commission's guidelines were followed. Commission staff reviewed material prepared by each task force, suggesting to the Commission and to the task forces modifications, additions, and deletions of material. Commission staff members attended each task force meeting and provided insight to the task force on the requirements of the Commission. In many instances Commission staff members drafted standards for the task force reports.

In October 1971 the Commission staff assumed full responsibility for completing the *Report on Community Crime Prevention* and much of the material in that report was developed under the direction of the Commission staff.

In addition the Commission staff had sole responsibility for producing for the Commission the *Report on the Criminal Justice System* and the final report of the Commission, *A National Strategy to Reduce Crime*. And the Commission staff edited and completed final preparations on each of the Commission reports prior to printing.

Under the direction of the Executive Director, a Publications Unit was formed to prepare manuscripts for the printer. The unit was established in October 1972 and was composed of professional journalists. This group processed copy submitted to it by the Commission staff and prepared it for production by the Government Printing Office. A professional design firm developed the concept of the cover art and was responsible for selection of type and layout.

The chairmen of the Commission's task forces attended Commission meetings and actively participated in its discussions. They did not participate in Commission voting. The reports of the various task forces together with the work performed by the Commission's own staff provided the Commission with its basic working material.

Under this structure, the Commission's work was decentralized and subject to a series of independent reviews. The majority of task force members were drawn from State, local, and private agencies. The bulk of the staff and consultants for the major task forces came from outside Washington, D.C. Two task forces, those on Police and Corrections, were headquartered in Los Angeles, Calif., and Austin, Tex., respectively.

The wide diversity of geographic representation on task forces and staffs contributed to the expression of a variety of viewpoints and provided access to a number of important information sources.

While the Commission did not view its task as primarily survey-and-study, several surveys were nonetheless undertaken by the Commission and task force staffs. These included, for example, a survey of several hundred criminal justice agencies concerning innovative programs, and a survey of State and trial court administrators concerning characteristics of contemporary court administration. Each of the task forces initiated contacts with professional associations and individual criminal justice agencies. The Police Task Force alone contacted

hundreds of small, medium-sized, and large police departments throughout the country.

Considerable volunteer effort was contributed by staff from agencies under the direction of particular Commissioners and task force chairmen. Among the agencies headed by Commissioners or task force chairmen whose personnel were involved in the Commission's work were the Los Angeles Police and Sheriff's Departments, the Dallas Police Department, the New York State Narcotic Addiction Control Commission, the Georgia State Department of Offender Rehabilitation, the National Council on Crime and Delinquency, the District Attorney's Office of Philadelphia, Pa., the Metropolitan Police Department of Washington, D.C., and the Michigan State Police.

A number of Federal agencies provided valuable assistance to the Commission, including the Office of Criminal Justice, the Federal Bureau of Investigation, the Bureau of Prisons, and the Community Relations Service of the Department of Justice; the National Institute of Mental Health and the Youth Development and Delinquency Prevention Administration of the Department of Health, Education, and Welfare; and the Manpower Development and Training Administration of the Department of Labor. All offices of LEAA, and particularly the National Criminal Justice Information and Statistics Service, the National Institute of Law Enforcement and Criminal Justice, and the Office of Criminal Justice Assistance, contributed papers, suggestions, information, and staff assistance.

The full Commission met eight times for 2- to 4-day periods during the course of its work. On numerous occasions, however, individual Commissioners consulted with and advised Commission staff and the task forces. During the latter half of 1972, the Commission met in a series of meetings to review and approve reports from the task forces as well as those from the Commission staff itself. Every standard in the Commission's reports was debated and voted upon by the full Commission.

In a number of cases, standards presented by task forces or Commission staff were modified or rejected. In some areas, more than one task force presented similar recommendations. The Commission allowed overlapping between reports so that each report could stand by itself.

Each standard adopted by the Commission was subject to approval by a majority vote; however, not every Commissioner agreed with every standard adopted by the Commission or with the narrative supporting each standard.

Task Force Members

Police Task Force

Chairman

Edward M. Davis
Chief of Police
Los Angeles Police Department
Los Angeles, Calif.

Vice Chairman

Dale Carson
Sheriff, Jacksonville, Fla.

Arthur L. Alarcon
Judge, Superior Court
Los Angeles, Calif.

George A. Bowman, Jr.
County Judge, Children's Court Center
Milwaukee, Wis.

William Cahn
District Attorney of Nassau County
Mineola, N.Y.

Benjamin O. Davis, Jr.
Assistant Secretary for Safety and Consumer
   Affairs, Department of Transportation
Washington, D.C.

Don R. Derning
Chief of Police, Winnetka, Ill.

Alfred S. Ercolano
Director, College of American Pathologists
Washington, D.C.

David Hanes
Attorney, Wilmer, Cutler & Pickering
Washington, D.C.

Clarence M. Kelley
Chief, Kansas Police Department
Kansas City, Mo.

David B. Kelly
Superintendent, New Jersey State Police
West Trenton, N.J.

Charles Kingston
Professor of Criminalistics
John Jay College of Criminal Justice
New York, N.Y.

Donald Manson
Policy Analyst, Center for Policy Analysis
National League of Cities
Washington, D.C.

John R. Shryock
Chief, Kettering Police Department
Kettering, Ohio

177

Joseph White
Executive Director
Ohio Law Enforcement Planning Agency
Columbus, Ohio

Courts Task Force

Chairman

Daniel J. Meador
Professor of Law, University of Virginia
Charlottesville, Va.

Vice Chairman

Stanley C. Van Ness
Public Defender
State of New Jersey
Trenton, N.J.

Arthur Azevedo, Jr.
California State Assembly
Office of Assemblyman Bill Bagley
Sacramento, Calif.

William O. Bittman
Attorney, Hogan and Hartson
Washington, D.C.

William L. Cahalan
Wayne County Prosecuting Attorney
Detroit, Mich.

John C. Danforth
Attorney General of Missouri
Jefferson City, Mo.

William H. Erickson
Justice, Supreme Court of Colorado
Denver, Colo.

B. J. George
Professor of Law, Wayne State University Law
   School
Detroit, Mich.

Edward B. McConnell
Administrative Director of the Courts
Trenton, N.J.

Tim Murphy
Judge, Superior Court, District of Columbia

Frank A. Orlando
Presiding Judge, Juvenile Court of Broward County
Fort Lauderdale, Fla.

G. Nicholas Pijoan
Director, Division of Criminal Justice
Denver, Colo.

Donald E. Santarelli
Associate Deputy Attorney General
Department of Justice, Washington, D.C.

William M. Slaughter
Litton Industries, Inc.
Beverly Hills, Calif.

George A. Van Hoomissen
Dean, National College of District Attorneys
University of Houston
Houston, Tex.

Corrections Task Force

Chairman

Judge Joe Frazier Brown
Executive Director, Criminal Justice Council
Austin, Tex.

Fred Allenbrand
Sheriff, Johnson County
Olathe, Kans.

Norman A. Carlson
Director, U.S. Bureau of Prisons
Washington, D.C.

Hubert M. Clements
Assistant Director, South Carolina Department of
   Corrections
Columbia, S.C.

Roberta Dorn
Program Specialist
Law Enforcement Assistance Administration
Washington, D.C.

Edith Flynn
Associate Professor, University of Illinois
Urbana, Ill.

Eddie Harrison
Director, Pre-trial Intervention Project
Baltimore, Md.

Bruce Johnson
Chairman, Board of Prison Terms and Paroles
Olympia, Wash.

Lance Jones
District Attorney
Sheboygan County, Wis.

Oliver J. Keller, Jr.
Director, Division of Youth Services
Tallahassee, Fla.

George C. Killinger
Director, Institute of Contemporary Corrections and
    Behavioral Sciences
Sam Houston State University
Huntsville, Tex.

William G. Nagel
Director, The American Foundation, Inc.
Philadelphia, Pa.

Rita O'Grady
Director, Family Court Center
Toledo, Ohio

Sanger B. Powers
Administrator, Division of Corrections
Madison, Wis.

Peter Preiser
State Director of Probation
Albany, N.Y.

Rosemary C. Sarri
Professor, National Assessment Study of Correc-
    tional Programs for Juvenile and Youthful
    Offenders
University of Michigan
Ann Arbor, Mich.

Saleem A. Shah
Chief, Center for Studies of Crime and Delinquency,
    National Institute of Mental Health
Rockville, Md.

John A. Wallace
Director, Office of Probation for the Courts of New
    York City
New York, N.Y.

Martha Wheeler
President, American Correctional Association
Superintendent, Ohio Reformatory for Women
Marysville, Ohio

Community Crime Prevention Task Force

Chairman

Jack Michie
Director, Division of Vocational Education
Lansing, Mich.

Martha Bachman
Hockessin, Del.

Ronald Brown
General Counsel, National Urban League
New York, N.Y.

Paul D'Amore
Vice President for Business & Finance
Marquette University
Milwaukee, Wis.

Adrian G. Duplantier
State Senator, Orleans Parish
New Orleans, La.

Carl V. Goodin
Chief of Police
Cincinnati, Ohio

Mamie Harvey
Youth Services Administration
New York, N.Y.

Richard A. Hernandez
Attorney
Los Angeles, Calif.

Gary Hill
The United States Jaycees
Lincoln, Nebr.

Eugene Kelley
Security Manager, Bendix Corporation
Newark, N.J.

Oliver Lofton
President, Priorities Investment Corporation
Newark, N.J.

Henry Mascarello
Executive Director
Massachusetts Correctional Association
Boston, Mass.

Harry L. McFarlane
Manager of Security, J.C. Penney Company, Inc.
New York, N.Y.

Advisory Task Force Members

Civil Disorders Advisory Task Force

Chairman

Jerry V. Wilson
Chief, Metropolitan Police Department
Washington, D.C.

George Beck
Deputy Chief
Los Angeles Police Department
Los Angeles, Calif.

Herbert R. Cain, Jr.
Judge, Court of Common Pleas
Philadelphia, Pa.

Gerald M. Caplan
Professor, College of Law
Arizona State University
Tempe, Ariz.

Thomas Gadsden
Civil Rights Division, Department of Justice
Washington, D.C.

Edward A. Hailes
Executive Director
Opportunities Industrialization Center
Washington, D.C.

Maynard H. Jackson
Vice Mayor
Atlanta, Ga.

Wayne A. Kranig
Chief, Law Enforcement Division
California Office of Emergency Services
Sacramento, Calif.

Robert E. Levitt
Majority Floor Leader, House of Representatives
Canton, Ohio

Norval Morris
Director, Center for Studies in Criminal Justice
School of Law
University of Chicago
Chicago, Ill.

Eugene J. Quindlen
Assistant Director for Government Preparedness
Executive Office of the President
Washington, D.C.

William A. Rusher
Publisher, *National Review*
New York, N.Y.

Community Involvement Advisory Task Force

Chairman

George B. Peters
President, Aurora Metal Company
Aurora, Ill.

Victor Henderson Ashe II
Knoxville, Tenn.

Sidney H. Cates III
Deputy Chief for Administration
Department of Police
New Orleans, La.

Patricia Costello
Northshore Youth Counselling Service
Milwaukee, Wis.

Sarah Jane Cunningham
Attorney, Cunningham and Clark
McCook, Nebr.

Ephram Gomberg
Executive Vice President
Citizens Crime Commission
Philadelphia, Pa.

Benjamin F. Holman
Director, Community Relations Service
Department of Justice
Washington, D.C.

Wayne Hopkins
Chamber of Commerce of the United States
Washington, D.C.

Kenneth B. Hoyt
Director
Specialty Oriented Student Research Program
University of Maryland
College Park, Md.

Steve E. Littlejohn
Harvard College
Cambridge, Mass.

Margaret Moore Post
Indianapolis News
Indianapolis, Ind.

Gary Robinson
Assistant Secretary
Executive Office of Human Services
Boston, Mass.

Edward J. Stack
Sheriff, Broward County
Fort Lauderdale, Fla.

William H. Wilcox
Secretary, Department of Community Affairs
Harrisburg, Pa.

Drug Abuse Advisory Task Force

Chairman

Sterling Johnson
Executive Director, New York City Civil Complaint
Review Board
New York, N.Y.

Edward Anderson
Bureau of Narcotics and Dangerous Drugs
Department of Justice
Washington, D.C.

Kenneth Biehn
Assistant District Attorney, Bucks County
Quakertown, Pa.

V. C. Chasten
Daly City, Calif.

Judianne Densen-Gerber
Executive Director, Odyssey House
New York, N.Y.

Jeffrey Donfeld
Assistant Director, Special Action Office for Drug
Abuse Prevention
Washington, D.C.

Robert L. Dupont
Director, Narcotics Treatment Administration
Washington, D.C.

Allan Gillies
Eli Lilly and Company
Indianapolis, Ind.

Frank Lloyd
Director, Medical Services, Methodist Hospital
Indianapolis, Ind.

Bruce Martin
Project Director, Regional Institute for Corrections
Administrative Study
Boulder, Colo.

Bernard Moldow
Judge, New York City Criminal Court
New York, N.Y.

William M. Tendy
Assistant Director
New York Organized Crime Task Force
White Plains, N.Y.

W. Elwyn Turner
Director of Public Health, County of Santa Clara
San Jose, Calif.

J. Thomas Ungerleider
Assistant Professor of Psychiatry
University of California at Los Angeles
Los Angeles, Calif.

Yaras M. Wochok
Assistant District Attorney
Philadelphia, Pa.

Education, Training, and Manpower Development Advisory Task Force

Chairman

Lee P. Brown
Director of the Law Enforcement Programs
Portland State University
Portland, Oreg.

Morris W. H. Collins, Jr.
Director, Institute of Government
University of Georgia
Athens, Ga.

Jay Edelson
Social Science Research Analyst
U.S. Department of Labor
Washington, D.C.

Donald E. Fish
Bureau Chief, Department of Community Affairs
Police Standards Board
Tallahassee, Fla.

Ernest Friesen
Executive Director, Institute for Court Management
University of Denver Law Center
Denver, Colo.

John B. Hotis
Inspector, FBI Academy
Quantico, Va.

John Irving
Dean, Law School, Seton Hall University
Newark, N.J.

Conrad F. Joyner
College of Liberal Arts, Dept. of Government
University of Arizona
Tucson, Ariz.

Charles V. Matthews
Director, Center for the Study of Crime, Delin-
quency and Corrections
Southern Illinois University
Carbondale, Ill.

Frederick Miller
Executive Director, Opportunities Industrialization
Center Institute
Philadelphia, Pa.

Gordon Misner
Director, Administration of Justice Program
University of Missouri
St. Louis, Mo.

Richard A. Myren
Dean, School of Criminal Justice
State University of New York
Albany, N.Y.

James P. Quinn
Indianapolis, Ind.

Alfred F. Smode
Executive Scientist, Dunlap and Associates, Inc.
Darien, Conn.

Information Systems and Statistics Advisory Task Force

Chairman

John R. Plants
Director, Michigan State Police
East Lansing, Mich.

C. J. Beddome
Assistant Chief, Administrative Division
Arizona Department of Public Safety
Phoenix, Ariz.

Gerald B. Fox
City Manager
Wichita Falls, Tex.

George Hall
National Institute of Law Enforcement and Criminal
Justice, Law Enforcement Assistance
Administration
Washington, D.C.

Scott W. Hovey, Jr.
Director, Bureau of Services
St. Louis Police Department
St. Louis, Mo.

Joan E. Jacoby
National Center for Prosecution Management
Washington, D.C.

James A. McCafferty
Assistant Chief, Division of Information Systems
Administrative Office of the U.S. Courts
Washington, D.C.

Vincent O'Leary
Professor of Criminal Justice
State University of New York
Albany, N.Y.

Larry P. Polansky
Chief Deputy Court Administrator
Court of Common Pleas
Philadelphia, Pa.

Donald R. Roderick
Inspector, Uniform Crime Reports
National Crime Information Center, FBI
Washington, D.C.

Juvenile Delinquency Advisory Task Force

Chairman

Wilfred W. Nuernberger
Judge, Separate Juvenile Court
Lincoln, Nebr.

Gary Abrecht
Metropolitan Police Department
Washington, D.C.

Mary Ellen Abrecht
Metropolitan Police Department
Washington, D.C.

Robert C. Arneson
Director, Law Enforcement Planning Commission
Boise, Idaho

Allen F. Breed
Director, Department of Youth Authority
State of California
Sacramento, Calif.

William S. Fort
Judge, Court of Appeals
Salem, Oreg.

Sanford Fox
Director, Center for Corrections and the Law
Boston College Law School
Boston, Mass.

Robert J. Gemignani
Commissioner, Youth Development and Delinquency
    Prevention Administration
Department of Health, Education, and Welfare
Washington, D.C.

Thomas N. Gilmore
Senior Research Analyst, Wharton School of Finance
    and Commerce
University of Pennsylvania
Philadelphia, Pa.

William H. Hansen
Chief of Police
Sioux City, Iowa

Milton Luger
Director, Division for Youth
New York State Youth Commission
Albany, N.Y.

James E. Miller
Director, Juvenile Delinquency
Indiana Criminal Justice Planning Agency
Indianapolis, Ind.

Wayne R. Mucci
Special Services for Children
Bureau of Institutions and Facilities
New York, N.Y.

Paul Nejelski
Project Director, Juvenile Justice Standards Project
Institute of Judicial Administration
New York, N.Y.

Margaret K. Rosenheim
Professor, School of Social Service Administration
University of Chicago
Chicago, Ill.

Stanton L. Young
Oklahoma City, Okla.

Organized Crime Advisory Task Force

Chairman

William L. Reed
Commissioner
Florida Department of Law Enforcement
Tallahassee, Fla.

Annelise Anderson
Palo Alto, Calif.

G. Robert Blakey
Chief Counsel, Subcommittee on Criminal Law and
    Procedure
U.S. Senate
Washington, D.C.

Harry Lee Hudspeth
Attorney at Law
El Paso, Tex.

Wallace H. Johnson
Special Assistant to the President, The White House
Washington, D.C.

John F. Kehoe, Jr.
Commissioner of Public Safety
Boston, Mass.

Aaron M. Kohn
Managing Director, Metropolitan Crime Commission
New Orleans, La.

William Lucas
Sheriff, Wayne County
Detroit, Mich.

John J. McCoy
Chief Deputy, Riverside Sheriff's Department
Riverside, Calif.

William J. Scott
Attorney General of Illinois
Springfield, Ill.

Research and Development Advisory Task Force

Chairman

Peter J. McQuillan
Judge, New York City Criminal Court
Flushing, N.Y.

Peter B. Bensinger
Director, Department of Corrections
Springfield, Ill.

Milton U. Clauser
Provost, Naval Postgraduate School
Monterey, Calif.

Phillip Lacey
Attorney, Butler, Binion, Rice, Cook and Kuepp
Houston, Tex.

Peter P. Lejins
Director
Institute of Criminal Justice and Criminology
University of Maryland
College Park, Md.

Evelyn Murphy
Consultant on Social and Economic Policies
   Programs and Research Methods
Watertown, Mass.

Joseph D. Nicol
Professor, University of Illinois
Chicago, Ill.

Dallin H. Oaks
President, Brigham Young University
Provo, Utah

Frank J. Remington
Professor, School of Law
University of Wisconsin
Madison, Wis.

Henry Ruth
Director, Mayor Lindsay's Criminal Justice
   Coordinating Council
New York, N.Y.

Bernard A. Schreiver
Schreiver & McKee Associates, Inc.
Washington, D.C.

Daniel L. Skoler
Staff Director, Commission on Correctional Facilities
   and Services
American Bar Association
Washington, D.C.

Paul M. Whisenand
Professor, Department of Criminology
California State College
Long Beach, Calif.

Task Force Staff Members, Advisers, Consultants, And Contributors

Police Task Force Staff

Executive Director

Vernon L. Hoy

Assistant Director

Taylor L. Searcy

Research and Editorial Staff

Ronald C. Banks
Jeremy I. Conklin
William J. Cox
Robert S. Earhart
Laurence E. Fetters
Newsom J. Gibson
Louis J. Reiter
Charles A. Sale

Research Assistants

David G. Brath
Michael K. Hooper
Don G. Letney
John D. Madell
Stephen R. Staffer
John Swan
Anthony R. Toomey

Administrative

Amy F. Aki
Lydia Anderson
Barbara Bonino
Terry Gallegos
Susan H. Hennis
Susan Sullivan

Consultants

George Eastman
International Association of
  Chiefs of Police

Courts Task Force Staff

Staff Director

Harvey Friedman

Editor and Co-Director

George E. Dix

Professional Staff

Paul Garofalo
William P. Redick
Arlene T. Shadoan

Editorial Assistants

Walter E. Dellinger, III
Daniel L. Rotenberg
David B. Wexler

Clerical Staff

Florence K. Fisher
Eleanor H. Kett
Hilda M. O'Neill
Katherine L. Watson

Research Assistants

Mary S. Burdick
James C. Doub
Jerome James
Jerry Kahn
Neil S. Kessler
Norman Leopold
Michael Needham
William E. Persina
Barbara F. Sachs
Mary Lee Stapp
Rodney J. Streff
Randall E. Wilbert
Charles J. Willinger, Jr.

Contributors

Carl Baar
Ernest L. Bailey, Jr.
Herbert Beaser

Martin Belsky
John M. Cannell
James Cogan
Walter W. Cohen
Gary V. Dubin
Elyce Z. Ferster
Ernest C. Friesen, Jr.
James N. Garber
Marshall Hartman
H. Paul Haynes, Sr.
William R. Higham
Laurance M. Hyde, Jr.
Joan E. Jacoby
James Lacy
Jerome F. Lieblich
Arnold M. Malech
Donald M. McIntyre
William S. McKee
Raymond T. Nimmer
Thomas B. Russell
Shelvin Singer

Advisers

James Beck
Winslow Christian
Richard A. Hauser
Axel Kleiboemer
Kirksey M. Nix
Michael O'Neil
Monrad G. Paulsen
Peter Ruger
Mark Sendrow
Lee R. West
Charles R. Work

Corrections Task Force Staff

Executive Director

Lawrence A. Carpenter

Assistant Director

Marilyn Kay Harris

Staff Director

Ernest A. Guinn, Jr.

Technical Writer

Francis Smith Dodds

Administrative Assistant

Faye Hanks

Staff Associates

Harvey Perlman
Billy L. Wayson

Contributors

William T. Adams
Melvin T. Axilbund
Lewis P. Brusca
John P. Conrad
Edith Flynn
Norval Morris
Frederic D. Moyer
William G. Nagel
Vincent O'Leary
Clarence Schrag
Richard G. Singer
Robert L. Smith
John A. Wallace

Advisers

Bill Anderson
William E. Baughman
Allen F. Breed
Milton Burdman
Joan Carrerra
John P. Friedman
Kenneth K. Henning
Hazel Kerper
Barbara Knudson
Robert J. Kutak
Joseph S. Lobenthal, Jr.
Richard E. Longfellow
Milton Luger
Ellis C. MacDougall
W. Donald Pointer
Francis J. Prevost
Sue Shirley
Daniel L. Skoler

Community Crime Prevention Task Force Staff

Staff Director

Louis Rome

Associate Staff Director

Kenneth D. Hines

Lori Blevins
Donald Brezine
Richard Friedman
Eleanor Hellrung

Roslyn Mazer
Patricia McLaughlin
Gail Miller
Dorothy Neubauer
Judith E. Rapp
Adelaide Reid
Rachel Shugars
Judith Zeider

In-Office Consultants

James Fleck
Bryon Mills
Joseph Phelan
Ruth Ann Rudnick

Law Student Researchers

David Callet
Paul R. D'Amoto
James A. Gass
Mark R. Kravitz
Karen M. Radius

Contributors

David Adamany
John Adams
Herbert Alexander
John F. Allbright
LaVerda O. Allen
Randolph Blackwell
Bruce Brennan
James A. Brennan
Leon Brill
Carl Chambers
John Duguid
Elaine Duxbury
William Falcon
John Favors
O. C. Foster
Maurice D. Geiger
Pearldean Golightly
Jerald D. Hampton
Robert Harris
L. Bert Hawkins
Wallace T. Homitz
Leon Hunt
Francis Ianni
Peter A. Jaszi
Ernest Jones
Michael Kantor
Russell Leedy
Donald Levine

Donald McCune
Harold Meiselas
Hubert Molina
Bruce Monroe
William Moore
Donald F. Muhich
Erasmus C. Ogbuobiri
Joseph Price
Charles S. Prigmore
Stephen H. Sachs
Ralph Salerno
Nicholas Scoppetta
James Shonkwiler
Neil M. Singer
Robert L. Smith
Neil Sullivan
Robert Taggart III
George Washnis
Malcolm H. Wiener
Kenneth F. Wilhoite
Ben Zimmerman
California Youth Authority
Manpower Administration, U.S. Department of
    Labor, for financial assistance
Narcotic and Drug Research, Inc.

Advisers

Howard Aldrich
Robert Atkins
Howard Braun
Albert Biderman
Lee P. Brown
Patricia Caesar
Orin C. Church
Eli Cohen
Martin B. Danziger
Hollis Devines
Robert Howe
Harold R. Johnson
Aaron Kohn
H. Joseph Meyer
M. Jean Miller
Perry Norton
Lloyd Ohlin
Vincent O'Leary
Howard Rogers
Charles C. Rohrs
John Rush
Wilbur Rykert
Ruben Schofield
Dwight C. Smith, Jr.
Edwin F. Toepfer
Mathew Wright

Information Systems and Statistics Advisory Task Force Staff

Staff Director

Paul K. Wormeli

Project Coordinator

LeRoy B. McCabe

Ronald E. Biggie
Donald F. King
Steve E. Kolodney
Robert L. Marx
Ernest A. Unwin
David R. Weinstein
Michael A. Zimmerman

Contributor

Paul M. Whisenand

Advisers

Ronald C. Allen
Lloyd A. Bastian
Wayne P. Holtzman

Criminal Justice System Contributors and Advisers

Planning for Crime Reduction

Contributor

Ralph M. Gutekunst, Jr.

Advisers

Richard Glynn

Peter R. Gray
Nicholas Roberts
Arnold Rosenfeld
Henry S. Ruth, Jr.
Allen Schick
Joseph L. White

Criminal Justice Education

Contributors

William T. Adams
Charles P. Smith

Criminal Code Revision

Contributor

B. J. George, Jr.

Victimization: Appendix A

Author

Anthony G. Turner

Encouraging Change: Appendix B

Author

Paul Solomon

Program Measurement and Evaluation: Appendix C

Authors

Howard H. Earle
Rosemary Hill
Richard P. Krank

Index

*Footnotes and Synopses of
Standards and Recommendations
have not been indexed.*

W

Wainwright, Louis: 113
Warren, Earl: 144
Wallace, George C.: 139
Washington, D.C.
    Major Violator Program: 89
    Minority group officers: 75
    Pretrial Justice Program: 47
    Project Crossroads: 95, 96
    Release on recognizance study: 27
    Streetlighting: 64
    Traffic offenses: 137
Watergate: 20
Wilmington, Del.: 58

Wisconsin: 31, 34
Witnesses: 108
Women: 85, 125
Worcester, Mass.: 51

Y

Youth: 16, 17
Youth Advocacy Program (South
    Bend, Ind.): 51
Youth Development Service (Billings,
    Mont.): 51
Youth for Service (San Francisco,
    Calif.): 56

Youth Services Bureau
    Accessibility to: 54
    Diversion and: 54
    Funding for: 54
    Legislation for: 54
    Number of: 51
    Role of: 51
    Source of clients: 54
    Voluntary nature of referrals: 55
Youth Service Bureau of Greensboro,
    Inc. (Greensboro, N.C.): 54
Youth Service Project (San Antonio,
    Tex.): 54

Photo Credits

The Commission wishes to acknowledge the many agencies and individuals who supplied photographs to illustrate the reports of the Commission. The Commission regrets that it was not able to use all of those photos.

☆U.S. GOVERNMENT PRINTING OFFICE: 1973 O—507-114

For sale by the Superintendent of Documents, U.S. Government Printing Office
Washington, D.C. 20402 - Price $2.55
Stock Number 2700–00204